within freedom found

A MEMOIR

BY SARA TREVELYAN

Scotland Street Press
EDINBURGH

Published by Scotland Street Press 2017

2 5 7 3 12 9 7 5 3

Copyright © Sara Trevelyan 2017

The right of Sara Trevelyan to be identified as the author of this work has been asserted in accordance with Section 77 of the Copyright, Designs and Patent Act (UK) 1988

All rights reserved. No part of this publication may be reproduced, distributed, or transmitted in any form or by any means, including photocopying, recording, or other electronic or mechanical methods, without the prior written permission of the publisher/author, except in the case of quotations embodied in critical reviews and certain other non-commercial uses permitted by copyright law. For permission requests, write to the publisher/author.

First published in Great Britain in 2017 by
Scotland Street Press
Edinburgh
www.scotlandstreetpress.com

Cover Design by Bookmark Studio
www.bookmark-studio.com
ISBN: 978-1-910895-07-8

Typeset in Scotland by Bookmark Studio
Printed and bound in Poland

I want to appreciate those who have been my friends, companions, teachers, and mentors who have helped me become who I am today. A special place has to go to my husband of twenty years, my life partner and soul mate Jimmy Boyle, who gave me so much and then left me, as he followed his own path. This has been a strange paradox in my life, but it has forced me to become self-reliant.

I am dedicating this attempt to express the wholeness in my life, and describe the path that I have walked to discover it, to my two children, Suzi and Kydd. They are the light in my heart and soul and the ones who I will hand the baton of life to when I leave. May they carry it well, knowing their roots and feeling the breath of spirit beneath their wings. May they know what it is to be FREE as they follow their own unique paths and calling into a future which is theirs to create.

Hymn to Freedom

When every heart joins every heart, and
together yearns for liberty,
That's when we'll be free.
When every hand, joins every hand and
together moulds our destiny,
That's when we'll be free.
Any hour, any day, the time soon will come
When we will live in dignity,
That's when we'll be free.
When everyone joins in our song and together
singing harmony,
That's when we'll be free.

- Oscar Peterson

My Father gave me this beautiful piece of music by Oscar Peterson during the time leading up to my marriage when I was visiting Jimmy Boyle in the special Unit in Barlinnie Prison.

I recently discovered that it also has words to accompany it. These express for me the essence of freedom, as we can come to experience and live it.

The music and the words sum up my journey from start to finish; the quest for freedom lies at the heart of life, it is a quest for us all, it is the yearning at the heart of creation.

Contents

Introduction					xi

PART 1 – DIFFERENT WORLDS

1. First Encounter					1
2. Beginnings – A World Apart			9
3. To Australia and Back Again			15
4. Barlinnie Special Unit – A Spark is Kindled	26
5. Glasgow No Mean City				35
6. Breaking the News – Getting Married		46

PART TWO – TWO WORLDS MERGING

7. Married – With the World's Press Looking On	59
8. Early Days of an Unusual Marriage		67
9. Many Rivers to Cross				79
10. Last Days in the Special Unit			86
11. Stand by Me – Saughton Prison, Edinburgh	96
12. Freedom Coming				111
13. Release – the Gate Opens			119
14. Freedom at Last and First Baby			135

PART THREE – EMERGENCE OF THE NEW

15. Launching the Gateway Exchange	149
16. Another New Arrival – Feeling the Pressure	163
17. Funding Crisis and Change of Direction	177
18. A Move to the Suburbs	191
19. Spiritual Emergence	202

PART FOUR – IN SEARCH OF SELF

20. The Challenges of Emergence	217
21. The Stormy Search	230
22. Moving Ever Further Apart	241
23. Being of Light	250
24. Increasingly on my Own	261
25. Approaching The Edge	268
26. The Broken and the Unbroken	280
27. Millennium and Divorce	294
28. Quest for a New Identity	305
29. A Final Word	315
Afterword	319

Introduction

At the end of the 1970s I met, and fell in love with one of Scotland's best-known prisoners, Jimmy Boyle. Our two very different worlds collided in an unexpected way and led me to unexpected places.

Our first unlikely meeting happened as a result of picking up and reading a book, which he had written, called *A Sense of Freedom*. It was an extraordinary and unprecedented achievement for a prisoner to publish a book while still serving their sentence. It should basically never have happened. Had the authorities had their way the manuscript would have been kept securely within the prison walls. His words though had a rawness and power, which gave them wings. A way was found to bypass the labyrinthine security controls of the prison system, and the manuscript found its way into print. This book, which became a best seller, was like a clarion call voice from the underbelly of society.

Reading this book for the first time had consequences which I couldn't have imagined or foretold. It became the catalyst that propelled me onto a journey which would completely transform me. Then, as now, I was an innocent in this world of hard man violence. I came from another strand of society altogether. At the time when we met I was a junior hospital doctor, and my family name Trevelyan had associations with class and privilege. My life had been cushioned in many ways. I had never known the hard edge of poverty or the crushing experience of imprisonment. I spent my teenage years on the sunny beaches of Australia. In my wildest dreams I could never have imagined myself living in Scotland becoming the wife of such a notorious prisoner.

In lots of ways this left me unprepared to enter his world and potentially vulnerable to my own naivety. I always believed though that my decision to get married to Jimmy, was the right one for me to be making. It was brave, in some people's view foolhardy, others might have considered me downright mad, but I knew deep in my own heart that this was the man I loved and wanted to marry. I had no hesitation or doubt.

Our unlikely marriage attracted considerable press interest – in today's jargon, it went viral. The event is still remembered, although many these days wouldn't have even heard of Jimmy Boyle or the Special Unit – certainly this is true of the younger generation.

Given the circumstances, it was an extraordinary choice to be making. Why did I fall in love with this man who was, according to his official record, a convicted murderer and serving a life sentence? How could this relationship grow and develop behind the prison walls? Why did we decide to get married while he was still in prison without even a release date?

The answer to these questions was partially explained by the unique conditions provided by the ground-breaking Special Unit, which allowed us an unusual amount of time and freedom to get to know each other. This was a brave experiment created to respond to a situation of recurrent violence amongst long-term prisoners in the late 1960s.

*

The harsh conditions that prevailed in the Scottish Prison system at that time resulted in escalating protests and serious injuries to both prison staff and inmates. This small unit, in what was formerly the women's section of Barlinnie Prison, became internationally renowned for its revolutionary work with a small group of prisoners who had been involved in these protests. The liberal regime that evolved challenged some of the most basic tenets of the prison system. The best known of the prisoners in the Special Unit in the 1970s was Jimmy Boyle.

After receiving a life sentence, with a minimum of fifteen years to serve, he had gone all out to fight the system. During his time in prison he earned further notoriety from the leading role he played initiating and participating in this series of violent protests. In the progressive regime offered by the Special Unit, he showed a dramatic capacity to reform his behaviour, and his talents in both writing and sculpture emerged to an astonishing degree, as did those of others, when he found himself in conditions where they were encouraged.

I unexpectedly found myself at the heart of this time of experimentation in the prison system. Through my love for Jimmy I was propelled in an all-consuming way into the intensity of the Special Unit. The events and experiences of that time were beyond anything I had known previously.

This is my attempt to do justice to the story of how we met, how this time impacted on both of us and also to give a description of what followed, up to the point where it all ended in the year 2000. Jimmy wrote about his years in the Special Unit in *The Pain of Confinement,* his sequel to *A Sense of Freedom.* Possibly to protect me, he said little about our relationship, and this book finishes abruptly at the point where he is released. There is nothing comprehensive to tell the story of what this passage to freedom held for both of us, and what followed after his release.

*

During this time, without seeking or intending to, I found myself experiencing a profound opening to what I call my deeper spiritual essence. This challenged me to the depths of my being in a different way. It contributed to the ending of our marriage and birthed me into a new time following the calling of my soul. Through this a very different journey began for me, which is my own continuing passage into finding freedom.

It is perhaps easier to relate to freedom as a physical state and condition – this is very real and a true gift as I experienced most unforgettably at the moment of Jimmy's final release after fifteen years of imprisonment. There is a different kind of freedom though which most of us are much less aware. This is the freedom that comes from within, it is part of our inner nature and at the core of who we are. This is what emerged powerfully for me during these years of inner transformation.

Following the promptings of my inner voice resulted in my exploring different spiritual approaches and eventually led me to the Findhorn Community in the north of Scotland. This was a community I had first heard about in the 1970s. When I rediscovered it I knew that I had found a place where my soul felt at home, and this is where I have embarked on writing this account.

The catalyst for finally starting on this work was Jimmy's seventieth birthday, which took place in 2014. This occasion created an incentive to open up old boxes of photographs and diaries I had brought with me to Findhorn. Suddenly all the memories came flooding back.

Chapters of my life, which I had set aside and which had remained buried in these boxes since the time of our separation started to push their way back into my awareness. The past came alive for me in a way that felt empowering and vivid. It was as though my former self wanted to spring back and reclaim the life that I had lived. It felt as though these ghosts of the past were insisting on not being forgotten.

Jimmy is a different person now to the man who I met in his prison cell at the end of the 1970s. His life has transformed in ways he probably never imagined it could. The experience of living through the changes that overtook us has brought me to where

I am today. As Jimmy warned me when we chose to marry, the journey hasn't been an easy ride. I have been pushed to deep places in myself, but eventually to a place where I know love doesn't break... it might change its form, but in its most profound essence, love is eternal. This kind of love, love from the soul, which is what I experienced with Jimmy, never dies. When we can open our hearts to experience this as our true nature, we can finally experience *freedom*. It's a journey to reach this place and what follows is my journey towards the living and celebrating of this truth.

I have written this memoir initially for our two children, so that they can know this story from my side, and can hopefully benefit from this. I believe that it has a wider relevance, especially with the current calamitous crisis in prisons, so I am hoping that it will reach those who have a genuine interest in these issues and in their impact on personal relationships. I would like to affirm the timeless truth that no matter what unexpected rolls of the dice we might encounter, our greatest challenges can become openings to new opportunities.

This account is personal, I have bared my soul in the telling of it, but I dedicate it to all those who dare to follow their hearts, who seek love, with all its ups and downs, and risk setting themselves free to discover the mystery that lies at the heart of life.

Sara Trevelyan, 2016

PART ONE

DIFFERENT WORLDS

1. First Encounter

In my late twenties I graduated as a doctor from St Thomas's Hospital in London. I was feeling unfulfilled and energetically drained, and my first medical job in a busy south London hospital was a stressful experience. All this contributed to a decision to apply for a very different kind of job in a small hospital in the far north of Scotland as my next step. I wouldn't have embarked on such a radical move to the other end of the country if I hadn't had another purpose in mind.

I had read about a community to the east of Inverness called Findhorn: a spiritual community where apparently magical influences were at work and where people communicated with invisible beings. These unconventional practices had extraordinary results giving rise to giant cabbages, vegetables and flowers, flourishing on the arid sand dunes. These achievements attracted considerable interest in New Age circles, leading to the growth of a radical and innovative community. Findhorn was supposedly a place to experience these other-worldly realities beyond the surface appearances of life.

What I had read about the community sparked my interest and, despite the fact that most of this was in complete contradiction to my outer life, I decided that I would like to explore this further. This was how I came to uproot myself from London towards the end of my twenties and with all my possessions packed into the back of my VW Beetle car, I set off on the long drive north to begin a new chapter in Inverness. I couldn't have named what I was seeking, but it felt like some kind of unquenched thirst and hunger for new horizons.

My choice to listen to my inner voice has certainly brought its challenges, but overall it has proved a reliable guide in my life. Here it was calling me, launching me into a new chapter of which I had no inkling at that time. What I was about to embark on proved very different to anything that I could have anticipated or expected.

I had few regrets about leaving the big city behind and my spirits soared as I caught sight of the snow-covered mountains. Peaks appeared, pristine and magnificent, as I ventured north into the wild and spectacular landscapes of the Highlands. I felt cleansed from the pressures of city life. The stress of endless nights on call in my previous job fell away from me. Everything that had felt dark and difficult seemed to be behind me. I took deep breaths of the bracing northern air and opened to a new phase beginning.

Work at the Royal Northern Infirmary, situated alongside the banks of the River Ness, flowed at an easy pace, like the meandering currents of water gliding downstream. People were amiable and friendly and my nights in my new Ear Nose and Throat job were wonderfully peaceful. I saw this as a time to regather myself after a few fairly tumultuous years living and studying in the heave and thrust of the culturally diverse environment of urban London. I felt an inner serenity and harmony returning, and looked forward to exploring the dramatic and inviting landscapes of the hills and glens close by.

I was aware of concerns which were starting to present themselves in terms of where life was leading me. I had recently ended a long term relationship, the advantage of which was that I was free to leave London. I was aware of feeling very much on my own, but had a basic trust that things would work out. In a letter that I wrote to my mother at that time I refer to this, saying that I am leaving questions such as marriage, children and my future in the hands of 'fate'. I had somewhere within me a sense of an invisible thread, which always seemed to guide my life. 'Fate' certainly was about to take hold of me but I had no notion at all what lay ahead.

*

A seemingly everyday choice became one that started me on the journey which would come to shape everything that followed. I was standing at the bookstand in Inverness Railway Station when a book called *A Sense of Freedom*, with a striking red and black cover, jumped out at me. I hadn't heard of the name of its author, Jimmy Boyle, before but it looked as though it would be interesting, so I bought the book, took it back to the hospital where I was working at the time and started reading it. I couldn't put it down. I read it from cover to cover in a matter of days.

This book was my introduction to Jimmy. It was an account of his life and upbringing in the Gorbals, which he described in vivid detail as 'the armpit of Glasgow.' He was born in May 1944 and was one of a family of four boys, brought up by his mother who worked from early morning until late at night as a cleaner. His father died when he was very young and early on Jimmy took to the streets where he became involved in thieving and gang fights.

He saw emulating the hard men round about him as a way to escape the harsh conditions of poverty, which was such a blight on his life. He was first arrested at the age of twelve and over the years was an inmate in a succession of penal institutions – remand homes, approved schools and borstal. The harsh discipline terrified him initially, but his fear soon became masked by bravado as his reputation and street kudos grew each time he ended up in one of these locally notorious places.

As a young adult he became an enforcer for protection rackets, and became progressively involved in street violence. There were many casualties as a consequence of his mindless and headstrong determination to stay ahead of the game and defeat his rivals. He was close to his mother and repeatedly promised to curtail his behaviour, but he failed each time. He was eventually prosecuted in two abortive murder trials, before being sentenced in 1967 to life imprisonment, with a fifteen-year minimum tariff, for the murder of another criminal, Babs Rooney.

This is a murder he claimed he was innocent of, but in his own words 'the cops were out to get him' and on this occasion they succeeded. His long sentence effectively ended his career as a well-known hard man on the streets.

★

In prison he refused to accept the authority of the prison staff and fought them at every opportunity. In the book he describes graphically the harsh conditions in Scottish prisons in the late 1960s and early 1970s. Early on he became involved in protests, fighting the system, which in his view was oppressive and brutal. The authorities responded, meting out ever harsher punishments which merely intensified his determination to go all out to deny them the satisfaction of breaking him.

He eventually ended up with others on a dirty protest and spending years in solitary confinement in the cages in Inverness Prison. The book ends with him being transferred into the Special Unit, which was where he was miraculously offered a wholly new chance at life – he found himself being treated respectfully by prison officers and the book ends with a memorable experience when he is handed a pair of scissors to open a parcel, something which would never have happened in the mainstream prison system. Trust is the key which opens a new door for him.

He says clearly in the book that he wrote it with the intention of warning young people that there was nothing glamorous about getting involved in crime and violence. In this searing account of his life in juvenile institutions and prisons his other message is that, just as he has been held to account for his actions, the authorities should also be held to account for the extreme brutality existing at that time in the closed world behind the prison walls. In his view, imposing ever harsher punishments merely provoked riots and other protests as prisoners took increasingly desperate measures to resist. The Special Unit, with its different approach, seemed to offer a potential solution to an otherwise intractable state of affairs.

He finishes the book saying:

> 'As far as my past goes, I don't think that it should be forgotten about or swept under the carpet as though it doesn't exist. It does exist and is very much a part of me. My own personal experiences have taught me that mistakes are very much a part of living. Certainly we must try to learn from them, as in this instance, and use this knowledge to let others see what can happen. I dread the thought of other kids going through my experience in order to gain the insight I now have....Certainly I have caused much suffering and have suffered, but the disease is much larger and older than me. An environment has been created that has encouraged change and that is what must be looked at.'

Reading this book had a profound effect on me, as it did for many others. The world that he was describing was in lots of ways unfamiliar and alien to me, and the violence disturbing. The message, though, was an important one and re-awakened my feelings of injustice about what was happening in British prisons at that time. I had read accounts written by other prisoners, but this was by far the most articulate and persuasive call for reform that I had seen.

Its argument that those in charge of the criminal justice system should be held to account in the same way as those who offend are, was in my view completely appropriate.

Normally I wouldn't have taken things any further, but shortly after reading this book I received a letter from one of my friends in London whom I had met when I was involved in a campaign to get control units (units that were designed along the lines of putting prisoners into conditions of sensory deprivation) closed down. I was a medical student when I first heard about these units, which involved sensory deprivation, twenty-four hour continuous lighting and complete sound proofing; they were designed to put an individual under maximum stress so that they would break down within a short time.

A group of us, medical students and doctors, considered that the involvement of trained doctors in a system designed to inflict such extreme punishment was contravening the Hippocratic oath. We were deeply concerned about medical collusion in sanctioning the use of such extreme punishments. Our campaign was successful as these infamous units were closed down shortly afterwards.

At the time when I left London I felt thoroughly burned out. My energies were drained after completing my first six month house job and I was planning to take a break from my campaigning days for a while – exchanging the intensity of meetings discussing tactics and focusing on abuses of power in the prison system and other sections of society, for weekend explorations of the spectacular scenery of the Scottish Highlands.

In her letter, my friend Liz mentioned that she had made a visit to the Special Unit in Glasgow where she had met a prisoner called Jimmy Boyle. I was immediately curious. She described him as a good looking 'macho man'. This didn't attract me, I was a feminist after all, but his book had impressed me so much that I decided I would write to Jimmy and ask if I could visit him and see the Special Unit myself. This isn't anything I would normally do, but in this instance it was as if something inside was pushing me to go beyond my normal shyness about approaching a complete stranger in this way. To my surprise I received a brief acknowledgment to my letter and an invitation to visit.

★

In early December 1977 I left the hospital at dawn to take the train south to Glasgow. From there I took a bus to Barlinnie Prison. This notorious prison is situated on the outskirts of the city centre of Glasgow. It is a forbidding, grim and austere looking building surrounded by a high wall and perimeter fence. What I remember of this first visit was passing through the imposing and heavily fortified entrance to the main prison, and then being conducted across a yard to a small locked doorway in a high wall, which opened onto a courtyard and two storey building, which had originally been the women's section in the prison.

I was escorted into this building and then upstairs to meet Jimmy in his cell. I had imagined meeting him in some kind of institutional setting like a hostel. I was completely unprepared to be invited into his cell, which was attractively decorated with green floral print William Morris wallpaper. Matching curtains framed a small high up barred window. Shelves containing books and other personal items lined one of the walls.

Jimmy, dressed in his denim dungarees, welcomed me standing beside his bed. He invited me to sit down on it, next to a table set for lunch. He had prepared what he called a 'Gorbals Salad', along with a freshly baked loaf of bread he had made himself.

I was delighted to be offered such a healthy spread. His face was fresh and alive. He was physically smaller than I had expected, but his compact physique was bursting with physical strength and energy. He spoke rapidly in a strong Glasgow accent. I was swept away on the stream of his words, and it seemed we instantly connected. Despite the differences in our backgrounds and circumstances, we understood each other. He had seen me on a Brass Tacks television programme defending the right of Myra

Hindley (jailed for the infamous Moors Murders of children, in Britain) to be considered for parole and had admired the stance I had taken on this controversial issue.

It was a remarkable first meeting. I went away inspired and impressed that here was someone who had the capacity to articulate all that was wrong with the present prison system, while describing how the Special Unit was showing what could be achieved with a completely different approach.

After this visit I received a card with Christmas wishes on it, signed Jimmy. I was surprised and pleased to receive this but there was nothing to suggest any continuing contact so things were left there.

My initial reason for coming to Inverness had been its geographical proximity to the Findhorn community. Before my encounter with Jimmy's book, I had ventured east along the coast, heading through the gently undulating agricultural landscapes of Moray for an initial visit. I will touch on this at a later point. My experiences were pleasant but like the flatter quality of the landscape, didn't outwardly inspire me to any great extent.

The magic remained hidden to my un-awakened senses. My attention was more drawn to this new spark which was at that moment embedding itself in my inner landscape – a live ember which would rest there waiting for the next mysterious touch of fate.

2. Beginnings – A World Apart

I returned to work at the Royal Northern Infirmary, which was a fairly predictable routine of ward rounds, and assisting with minor surgical procedures. The institutional life, which involved living in a small hospital room, was lonely at times after my heady days of sharing a communal house in London. What this gave me was plenty of time to reflect. I enjoyed regular walks alongside the smooth flowing waters of the river Ness. This brought me an inner clarity I had lost during my years of living in London.

The life and the circumstances I was born into in 1950 were completely different to the tenement slum conditions Jimmy was exploring at that time with such boyish enthusiasm. I arrived into the world in an upstairs room in my grandparents stately white house in Westmorland (now called Cumbria) – a mere two hours' drive south of Glasgow but worlds apart at that time due to the absence of a motorway, let alone the imprisoning nature of social norms.

The terrace in front of the house overlooked a large and pleasant garden with a view beyond onto the green woods, fields and rock- strewn fells of the Lake District. It was an idyllic setting. My parents were John Trevelyan and Joan Scot (my mother's maiden name).

My mother was thirty eight when she had me and coming towards the end of her childrearing years. She had recently married my father, a marriage encouraged by my grandparents, as three years previously she had given birth to my brother in a nursing home in Devon. This had been arranged to deal with an awkward and socially embarrassing situation.

My mother was intelligent, one of the earliest women in England to graduate as a doctor, and she had worked at the Birmingham Fever Hospital in the post-war years. She had met my father when he was Westmoreland's director of education. This was in the days before his job as Secretary to the British Board of Film Censors made him publicly known. He was married at the time, but this first marriage ended some years later. His wife Kay had lost two babies due to suffering from eclampsia in her pregnancies. This double tragedy caused problems in their marriage. Counselling and support services were not available at that time and both of them sought to escape their unhappiness by having affairs.

My father met up with my mother almost accidentally after looking through his notebook of addresses and phone numbers, then calling her. My mother happened to answer and accepted his invitation to dinner. She was at a low place in her life as she had recently ended an affair with a man well known in the medical establishment. He had ended this fearing that it would prejudice his career.

This was someone she had been very much in love with but he was married and social norms could not be undone with the ease that they are today. Both my parents were depressed and miserable when they met and by my mother's account my father was actually suicidal at this time. Drawn together by their mutual unhappiness, the affair continued and early on she became pregnant.

My brother James was born in 1948 in a nursing home in Exeter. Giving birth without the support of family or friends must have been a difficult experience for her and it was one she never spoke about afterwards. My father, deciding that there was no future in his first marriage, moved in with my mother and shortly afterwards agreed that they should get married to ease the tensions with my grandfather.

All of this is quite a saga and explains the fact that, although the outer conditions into which I was born were tranquil and idyllic, there were hidden shadows and fault lines which would erupt dramatically later on in my childhood.

Memories of my early childhood years are mostly of a large house that my parents bought in Kent. This also had a beautiful garden surrounding it and I spent many happy hours exploring. My father came and went as he spent part of the week in London, which was where, after a spell of freelance work, he had become a part time examiner for the British Board of Film censors. What I didn't realise until reading a memoir which he wrote before the end of his life, was that throughout my early childhood he was having an affair with his secretary Jean. He was leading a 'double life' – having two wives and two homes. As I played innocently in the sunshine in the garden with my brother I was oblivious to these hidden shadows.

He described his marriage to my mother as a marriage of convenience and not a 'love match'. I'm not sure that this was how my mother experienced it as she pleaded with him to end his affair, but despite promising to do this he covertly resumed his relationship with Jean. At a young age my brother was sent off to boarding school, while my mother took on my early lessons at home. This was not a happy experience for me as she was overbearingly strict and not at all fun-loving.

In fairness to her she must have been deeply unhappy at the time. As an intelligent woman, finding herself isolated and alone living in the country must have been very unfulfilling. Things were of course made worse when she started to hear rumours of the affair my father was having with his secretary.

*

My life, sheltered and protected as it was, couldn't have been more of a contrast to Jimmy's. Contact with other children was limited as I didn't start school until I was eight. Life was quiet and predictable, spent largely in the garden where my most vivid memories are of daffodils, primroses, and cherry trees.

My only exposure to any kind of law-breaking came through the early television programme Dixon of Dock Green. In each episode a kindly looking policeman in his London bobby's hat would solve petty crimes with a combination of common sense and human understanding. It was a far cry from the approach to law and order on the streets of Glasgow that Jimmy describes in his early years.

My life took on a different rhythm when, at the age of eight, I started school. As a late starter I was all at sea at first and had quite a bit of catching up to do but I settled into my class and made my first ever friend, Johanna, who had a mop of soft curly hair, a chubby face, and warm twinkly eyes. I had just settled into this new routine when things suddenly erupted and my familiar, safe life came to a sudden and dramatic end.

The event that changed everything shortly after I had turned nine was my parents' decision to get divorced. My mother broke the news to me one memorable afternoon after I had arrived home from school, when I was having my afternoon snack. She told me that our lives were about to change. My father wasn't coming back home. I would not be going back to school and the three of us were going to go to a place called Australia. This news landed like a sudden unexpected bombshell. All that I can remember is that my stomach turned a gigantic somersault! Then blank...

Apparently I cried for twenty-four hours, then accepted the changes, but shut it all deep inside myself. I spoke to no one because I had heard from my mother that it wasn't safe to do this. There was something *secret*, and therefore shameful about everything that was happening. This was the way children were given this kind of news in those days – it was simply a matter of this is what is happening and we will have to get used to it. There was no time or space for questions and no safe place to feel the emotions.

My mother must have had more than enough of her own to cope with, let alone the responsibility of making all the arrangements for our coming move across the world. At that time there was an enormous social stigma attached to divorce. As a child all I knew was that something shameful and dreadful had happened which, at all costs and as far as possible, shouldn't be shared with others. I took this very literally and apparently spoke to no-one.

It is impossible to know what I felt about the sudden absence of my father from our lives. My feelings of hurt sank into some deep place inside me. I had been physically and emotionally close to him. He represented stability, love, and safety to me and was the one whose warm body would enclose mine when I snuggled next to him in bed. This cosy relationship was suddenly and wrenchingly torn apart. Later on in my life when I became conscious of my feelings of abandonment and pain, I found myself feeling outraged and hurt that he never came to say goodbye.

The situation which had brought things to a head was that Jean, his secretary who he had been having an affair with all these years, had become pregnant with twins. In his memoir my father says that he was faced with an impossible situation. My mother having faced her father's disapproval before, and fearing publicity because of my father's new appointment as Secretary to the British Board of Film Censors, must have decided that she had no option but to accept the situation and asked him to leave.

She told him that he couldn't let Jean go through this alone. Perhaps on her mind was her own experience of giving birth to James in the nursing home. It must have been a painful final encounter and resulted in my father leaving the next day.

The sudden, deep and unexpected loss of him was the first major challenge in my life. Jimmy had lost his father at a younger age than I lost mine. This was a disturbing event in his life as his own father died as a consequence of violence, which must have had a devastating effect on him. Such losses and our responses to them define and shape us. Like me, he never spoke much about it afterwards.

My experience shaped and coloured choices which I have made since – it wasn't surprising that I would seek a path which would involve healing, for the hidden wounds which I carried inside as a result of these difficult experiences in my childhood took many years to access and heal. Divorce became one of my least favourite words and I strongly intended never to repeat this experience in my own lifetime.

Sadly I failed in this respect, but much water was to pass under the bridge before I reached this same threshold forty years later in my adult life. Meanwhile I was about to be catapulted out of my safe childhood cocoon and transported across the globe to begin a new life on the other side of the world.

3. To Australia and Back Again

These days many people travel to Australia – it is a mere twelve to eighteen hour flight away, depending on which side of Australia you are flying to. With relatively low cost air fares this is a popular destination for those wanting to escape the grey skies and rain of the British Isles and seek the sun, light, and warmth of the southern hemisphere.

In 1959, when we made this journey, we sailed on an ocean liner across the Atlantic. We crossed Canada by train. We boarded another ship on the West coast of America, then sailed across the Pacific, docking at Tahiti and New Zealand on the way. I think the whole journey would probably have taken us about six weeks. We stayed for a short period in Sydney where I remember gazing up at the vast Sydney Harbour Bridge and watching the ferries steaming backwards and forwards across the bay. My mother wasn't much impressed so we took a flight across the continent to Perth on the West Coast.

What was in my Mother's mind as she took us on this journey to the other side of the world? She said that she had considered different options, Canada and South Africa, as well as Australia. I think her primary motivation was that she wanted to get away – away from the shame and stigma of divorce, away from any publicity.

My father had recently been appointed as Secretary to the British Board of Film Censors and he was about to become famous through this public role, but at that early time he wasn't sufficiently well known for the news of his divorce to generate headlines. It seems to me that this unexpected trajectory across the globe could only have been an expression of my mother's pain, the pain that she tried to withhold from us, but which was expressed in these kind of displaced ways.

I'm sure that if it had been possible to travel further she probably would have because our final resting place, the Ocean Beach Hotel, with its brash and noisy beer swilling clientele, alongside what is still one of Perth's most popular beaches, was an incongruous choice for a cultured English woman like my mother. My brother and I were enrolled at a local state primary school nearby where we were ridiculed for our 'pommy' accents. Over time though we settled and moved into a new home, a sedate suburban bungalow in the suburb of Nedlands.

I attended a private school, Methodist Ladies College, which was also situated in the suburbs and my brother attended the Church of England boys school next door. Our lives settled into a relaxed suburban rhythm – there was only one unacknowledged shadow and that was that our family was different. I was all too aware of my father's absence – my mother didn't have a husband, and my brother and I didn't have a father. I dreaded the question at school: 'What does your father do?' This would result in me feeling full of shame and embarrassment.

As far as was possible I tried to hide this aspect of our lives by not talking about it, burying it deep inside. I imagine that this is what many children do with experiences that they don't comprehend, and don't know how to talk about. These days there is a lot more expertise available in this area, and services to support children affected by family breakdown and divorce – in those days there was none.

Gradually we adapted to our new environment in this remote capital city. Although a complete contrast to the life we had led during my early years in Kent, Perth soon came to feel like home. I loved the outdoors, the warmth of the sun, the long summers, the freedom I experienced and the easy going pace of life. I especially loved the sparkling waters of the river, the beach with its rolling, white-capped waves and white sand, and having friends to play with.

As the 1960s started I sprouted into adolescence, had my hair cut into a fringe and became infatuated with the Beatles. Their harmonies and songs accompanied my early experiences of falling in love. As a small family of three we successfully landed and rooted ourselves 'Down Under'. Life seemed full of promise and England seemed very far away.

This was literally on the other side of the world from the grey, rain slashed streets of Glasgow where, during these years, Jimmy was creating mayhem, establishing a reputation for himself as an incorrigible street-fighter and becoming an increasingly well known gangster.

Our lives were so contrasting and physically far apart that it would have been thought inconceivable our paths would ever cross. While things moved towards the fateful courtroom climax for him when the judge, with a resounding voice announced his life sentence, I was looking forward to newly expanding horizons as I finished my school days.

*

My youthful life was happy and carefree. I had a few memorable skirmishes with teachers and at home when I entered my more rebellious phase. I was a real beach lover and idled the summers away basking on the white sands at Cottesloe, deepening my sun tan, sporting my first bikini and learning to surf the waves. My first post-school experience was a trip with a friend across the vast expanses of Australia to Surfers' Paradise. Not feeling any enthusiasm for prolonged studies I decided to begin a training in Physiotherapy.

This proved unsatisfying so I applied to go to university to study politics, economics and psychology. This was a failure as well. Like having three strikes, I knew that my third choice had to be the 'right' one. After thinking long and hard I decided to follow in my mother's footsteps and study medicine.

Underneath the surface comforts of my life I felt unfulfilled and restless. I craved the excitement of wider horizons. I had a moment of clarity when I decided not to enrol on a medical training in Australia, but to travel back to the UK. I felt as though some invisible thread was drawing me back to the country I had left when I was nine.

A passage was booked for me on the S.S.Arcadia, one of the large ocean going liners, which was the way most people travelled back to the 'Mother Country' in those days. I set sail waving goodbye to my mother and friends. In a photograph taken of them standing on the dockside they all looked very sad. Looking down on them from a long way above, leaning over the side of the deck waving at them, I was excited to be setting out on what felt like an incredible adventure. It felt right to be leaving. Part of me knew that I was saying goodbye to everything my life had been about up until then. This was a very final decision. I wouldn't be coming back.

*

The voyage was an experience in itself. Reality started to come home to me once I arrived at my grandparents' house and then travelled south to London. The relatives who I stayed with initially were kind and hospitable, but apart from the closeness I felt with my grandparents, it seemed I had little in common with them. I hankered after the beach and took a train to the south coast only to discover that I was walking on pebbles not sand, and the water was grey rather than sparkling and blue.

I turned my attention to enrolling at medical school but discovered that my Australian leaving qualifications were considered insufficient. I therefore spent my first year studying at a tutorial college. These were called 'crammers' as their only purpose was to get us through the exams with a good enough pass grade.

The glamorous image I had tried to cultivate was stripped away in the company of other students much younger than me. London was a huge metropolis and I felt crushed at times by my insignificance amongst so many thousands of people. It didn't take long to discover how lonely it is possible to feel in a big city. In some ways there was tremendous freedom about suddenly finding myself anonymous, but inside all I felt was panic. I met people through introductions and encounters, and explored many different parts of the city, but I didn't, for a long time, feel any sense of belonging.

It was during this time that I resumed my relationship with my father after a stay of ten years in Australia. He was one of the few sources of comfort for me. He welcomed me back with a deep fondness and affection. We didn't talk about what had happened in the past. Our relationship felt the same, although his circumstances had changed. He was living in a small house in Dulwich and I visited him regularly there.

Some years previously Jean, the mother of his twin boys, had been diagnosed as having multiple sclerosis. I don't have many memories of her but I could see that the situation was dreadful. I met the twins but was never close to them as they were sent away to boarding school. Things deteriorated with Jean ending up in a nursing home, where she eventually died in November 1972.

A couple of years later Dad married Rosalyn, his fourth wife. His life was a succession of deeply unhappy marriages and it seemed that he sought refuge in the endless cigarettes he smoked, as well as his regular nightly glass of whiskey. My sensitivity to his ongoing personal problems meant that I didn't ever think to ask him why he had left us. I knew that he loved me and this acted like an anaesthetic balm, erasing the painful memories.

I was eventually accepted into medical school at St. Thomas's Hospital. This was a prestigious setting to begin my medical training. The hospital was located opposite the houses of parliament and has a rich history. It was, and continues to be, one of the top hospitals in the country. My uncle who was also in the medical profession and who had a distinguished career, put in a word for me, and it was almost certainly because of this that I was offered this place. I then embarked on a six-year training.

*

Having cut myself adrift from my family, friends and support networks at home in Perth, I struggled through these years, the biggest challenge being loneliness, and a deep feeling of alienation. I didn't feel 'English' and I felt I had little in common with my family who seemed to live in a cocoon of privilege, protected by the wealth they had inherited, but who for the most part had little social awareness, or so it seemed to me.

I became drawn into left-wing politics, which appealed to my keen awareness of social injustice and found common ground with different oppressed groups. I was influenced by the women's movement which was flourishing at this time, and I tried to catch the tail end of the sixties, wearing an Afghan coat, platform heels and flares, followed by a phase of wearing Indian dresses.

I was fortunate that I had resources to buy a flat, so I eventually established a new home. At the hospital I struck up a lasting friendship with one of the senior nurses, Pam, whom I invited to move into my flat with her partner Dave. Their warmth, good humour and kindness helped enormously through these years. Through this time in Cornwall Gardens I made new friends and we had a regular flow of visitors, often from other countries, which allowed me to begin feeling part of a community of like-minded others. The sense of home and comradeship, especially with others who I met through the many left wing political groups that were active at that time, helped to support me through my years of medical training at St Thomas's.

It was through my father that I had my first opportunity to visit a prison. Prisons had played no part in my life before this, I wasn't even interested in reading about them. My father though, was influenced early on by his own father who was a church vicar. He memorably said that the most important part of his work was not taking services, but helping people in need. In his own life my father developed a strong commitment to supporting unpopular causes. He corresponded regularly with a number of prisoners.

Through his role as film censor he knew many people from different backgrounds, as well as those involved in public life. One of these, an old school friend, was Lord Longford. It was through him that he was introduced to Myra Hindley, who with her partner Ian Brady was convicted of the notorious and appalling Moors murders in 1966.

Dad was one of a small number of respected individuals who were approached to support efforts being made to enable Myra to have access to education in prison, with a view to her eventually being able to apply for parole and release. He never believed that this goal would be achieved, as he felt no Home Secretary would have the courage to stand up to hostile public opinion. This belief didn't detract from his support for Myra, and others like her on life sentences, to be offered humane conditions of confinement and to be able to develop their positive talents and abilities. He thought that it might help Myra to be visited by a woman closer to her in age, and this was how I became involved.

I had been out of the country when Myra Hindley and Ian Brady were arrested and charged with these shocking crimes. I hadn't been exposed to the lurid and sensational publicity surrounding this dreadful case. As I felt very much in sympathy with my father's humane outlook on life, I agreed to his suggestion that I visit her.

This resulted in me making the first of many visits to see Myra while she was in Holloway Prison.

The woman who I met had dark hair and fine features. She looked nothing like the 'bleached blonde monster' image of her so often displayed in the popular press. She spoke quietly and, like my father, smoked heavily. I don't know what I expected, but I met someone who it was not difficult to strike up a rapport with – she told me about her daily life in prison and was well informed about a number of current issues. We didn't for a long time discuss her past. My role was initially quite straightforward and that was to befriend her and help her to maintain a healthy link with the outside world.

Through my involvement with Myra and my regular visits to Holloway, I met other ex-prisoners and I became involved and interested in some of the prison reform groups active at that time. All of this extended my social education and fed my reformist views. The early 1970s was a time of radicalism and challenging the system. These were the formative experiences which introduced me to the world of prisons and which paved the way for me feeling such a deep connection with Jimmy when I first met him.

*

I extended my own social horizons in another unconventional way, when after a relationship ended I moved out of my flat and into a squat. This world contrasted with the other part of my life spent attending lectures, tutorials and ward rounds in the conservative milieu of St Thomas's Hospital.

A bridge of sorts was built between these two very different worlds when I was invited to join some of my newly qualified medical friends who were in the process of setting up a radical community-based medical practice while living in a commune in south London.

It was a time of experimentation and of sex, drugs and rock

and roll. I probably owe it to my determination to complete my medical training and start my career that I survived this time relatively unscathed. This was the era of psychedelic drugs, which were seen to offer a doorway to escape the prison of the mind and unleash all the creativity lying dormant in those who led conventional lives.

My experiences of having my consciousness expanded through the use of marijuana and LSD opened new doors for me, taking me into the expansive, vivid, and extraordinary world of heightened sense perceptions. Through this I was introduced to an awareness that what we perceive of as 'normal' consciousness is in fact only a small portion of the spectrum which is potentially available to us.

These experiences in some ways represented an early stage of 'awakening'. I dipped a toe in the water but decided that the potential hazards didn't make this a wise path for me to explore any further.

*

Instead I decided to expand my horizons in healthier ways. I did this through travel and had some memorable experiences, one of the most enriching being a choice to do an elective – a student medical posting – at a small mission hospital in West Bengal in India. This opened the floodgates for me – my first experience of visiting the East was a true revelation, which exceeded in heights and intensity anything which I had previously encountered. I did not become one of the many who followed the hippy trail to the East or who dropped out of society to join an ashram, but I came very close to this.

*

While I was having these relatively pleasant experiences, Jimmy was undergoing his darkest days – spending long spells in solitary confinement following his participation in ongoing riots and prison protests. His time in the dreadful conditions which existed in such places as the Inverness cages, extended his perceptions in ways which he has written about.

His route to having his mind altered and gaining glimpses of other realities came in this much harsher and potentially more detrimental way when he and others were exposed to hostile, barbaric and extreme conditions of sensory deprivation with all comforts being removed. Had he not found such a core of strength within himself these prolonged experiences could have resulted in permanent insanity.

I see now that this was a time of early spiritual seeking. Through my reading about meditation and yoga, and my journeys to the East, I was getting a sense of something which existed beyond the rational mind and mundane appearances of life, which offered a deeper source of nourishment and meaning. This was also the time when I first heard about Findhorn.

I graduated from St Thomas's Hospital and, as I had expected, I didn't land any of the house officer jobs which are the most competitively sought after in the central London hospitals. I started, instead, a six-month medical job in Croydon Mayday Hospital. The name of this hospital has now been changed, which doesn't surprise me.

The stresses of this job made me willing to consider a very different prospect for my next appointment, which was a six-month surgical placement.

Although I didn't know it at the time, I was on the point of making another very significant choice in my life which ushered in a completely new phase. It started in an apparently ordinary way with me sitting in the medical library with a current copy of the BMJ, leafing through its pages looking at the job advertisements. The one which 'jumped out' at me was for an Ear, Nose and Throat surgical appointment in the Royal Northern Hospital in Inverness.

I couldn't imagine that there would be many emergency nose

bleeds in the middle of the night and the other factor which appealed to me, as I have already mentioned, was that Inverness was close to Findhorn. I spotted a potential opportunity to visit through being based relatively close by. This was not exactly a choice designed to advance me up the career ladder, but it was clear and definite for me – this was it, I applied, was accepted, and set about preparing to leave London.

*

I welcomed the prospect of change as I was feeling overwhelmed by the stresses of city life. The situation in the commune where I was living had deteriorated. A good friend had died after taking an overdose of barbiturates. Other friends had departed for India but had left a trail of hurt and chaos behind them. I was exhausted after my six months job in general medicine in Mayday Hospital. This had been full of emergencies, and too many sleepless nights with my bleep constantly going off. I was ready to open to something completely different.

As with my decision to leave Australia, I didn't spend much time thinking about what lay ahead, I simply knew that this was the next step I had to take. The mysterious invisible thread had taken hold of me again.

4. Barlinnie Special Unit – A Spark Is Kindled

As I approached the end of my six months probationary job at the Royal Northern Infirmary I had an important decision to make. Where was I going to head next? Now as a fully qualified doctor my future felt wide open. As I was reflecting on this question someone at the hospital told me about a radically different psychiatric hospital in the Scottish Borders called Dingleton. Hearing that this was run along therapeutic community lines my interest was sparked, so this was where I applied to go. As if fate was leading the way, this was to be the stepping stone which would lead to me meeting up again with Jimmy.

The choice to apply for a job at Dingleton Hospital introduced me to the world of therapeutic communities. The person who pioneered this work in Scotland was Dr Maxwell Jones. The intention of this approach was to create 'a group atmosphere' which would promote the recovery and rehabilitation of patients. Treatment was no longer confined to the therapeutic hour but became a continuous process operating throughout the waking life of the patient.

The philosophy was essentially that people respond with their maximum potential when given opportunities for involvement and responsibility. This contrasted with the traditional medical model where the patient is largely the passive recipient of treatment administered by the doctor who is assumed to have all the necessary expertise.

To accomplish this vision and goal, Maxwell Jones had to re-order the hospital society and flatten the traditional hierarchical pyramid of authority to promote more interaction between patients, nurses, and doctors. This approach had been used successfully with disturbed adolescents in the 1950s in the Henderson Hospital in London. Maxwell Jones became physician superintendent of Dingleton in 1962.

When he arrived he took immediate steps to establish a therapeutic community not only in the hospital itself, but in the surrounding catchment area. Maxwell Jones' philosophy was that everyone should participate in patient care – this involved frequent meetings that included the entire hospital staff – doctors, nurses, social workers, rehabilitation workers, secretaries and even hospital porters and cleaners.

It was a radical approach.

I applied and was accepted for a position on one of the community psychiatric teams starting in April 1978. Maxwell Jones had moved on and the hospital was no longer as trailblazing in its approach as it had been during his time there, but it promised an opportunity to experience this open and inclusive approach in psychiatry. In a letter to my mother at the time I reflected on the mysterious coincidences and series of fateful encounters that had resulted in me getting this job at Dingleton. I was clearly choosing 'the road less travelled,' a far from conventional career path.

With such a strong bent in this direction it wasn't surprising that I was drawn to work in a hospital that aspired to challenge the traditional doctor/ patient dynamic and explore a more innovative approach. After arriving at Dingleton, which was situated in the rolling green hills of the Borders about an hour south of Edinburgh, I shared my initial impressions in another letter to my Mother:

> 'In hospital terms this is quite an exceptional place. The whole concept of therapeutic community involves running things on

an egalitarian basis – i.e. as you may have noticed on your brief visit, no one wears uniforms, and staff and patients alike are on first name terms. The general atmosphere is relaxed and friendly and the level of morale is exceptionally high.'

There were vestiges of the old ways apparent – student nurses tended to defer to their superiors, the general hospital staff tended to defer to the doctors and a paternalistic attitude was commonly adopted towards the patients – however, overall there was a genuine attempt to run the hospital in accordance with the ideal of universal contribution and participation.

I joined as a member of one of the community psychiatric teams. Our work involved visiting people in their own homes to make assessments. We worked in pairs, which was a valuable and supportive way to learn. We had opportunities for informal discussion and sharing of views as relationships deepened within the team. The aim was not only to relieve symptoms but also to help patients and their families deal with crises in ways which promoted emotional growth.

The emphasis as far as possible was to keep people out of hospital by identifying the underlying causes of the crisis, as well as potential sources of support. It was possible to get a much more comprehensive understanding of someone's living situation through seeing them at home, rather than in the clinical environment of a hospital. I still feel that this is an excellent model for community psychiatric care. Dingleton's rates of hospital admission as a consequence of this excellent crisis based service were considerably lower than the national average.

*

I became interested in the whole Therapeutic Community Movement, which was in its heyday at that time, and I attended a conference that helped me to deepen my understanding of this approach. Just before this I was able to make my second visit to the Barlinnie Special Unit. Some of the staff from Dingleton were involved in visiting the Special Unit because it was also run along therapeutic community lines and was considered to be an experiment of great interest.

The Working Party which was originally responsible for proposing this new unit had been influenced by Maxwell Jones's concept of therapeutic community. The small number of long term prisoners who were demonstrably not responding to the increasingly repressive sanctions – which included beatings by squads of baton armed prison officers, and solitary incarceration, often naked, and for protracted lengths of time, were to become the guinea pigs for a radically different approach.

The unit which would accommodate up to ten prisoners was intended to have an explicitly psychiatric orientation, making use of group counselling, drug therapy and creating a therapist/patient relationship between staff and prisoners. Such was the crisis of violence in Scottish prisons that this proposal had the full personal backing of the Secretary of State for Scotland, and the controller of Scottish Prisons at that time.

From the start there was some uncertainty among all those in charge as to what the daily routine should involve. The Special Unit opened in February 1973 in the former women's wing of HMP Barlinnie. The new unit had ten cells, a kitchen, the governor's office, an officers' meeting room, a surgery, the community meeting room and several rooms which were subsequently used as workshops for the arts. The room designated as the solitary confinement cell ended up being used as the sculpture studio. There was also an outside courtyard, where the sculpting of larger pieces was eventually to take place, a small garden, and a greenhouse.

The Unit, inevitably, began in an atmosphere of mistrust and suspicion; despite commitment to trying something new, prison staff and prisoners carried into the situation deeply conditioned attitudes they had acquired in the mainstream prison system. Some prison officers were also nurses. The prisoners to whom the informal, relaxed regime was at first understandably disorientating worried that the Unit was in actual fact merely a step towards transfer to the dreaded state mental hospital at Carstairs.

One particular prison officer, Ken Murray, a member of the Executive Committee of the Scottish Prison Officers Association (SPOA), who had been on the Working Party that proposed the Special Unit – took the lead in challenging the prisoners' perceptions. Jimmy was the first prisoner who responded in kind to the trust Ken Murray showed. The two built a bridge of friendship and slowly made the initially awkward and tense communication between the staff and prisoners possible.

The key that opened the door for the Special Unit's early success was this mere fact of prisoners and staff talking together. Regular community meetings were held in which the two groups learned to communicate honestly with each other, expressing frustration verbally rather than through the use of fists, showing vulnerability, and resolving conflicts through confronting unacceptable behaviour.

Although it started tentatively, with some awkward flashpoints along the way, a new climate emerged. The mutual suspicions and hostilities, all too prevalent in the mainstream, diminished.

The Unit was designed to be hospitable to visitors, and allowed extended visits from families and friends, without the barrier of the glass screen, which had divided them in mainstream prison settings. The arts became a very important aspect of life in the Special Unit. The regular flow of 'arts' visitors was central to the development of its strong creative ethos giving rise to arts festivals, poetry readings, dance performances and many other creative activities.

★

The fact that the arts flourished to such a degree in the Special Unit was unexpected, and little short of a miracle. In the early days the immediate problem of the Unit was that a small number of prisoners had a lot of time on their hands. The Special Unit inmates were completely segregated from the main prison and were therefore excluded from the usual prison work scheme. In an attempt to develop an interesting daily routine outside resources were brought in.

The inmates had all arrived at the Unit from long periods of solitary confinement, from outbursts of violent behaviour and from years of suspicion, hatred and mistrust. It was touch and go, and in all senses a daunting proposition, to introduce this small group of hardened inmates to the arts.

The arts had no place at that time in the prison culture and were regarded as 'cissy', or 'for toffs'. Joyce Laing, an artist and art therapist, who had experience of working with people in hospitals suffering from many different illnesses, was the person responsible for introducing the arts into the Special Unit.

The first five inmates, who included Jimmy, sat in an awkward semi-circle. She was introduced to them by the Governor and then left to it. The atmosphere was strained as she was left to chat about art – her early attempts to encourage them to take up painting, drawing or sculpting fell on stony ground. The breakthrough only came after she expressed her feelings of frustration and eventually just sat on the ground with a bag of sculpture clay modelling a head in relief with the prisoners watching.

One of the prisoners took up some of the clay in his hands and started working with it. When she rose to leave one of them looked up and asked, 'Going to leave some clay?' On the following visit a few pieces of sculpture, mostly heads, had been made.

Amongst them one piece completely captured her attention – a model of a roughly fashioned figure crouched behind a few rods of wire which surrounded it. It was titled *Solitary* and was one of Jimmy's first sculptures. Joyce later said of this piece: 'This I believe was the birth of the arts in the Special Unit.' It was a powerful expression of the experiences he had emerged from, and literally opened the floodgates for him.

From these beginnings of artistic creativity, the concern was to ease the way for others. A variety of art forms were embraced, the strength behind each step in developing creativity was the freedom of the daily routine, as well as the acceptance and encouragement by all the members of the community in each original creative talent as it emerged.

There were problems, challenges, and abuses of the liberal aspects of the Special Unit regime, with some inmates smuggling in alcohol and drugs. This led to negative publicity with the press calling the Unit the Nutcracker Suite and the Wendy House. There were negative attitudes on the other side of the wall in the main Barlinnie prison to deal with. One particular tragedy was the death from a barbiturate overdose of Larry Winters, an inmate in the Unit, which precipitated a serious crisis almost ending the experiment. It was a tribute to all involved, staff and inmates alike, that the Special Unit survived in the aftermath of this crisis.

In terms of the many challenges facing a therapeutic community located in the prison system there was clearly much to talk about. I am grateful to whomever it was who arranged for some of the staff at Dingleton Hospital to go as this was when I next had an opportunity to visit this extraordinary place. I dropped Jimmy a line to let him know that I would be with the party visiting and looked forward to seeing him again.

Many people are curious, understandably so, as to how my relationship with Jimmy began. One myth that seems to have prevailed around this is that we met through me being a psychiatrist working in prisons. This is certainly not true although this second encounter came about through my psychiatric job at Dingleton.

Along with colleagues I spent an intense and interesting day in heated discussion with the Unit staff and inmates, with Jimmy playing a prominent role. At the end of the meeting, as we were leaving, he suggested that I might like to come back and see him again. I visited the following day, this time on my own. What I can remember is that at a certain moment, when I stood up to leave, he stood behind me, folded his arms around me, and the rest, as they say, is history...

The spark was lit at this point. A passion in us both was unleashed which despite Jimmy's notoriety as a 'Hardman' and according to the popular press, 'Scotland's most violent man', swept me into the broad currents of love. The man I met was so far from the image portrayed by these labels that from the start I trusted him completely.

When our relationship became public knowledge I was perceived by many to be naïve, and I can look back on these events now and feel that certainly some of this was true. Sometimes naivety is a good thing though because I didn't let his reputation or background stop me from listening to and trusting my heart. The force and intensity of the love we both discovered for each other opened me to a whole new dimension of experience.

We continued getting to know each other in visits that happened when I drove up from the Borders and saw him in his cell in the Special Unit. We also wrote frequently to each other. Letters in which the flame of love sparked to and fro like live electricity. I was soon writing to tell my mother that I would be leaving Dingleton and moving to Glasgow at the end of September.

The reasons I gave for this included the fact that I wanted to enrol on a training programme in preparation for taking my membership exams. Dingleton was isolated and stood on its own in this respect – with no formal attachment to any other psychiatric hospital which meant that I wouldn't have been able to progress my training had I stayed on there.

Of course the real reason was that I wanted to move closer to the Special Unit so that I could continue visiting Jimmy. The bond between us had very quickly become as deep as an ocean.

5. Glasgow – No Mean City

Glasgow and Edinburgh are only an hour apart, connected by the M8 motorway, but like two competing sisters, their character and nature are completely different. Edinburgh is the more refined of the two – the city centre with its fine castle is its greatest treasure. Its citizens have a reputation for being respectable, it hosts the world famous Edinburgh Festival and Fringe each year which make it a mecca for tourists and for the performing arts.

The housing schemes are more peripheral and less omnipresent than in Glasgow. Glasgow is larger in size, with a reputation for wildness, acquired in the 1950s and 1960s. It is a city with strong socialist roots and a colourful working class history. Its people are fast-talking and friendly, generous and often have a quick sense of humour which is infectious. Both cities have a lot more than this to their character but at the time, when I first moved to Glasgow, I knew little more than this. A much more comprehensive and multifaceted picture was to unfold through all that lay ahead for me.

I moved into a hospital flat and started my new job at Gartnavel Royal. I liked the city and felt welcomed by people, appreciating their warmth and almost instantly feeling at home in this northern industrial city, which spans both sides of the River Clyde. The hospital though, in both appearance and approach, was a dramatic contrast to Dingleton – it was like a lurch back into the dark ages. It was formidable, a relic from the days of the Victorian asylum – menacing and imposing with ramparts and turrets. Even on a sunny day it looked starkly grey and cold.

My initial meeting at the start of my appointment took place in the medical superintendent's office. We met with a clinical tutor and one of the consultants. I was one of a group of six trainees. There was none of the cheerful informality of Dingleton. Here we were all introduced by our surnames. The welcome was brief and official. We were given guidelines for admissions procedure with particular emphasis being placed on identifying the boundaries of the catchment area. Shades of the prison house. The lines were drawn for us with it being made very clear that bureaucratic and institutional formalities took precedence over anything else. There was certainly no focus on communication with patients or how to ease the stress of an admission. I felt depressed and out of kilter with this traditionally-run institution from day one.

The next piece of bad news was when I learned that my first six months were to be spent working on the psycho-geriatric and long-term rehabilitation side. I could only speculate about why I was being sent to these 'back wards' first and was tempted to think that it might have been a way to put me somewhere where I would be least likely to cause trouble. Dingleton with its unorthodox and liberal culture was viewed as a kind of rebellious adolescent by the establishment side of psychiatry at that time. Here I was back in the fold and it seemed that I was about to have my wings as well as my mood clipped.

*

I moved out of my hospital flat into a bedsit as soon as I could. My working life was an ongoing challenge. I was assigned to Ward eight. The ceilings were high, the walls were painted in a dingy pastel colour, the floor was mostly lino, shabby and impregnated with multiple dousings of disinfectant. The smell of bleach was sometimes unbearably strong, almost as overpowering as the clouds of cigarette smoke which invariably filled the atmosphere with a dirty haze.

There was a feeling of chronic stasis about the ward, both in the lives of individual patients, as well as on the ward itself. It was like a ship with its propeller caught in the weeds, riding up and down on the passing waves but going nowhere.

I was in charge of fifty female patients, who used to sit wan and pale, slouched in their daytime chairs. With their voluminous files of notes they were in some ways like museum specimens. Collectively they were an indictment of the corrosive effects of long term chronic institutional care. I attended to immediate symptoms, and prescribed their medication, struggling to make sense of some of the drug regimes which, it seemed, could only contribute to a perpetual toxic overload in their frail systems. I tried to make summaries of their notes which spilled out of bulging folders.

It was a battle to keep my spirits up. I tried to give encouragement, and maintain a sense of humour. When all else failed it helped to be able to laugh at some of the eccentricities and imaginative phantasies of the patients – one long term patient dressed herself up each day, and sat with crimson lipstick and ornamental spectacles, fully believing that she was on an everlasting cruise.

I found it easier, and kinder, to indulge in her phantasy, admiring her capacity to create a reality which defied the stultifying boredom of the ward. I felt fortunate to be able to escape each day, wondering how anyone could survive the shabbiness, the cramped sleeping arrangements, the lack of comforts or privacy, the dreadful institutional food...it was so awful that any small attempt at change felt relatively pointless.

I felt sorry for the staff who did their best in these overwhelmingly stultifying conditions. I heard many negative feelings expressed about the ward: 'Nobody likes being here, its hell...it's a jail!'; the resentment and dislike were almost unanimous. Nonetheless, I noted that they all stayed.

It was not in fact a prison, the doors were not locked and the walls were imagined rather than real. This was the most fearful and threatening area for them to confront. The real reasons why they stayed had to do with shame, failure and a tremendous fear of the outside world. I found myself longing for an environment creatively designed to maximize their humanness and potential, rather than this forlorn and desolate stagnation where even the fittest would be lucky to survive. It felt as though I was getting introduced to all the worst aspects of what can happen in places designed to offer refuge and care, but overtaken by apathy, with staff and patients alike developing defensive mechanisms to deal with this.

I also found the trainee course for membership exams, for the most part, disappointing. The quality of a lot of the teaching was poor, the case presentations tended to be time consuming and tedious. I was struck by how much the emphasis seemed to be on a clinically nit picking process of arriving at a diagnosis, with an avoidance of what to me seemed the far more important question of how to treat the patient.

These were patients with fascinating social histories full of examples of trauma, bereavements, and other life stresses which had contributed to their eventual breakdown and hospital admission. The only recourse seemed to be to prescribe drugs, or in more severe cases administer ECT (electro convulsive therapy). The words therapy or healing, as far as my memory goes, were never mentioned. Across the board a defining separation was made – between 'us' and 'them'. It was this invisible divide, which society as a whole also extends to the prison system, which I was challenging through my ongoing relationship with Jimmy.

*

My visits at this point to the Special Unit were limited to twice a week, on Thursdays and Sundays. I felt very alone in between these times. When I was with Jimmy I felt embraced in all of who I was, lifted out of my depressed state of mind through his invariable optimism. The situation allowed us to 'meet' each other in a way I hadn't experienced previously – nothing was hidden.

'I don't feel that there's anyone apart from Jimmy who really knows 'ME'.'

Many people have commented that I must have 'helped' him a lot, but in these early stages of our relationship when we were getting to know each other, it often felt that it was the other way around. I was the one who was 'fragile' and lacked confidence. When I think back on my life I'm not surprised that with so many moves, and finding myself in such an altogether different environment to the one I knew previously, I was undergoing something of an identity crisis.

*

My new life in Glasgow then, apart from my time in the hospital, revolved around my relationship with Jimmy. This was wonderful, and at times all-consuming in its intensity, but it did pose a threat to my own separate sense of identity. What we shared, because of the circumstances that brought us together, involved far more contact with his friends and family than mine. With time, contacts with my family and friends in London became more distant. I was very much alone in this rain soaked northern city during those first few months.

Some of the people who I was introduced to through Jimmy though, were an immediate counterbalance to these kinds of feelings. I made regular visits to the home of his Aunt Peggy and her husband Alfie. They lived in a ground floor flat off a stair in the Gorbals. Their door was always open. Peggy with her weathered face and infectious smile was a solid and robust woman with a strictly no-nonsense approach to life. Alfie, a small impish looking man, with a fondness for a good drink, was always looking for ways to avoid Peggy's scrutinising gaze. Freddy, their youngest son, had tragically been run over by a bus in his late teens – he was left with a severe head injury, and walked with a stick and a limp.

Despite this he always had a joke to share. Peggy and Freddy had a stall in Paddy's market across the river. This was an extraordinary street market of Dickensian character selling an assortment of clothes, shoes, and household items of a quality no shop would ever consider, but the sellers would present them as if they were the greatest of bargains:

Shoes of different sizes, a vacuum cleaner without its motor and similar, hilarious unlikely options. In order to excel in this kind of market you had to be tough and have the gift of the gab to convince the potential buyer that they could find a use for the item. Peggy and Freddy were experts at this and crossed the river each day to pursue their trade.

Their lives were so different and far removed from anything I had experienced previously. They had little in material terms and had plenty of problems, but they had a great spiritual richness in their lives. Humour sustained them on a daily basis and this was never lacking. Despite our different circumstances in life there were never any barriers. I always felt completely welcome when I visited them. These people were to me 'the salt of the earth'.

I drove down to Castlemilk, a district which is situated in the south of Glasgow, and met with Jimmy's youngest brother Harry, his wife Margaret, and their twins Chris and Greg. With their short brown hair, freckled noses and cute smiling faces these two were identical. It was difficult to tell them apart. Despite the bleakness of the housing scheme in which they lived, the flat was immaculate.

At that time Harry and Margaret were a handsome couple, both slim, with dark hair and a well turned out appearance. As with Peggy and Alfie they warmly welcomed me into the family. Despite the support I received from all the close members of Jimmy's family and others through this time, it was a cultural difference of immense proportions and I often found myself struggling to bridge the contrasts.

Jimmy was a wonderful support but I often felt like an alien in these very different surroundings. I knew that I could never be part of life here in the same sense as those who had spent all of their lives in Glasgow. I had visited the more cosmopolitan Edinburgh and had been south to visit my friend Heidi in London. These experiences made me even more aware of how much it was taking to adapt to the atmosphere and culture of this earthy northern city.

I was aware that it would take time settling in and putting down more permanent roots. I really couldn't see how it would all work out, and I couldn't see life coming together in any particularly easy or natural way until Jimmy was released.

I wrote to my mother:

> 'Because of who and what Jimmy is, I am set apart from other people. I'm sure they don't know quite what to make of it...well, they seldom mention it...so sometimes I do feel very much on my own.'

I had taken my time before telling her about my relationship with Jimmy. When I finally did this she was warm in her response and very committed in her support. Her unexpected enthusiasm helped to keep my spirits up. She deserved a lot more appreciation for this than I ever gave her. I can only attribute it to her innately rebellious spirit and anti-establishment attitudes that she embraced our relationship with such trust from the beginning. Her support helped through this early time when I was often haunted by inner demons and felt very alone.

*

Jimmy could always lift my spirits in an instant. Through his time in prison he had developed an extraordinary strength and resilience, which helped him to survive his confined situation. He used his writing and his sculpture to express himself and to channel his feelings. Every minute of his day he kept himself occupied. He was also in frequent contact with many creative and talented individuals who, like me, had been in touch after reading his book.

It was an unprecedented achievement to manage to write this articulate and compelling account of his early life and prison experiences, let alone managing to get it published while he was still serving his sentence. It is a testament to the commitment and strength of support that he received from his publisher, Stefanie Wolfe Murray, that he was able to do this at all. His unique talent as a sculptor, which he had discovered in the Unit, had led to an ongoing friendship with Richard Demarco, who was one of the founders of the Edinburgh Festival.

As a well-known Edinburgh gallery owner and radical influence in the Arts world, he was able to arrange for groups of artists to visit the Special Unit and for exhibitions of Jimmy's work. It was exciting for me to meet some of these people and to be introduced to the extraordinary phenomenon that the Special Unit was in those days.

At a more personal level, Jimmy was usually fresh and strong, and our times together were deeply special for us both. We were very much in love. The circumstances though were challenging – as they led to intense bursts of closeness following which we were torn apart. Jimmy was always full of optimism about all the things he saw us doing in the future together.

Every moment was precious and we knew that this experience would prepare us for whatever was to come. He said something that touched me one day when we were talking: 'Adore the ordinary. Appreciate the insignificant' This said much about his intense feel for life – he was opening my eyes to a deeper and more vibrant experience of the world.

In this he was different from others I met. One day coming down the steps outside the front gate of the prison I commented on a spectacular and amazing sunset. I was with Margaret, who had been visiting a relative who had ended up in prison at that time. She carried on talking – it seemed that she just didn't 'see' what I was seeing. I saw how people numb themselves and literally close down their senses in order to survive the stresses of life.

I always felt fortunate not to have to do this, but I never forgot that my situation was privileged in so many ways – I didn't have to cope with worries about the bills, the 'weans', the stigma, and the numerous pressures that Margaret was facing, and which the majority of prisoners' families usually have to weather.

*

Some aspects of this world that I was being introduced to were like being taken into the underbelly of the city. I was treated to descriptions of people throwing themselves out of windows in a block of high flats in the Gorbals. Others had cracked up and had flung pots of paint or even all their furniture out through the air onto the pavements below. I also heard a tragic story of a young mother who ended her life by taking an overdose with her two children lying beside her.

It gave me some insight into the horrific social consequences of tearing down the fabric of the old tenements in areas like this and putting those displaced into high multi-story blocks. Architecture, when it takes no account of people's social needs, has a lot to answer for.

I was told that the violence was less than it used to be in the days of the street-fighting gangs. I heard descriptions from Margaret about some of the random violence to which people she knew had been exposed. This was quite blood curdling stuff. It could have fed my fears but I felt fortunate, as a consequence of my background and work, to be well removed from this world.

Of course I thought long and hard about the crime of which Jimmy had been convicted, as I have a deep abhorrence of violence. I had not had to survive the hardship of this urban jungle though and from this perspective I felt in no place to judge.

Jimmy always maintained that he hadn't killed Babs Rooney, but admitted that he had slashed him. He was less forthcoming than he might have been in his book about the circumstances resulting in this man's death because, as he has revealed in the afterword of the recently re-published edition of *A Sense of Freedom*, he did not want to be a grass. His adherence to this 'code of honour' prevented him from naming his co-accused, William Wilson, as being responsible for this murder.

Jimmy therefore ended up serving a life sentence with a recommended minimum of fifteen years for a crime he had been wrongfully convicted of. This has been a heavy cross for him to bear, but he freely admitted that he had brought this situation on himself and had been living a life where slashings and stabbings were a regular occurrence.

Recently when I re-read *A Sense of Freedom* I felt deeply uncomfortable about the many people Jimmy did injure during his street fighting years. Of course I should have thought about all of this a lot more before deciding to marry him, but love has a way of blotting out these less than comfortable truths.

*

Jimmy lost his appeal and served his sentence, refusing to take the, 'I've been wrongfully convicted' stance. His searing anger, which erupted in response to his many head on clashes with the authorities in his early prison years, must have been driven at least in part by a feeling of injustice - as well as his deep frustration with the dead-end choices he had made which put him where he was.

Through serving this long sentence, he ended up in circumstances which miraculously transformed his life. He was not alone in this – other inmates of the Special Unit, although small in number, also benefitted from the opportunities provided by the very liberal regime. The arts flourished in this environment, creating an opportunity for self-expression which had been long suppressed or denied.

A renewed sense of hope arose with an experiment which showed that genuine rehabilitation is possible with a different approach – a message which is as relevant today with the present crisis in prisons as it was back then at the end of the 1970s.

6. *Breaking the News – Getting Married*

My life continued with the ongoing routine of my hospital duties interspersed with visits to the Special Unit to see Jimmy. I was able to see him during the week in the evenings between seven and nine, and mornings or afternoons at the weekend. There was no restriction on how often I could visit so I went frequently.

The visiting conditions were particularly generous compared to the mainstream prison system in which visits are far more restricted and usually take place in noisy, smoke filled visiting rooms with no opportunities for privacy. This is a sensitive and controversial area, but as human relationships are often the key to successful rehabilitation, it seems more enlightened to take a progressive approach which encourages and supports, as far as possible, conditions which allow contact between prisoners and their loved ones to be restored.

This happened in the Special Unit to a degree unprecedented in Scottish penal history. Cell doors were not to be locked when visiting, but that was the only restriction. This allowed a level of intimacy greater than many couples experience, as it was free of all outer distractions. In addition to this Jimmy was able to get permission to be taken outside the prison for outings, called Special Escorted Leaves (SELs). These also relieved the pressure of his confinement considerably and gave him a much longed for opportunity to taste life out-with the prison walls.

Memories of this time at the end of the 1970s have been brought back to life by looking at some of the photographs that capture moments along the way as our courtship and love were progressing. In one of these pictures the two of us are walking hand in hand, down one of Glasgow's tree lined West End streets. The sun is shining and we are smiling happily with our heads turned towards each other. We are moving towards the camera with our bodies and hearts in synchrony with each other. We are together, but there is also space between us. This picture captures our ease together and our joy at this fleeting taste of freedom beyond the prison walls early on in our relationship.

In the other photo, Jimmy is standing in the courtyard of the Special Unit. His right hand is on the head of a figure he is sculpting. He is holding a chisel. In his left hand, resting on his thigh, he is holding a hammer. His foot rests on a piece of stone slightly above the ground. He is wearing a black T-shirt and dungarees. He is smiling in this picture too. He looks confident and relaxed. No trace of the despair and darkness that he has had to come through to reach this point in his life.

Jimmy is surrounded by the raw materials of his passion and work, blocks of stone, some of which are in the process of being transformed – just as he has been transformed by this space and place. The whitewashed walls and barred windows of the Special Unit block of cells are to his left. The green door leading to the main body of the prison is behind him. There is a high wall separating the two.

These two images capture the inside/outside dynamic of our relationship in those early days. The wall separated us through this time, but we were able to find ways to incubate our relationship within the close confines of his cell in the Special Unit.

*

As time passed we focused more and more on our future plans together. The immoveable obstacle was Jimmy's continuing confinement. At this time he had no definite release date. His fifteen-year sentence was due to end in 1982, but there were many who felt that he should serve extra time on top of this because of his participation in riots leaving some prison officers with serious injuries. In the circumstances the last thing we should have been thinking about was getting married, but love has a way of sweeping all other realities aside. I did know that it was a momentous decision that we were both taking.

The prospect of getting married hadn't featured at all in my life up until that time. I had never been able to picture myself as a traditional bride, dressed in a cascade of white, walking up the aisle. I could also never have imagined myself contemplating marriage in this kind of situation. God certainly moves in mysterious ways.

That this man and this place were to play such a central part in my life was so far outside of what I might have planned or envisioned for myself that it defies any logical analysis. Plenty of people tried to put interpretations onto my actions and, in a fairly obvious sense, I gave those who like to indulge in this something of a field day. For me there is only one way to describe this kind of meeting and marriage, and that is destiny – the hand of fate was clearly upon us.

As our meeting and marriage was equally inconceivable for someone of Jimmy's circumstances and background the same has to be true for him. Our wedding came together in a most unlikely way, and in a most unlikely setting. The only explanation I have is that it was divinely orchestrated and conceived – the forces and conditions transcended the odds of this physical world touching on that other mysterious dimension of life I choose to call the soul. To me it was, and remains, a marriage made in heaven.

I should add for the sake of clarity that Jimmy, at the time when I met him, already had two children with a woman he had been involved with before receiving his life sentence. This relationship took place in the all too short intervals between his times in prison.

His children James and Patricia had been taken occasionally to visit him in the early days of the Special Unit, although I didn't have the opportunity to meet them until after his release.

He had dedicated his book *A Sense of Freedom* to them and felt an enormous sense of regret that he hadn't been able to play any real part in their lives. This former relationship, as it never resulted in marriage, didn't present any obstacle to him taking this step with me.

As 1979 drew to a close we put in an application to the prison authorities to get married, and on December 20, just before Christmas that year, we had news that permission had been granted. It seemed that both the staff in the Special Unit as well as the official establishment were supporting our decision. Jimmy was even informed that as from the New Year he would be granted parole leave of one day out each week.

We were delighted and we celebrated. We had a strong sense that we were 'meant' to be together, there was no doubt or fear in either of us, and we hoped that everything would progress well from this moment on. Some close friends did try to warn us that we were 'taking on a hell of a lot,' marrying in Jimmy's present circumstances, and were concerned that he was being over optimistic in anticipating his release, but we were both resolute and in love – and love conquers all, doesn't it?

*

The date of our wedding was significant. It was largely Jimmy's choice; he wanted to get married in the first month of the new decade. Allowing time to apply for and place our wedding notices, we chose January 31, 1980, which was the only way we could squeeze our special day into this time frame.

With the benefit of hindsight, the timing was absurd for a wedding, given that January is one of the coldest and darkest months in Scotland, but it is a measure of how far this kind of awareness was from our thoughts that we never considered this. Neither did we consider for long the possibility of the press getting hold of our news, which was a much more serious oversight.

We decided to apply to get married at Balfron. This is a very small village a short distance from Loch Lomond. It was an area we had been able to visit on one of Jimmy's parole days out and it held special memories for us. We hoped that choosing to get married in this small out of the way place would ensure a quiet wedding. No chance!

> **1.1.80** From my diary: 'New Year's day (always a special time for me) dawned magnificently with the sun rising...a huge glowing red sphere making its silent and triumphant ascent into the clear blue frosty skies...a blaze of pink and gold light strikes the city which is still empty and silent, sleeping off the night before.'

This felt like a good omen for the start of this new decade and the promise it held. Jimmy welcomed me when I visited him in his cell with a special ceremony he had created with photos of us laid out, carnations, and fruit. I know that he was very much 'with me' as the bells rang...as I was 'with him' from my hospital room. I really appreciated his way of celebrating a special occasion. This created a sacred dimension, transforming the ordinary fabric of life into something potent with meaning.

I learned a lot from him and wrote, 'He is a very spiritual person.' That afternoon we filled in our marriage forms dating them with great pleasure, 1.1.80.

The following day we had lunch in Jimmy's cell in the Special Unit with Father Anthony Ross, the man who was going to perform the sacred part of our marriage. Father Anthony was a well-known and respected Dominican priest who for years had worked with the homeless and people on the margins of society.

He had contributed in the early days to the training programme for the staff of the Special Unit and had become a friend of Jimmy's through his regular visits.

With his open face, kindly, knowing eyes and flowing white hair he was a unique and exceptional man. He spoke with a soft Highland accent. He had dedicated his life to the church and to supporting those who were considered outcasts of society – the homeless, drug addicts, alcoholics, and ex-prisoners. He spoke to us about his work in different communities and said 'sometimes you need to put up with somebody stealing from you for a while before they grow through this phase.' Anthony was capable of a depth of compassion that few could equal.

*

In January the phone in my flat rang late one night and I found myself speaking to Phil Davies from the Sunday Mirror. I listened silently as he did all the talking. They had all the facts, when and where we were getting married, and even that Father Anthony Ross was going to conduct a special private ceremony at the flat afterwards. I was devastated. It came as a terrible shock and blow that our carefully made plans had somehow been leaked.

This was in the pre-phone hacking days, so we attributed this later to a leak coming from a close friend or even someone in the Prisons Department itself. The press had other confidential information as well and said that they had had it for some time – this included, worryingly, my phone number and address.

In the morning the press appeared at my door. Jimmy was appalled when I broke the news to him. He turned pale, stiffened and gulped, expressing a combination of frustration and fury. The disturbing implications of this unwelcome attention from the press were starting to dawn on me.

At this point I was starting to feel vulnerable; what had been a closely guarded secret, kept private and hidden between us, was now being exposed to others. Little did I know just how widely our 'secret' was to be shared. The implication of the press being hot on our trail was that we could no longer share moments like this. We struggled with what to do. Should we call the wedding off? Should we set a different date?

All options felt futile as the word was out now. Malky another prison officer we were close to, came in looking solemn, shaking his head. After considering the options, we decided to stick with our original date, but to change our plans. Jimmy's day out would be cancelled. We applied for permission for him to simply get leave to go with me to the registry office – after that we would have to come straight back to the prison. We would ask Anthony to come there instead. One decision that we were both very clear about was that neither of us could bear to cancel our wedding.

Fortunately Mum and Dad, who were both supporting us, were very understanding. Dad told me that the *News of the World* newspaper was running a story that I was pregnant. The press was having ball, but for the most part I managed to field their probing questions. Dad, who had had plenty of his own experience with the press, put a lot of this in perspective when he told me to remember that today's newspaper is tomorrow wrapping up the fish and chips. I was grateful for his experience and seasoned sense of humour.

I went across to the Gorbals to warn Peggy, Alfie, and Freddy that the news about Jimmy and I getting married would be splashed all over the press in the morning. When I first told them that we were planning to get married they had been absolutely delighted. When I added that Jimmy was getting a day out every week from now on their faces lit up.

'He couldn't get out soon enough for us' they said. Even with the threat of the press furore they were fantastic: 'Oh that doesn't matter, Hen'. Alfie, swaying under the influence, tells me how much he loves me. Freddy too. Peggy makes me a sandwich.

Freddy asks me with a grin if I'm pregnant and Peggy tells him to shut up! I love their open hearts and fireside...this is the warmest place I know right now in Glasgow.

I have deep love for these people with their generous hearts – they always welcomed me as one of the family and were unfailing in their good humour and support, never commenting on the differences between my life and theirs.

*

The following morning I got up early to go for a run and get the papers. The press again showed up outside my door asking if our plans are still on for Friday. I hesitated, not knowing how to reply, then said 'no comment'. Gordon Ayres from the *Daily Record* started to ask questions about the flat. Again I refused to comment. There was a moment of farce when I climbed into my car, planning for a quick getaway, but when I turned the key, the engine didn't start as my battery was flat.

I had the pleasure of inviting these annoyingly persistent hacks, and flushed looking photographer, to push me down the road. I was offered all sorts of inducements to give special access to our story. The only deal I would have been interested in was a promise of silence – but this clearly wasn't on offer.

The press pursued me to the hospital. The women on the switchboard were wonderful. They congratulated me and said that I was doing a very fine thing and showing a lot of courage. Otherwise some of the staff on the wards gave warm smiles and looks which showed their support – others assumed blank expressions. Only one, thank goodness, was overtly hostile.

Some of the nurses congratulated me, while others remained pan-faced, deliberately discussing other topics. Neither of my consultants said a word. Heading home I passed my neighbour from across the street and she hastily looked the other way. I noticed a chalk cross on the wall outside 139 Wilton Street – this was an ominous sign, which provoked a twinge of fear in me.

The following day another consultant, looking sheepish, made a comment about my name being in all the papers and went on to hint that this was obviously going to make it very difficult for me to pursue a career in psychiatry in Glasgow. I was very uncertain of my future plans at this point and told him this. Meanwhile many of the patients came up to congratulate me, as did the cleaners - who said that all the press do is talk a load of rubbish and they should mind their own business. The fact that they read these papers every day is beside the point – I appreciated them showing solidarity.

The pressure was intense on both me, and Jimmy. I collapsed in his arms and he held me, but it had been hard for him as well. His body was tense and his face strained. Fortunately there was a funny story, which gave us a bit of light relief when it was much needed. Jimmy's oldest brother, Tommy, told this to me the night before. He had overheard a conversation between two women on the bus he was on:

One said to the other: 'What do you think of James Boyle getting married then?'

Replies the other: 'Oh he's a right nut case, so he is...and so is she.'

The first one replies: 'So they are hen...what a carry on for goodness sake...etc...etc...'

At this point Tommy turned round and told them that I'm a fine girl, and Jimmy is one hundred percent as well, and that as a matter of fact, he is his brother. This apparently left them gaping.

All of Glasgow seemingly had their eyes on our wedding – the likes of it had never been seen before. Much as we had no wish to share this private occasion with so many, it was a question of keeping our faith in each other and making the best of it.

None of the outer furore detracted from what we were both holding in our hearts. This letter which Jimmy wrote to my mother and which, unknown to me, she kept expresses his gratitude as we reached the threshold of our special day.

Special Unit 24.1.80

Dear Joan,

Just to tell you that Sarah and I have been out together in the last few days. As you can imagine its been wonderful.

Yesterday I had lunch with her and then went to do some shopping on my own for next week, which was good as I was able to get some nice things for Sarah.

Joan, next week is almost upon us and I feel that I want to say something to you about it. As Sarah's Mum I want you to know that I will always try to be sensitive to her needs. I love her very deeply and want John and you to know that I'm very much aware of the importance of this step that Sarah and I are taking. She is a very tender person with exceptional qualities, some of which are attributes of yourself.

Both of us are aware of the commitment we are taking on, particularly at this time. We are very realistic in this. Still it is important for me to write to John and you, in order to express my appreciation for having brought someone such as Sarah into this world, therefore to my life. It would be all too simple to take this for granted. We'll call you on the day but you'll be with us in spirit throughout.

With love, Jimmy

PART TWO

TWO WORLDS MERGING

7. Married – with the World's Press Looking On

Our wedding, predictably, because it was such an unusual and controversial one, attracted a great deal of attention from the press. In contrast to the outer furore it was also a deeply personal experience. I found a typewritten description of it on the faded pages of an early journal, which had been stored and forgotten about in a box of folders.

Discovering this was the catalyst that reawakened my memories of this special day. I read them and finally found the strength to write about this time. Like a flame kindled back to life, as I relived the day my heart and soul were once again filled with warmth and deep love.

I felt a lot of tension and excitement in the build up to our wedding and woke very early that morning. I was full of memories and reflections about our relationship and everything that had brought us to the point of getting married. As it must be for others on the threshold of saying their wedding vows, it was a lot to take in. This was without taking account of our exceptional circumstances and simply not knowing what lay ahead. My thoughts were interrupted by a loud knocking on the door. It was 7.15 am…bastards!

I felt a rush of fear and nerves, as if I hadn't been feeling strung up enough before this. It was difficult to keep calm, and get ready, because my hands were sweaty and trembling. When Heidi, (one of my closest friends, who had come up from London to be one of our witnesses) and I went downstairs, the press were waiting in their hordes outside on the street. They obviously knew that this was the day. We didn't stop for comments but all the cameras were flashing and clicking frantically. One reporter asked if I was off to the prison to get married or going off to work?

What a question, did I look like I was dressed for work? (I can smile now as I see how completely unlike a traditional wedding set up this was. I was wearing an all in one aubergine coloured jump suit and over this I wore a brown coloured fashionably shaggy coat which I had acquired from Heidi – not exactly the white wedding image for sure. I was also about to drive myself to collect my husband-to-be from the prison in my own much loved Volkswagen Beetle.)

We drove down the street tailed by at least a dozen cars. We laughed. It was funny, my small, well-worn VW beetle being the focus of all this extraordinary attention. As we went through a set of traffic lights on the orange I breathed a sigh of relief, thinking that we'd managed to leave them all behind. But no, they all crashed through, ignoring the red. It was crazy…just crazy...

We drove to George Square to pick up Margaret who was to be another witness. When we stopped the press surrounded the car. I firmly shut the door on a female journalist who I had taken to calling 'the diamond queen'. Earlier she'd said: 'I warned you it would be like this... you should have taken our advice and let us handle it. Is there anything we can do now to help? We'd like to make things easier for you, all this carry on must be awful.' But she was one of the worst herself.

*

We drove on up to the prison, still with our incredible escort, with the three of us laughing, enjoying this bizarre experience. The road up to Barlinnie was cleared especially for us. The big electric doors opened and we were swallowed into the bowels of the prison. Waiting for us were Malky, Wattie (two of the prison officers who I knew well by that time) the Governor, and Jimmy. I was happy and relieved to see him. He looked so fresh, vibrantly alive, and seeing him I felt overwhelmed by my love for him. This was the man who was about to become my husband.

Heidi took the wheel and drove us out to Balfron, a small village just north of Glasgow. It was a truly extraordinary wedding procession. We had no idea even at that time how much press attention our wedding would end up attracting, with news of it spreading around the world. The weather was stormy at first, then it started snowing. This was a surprise but it gave the hills a white covering which made them look even more beautiful and spectacular. I was sitting in the back seat holding both of Jimmy's hands, with Margaret on the other side of me. Heidi and Malky were in the front. I felt his warmth and strength flowing into me. We looked at each other. It was our day.

When we got to Balfron there were again literally hordes of press waiting for us with cameras clicking as they surrounded the car. We had to push our way through. There were moments when I found it hard to stay calm, when it all started to feel too much. I lowered my eyes to disconnect from the fracas all around us. Inside we were greeted by a smiling female registrar, which helped me to relax. This was unexpected but I was happy that we were to be married by a woman. It was suddenly quiet.

We were taken into a plain ordinary room where four chairs had been set in front of a desk. We sat down and took the rings out. We both felt nervous. This was the moment. I can't remember too many details of the ceremony itself except that we were invited to stand and make our pledges to each other – the promises that would bind us together as man and wife.

Do you take this man to be your lawful wedded husband? Do you take this woman to care for in sickness and in health until death do us part?

The ceremony was prescribed and traditional. It was a sacred and profound moment. Of course we both said yes. It felt full of meaning to do this. Our voices sounded strong and when the moment came we were steady, sure, and focused.

*

With the benefit of hindsight of course we eventually broke these vows, but neither of us were able to see into the future or know that our paths would one day separate. On that day it truly felt as though we were bound together forever. Then came the moment when we were to put the rings on each other's fingers. There was an awkward pause as it was very difficult to get mine on. Once on it fitted perfectly. Then… we were married.

We jointly signed our marriage certificate. We were man and wife, for each other, our families and friends, and for the world. Mr and Mrs Boyle. The journalists and photographers with their cameras were waiting patiently outside in the cold, some jumping up, trying to peer into the windows. We sat for a while, hugging, kissing each other and taking our own photos. I felt very grateful to Heidi and Margaret for their supportive presence. We couldn't have made a better choice with our two witnesses. Malky, the third, was present more as a friend than a prison officer. He and Jimmy had been through many testing experiences in the Special Unit together.

As we stepped outside I had Jimmy's hand in mine. It was hard to know where to look and how to face the gathered press who were like uninvited guests. There was a barrage of cameras with everyone asking for comments. Jimmy's first words were, 'It's amazing.' I said: 'Its overwhelming' which it was. We got into the car as quickly as possible to escape the frenzied mob. Heidi had trouble getting into reverse, but we got away and as with the earlier drive out of Glasgow, we were tailed by a continuing escort of all the press cars.

With so much going on it was hard to take everything in. I knew that I loved Jimmy fiercely and intensely, but with the love came pain. I knew that the hardest part of the day for us both would be not being able to spend the night together.

Back at the prison the electric doors once again swung open and swallowed us up. We got out and walked back to the Unit, the first time I'd walked back alongside Jimmy. There was a sudden sense of quietness and peace as we returned to his cell. After the noise and confusion outside it was a pleasant relief to be free of the press for a while at least.

Jimmy had arranged flowers on the table in his cell. We lit candles and opened a bottle of champagne (allowed in as a special concession for our wedding day.) We exchanged our presents and toasted our future happiness and the positive success of our marriage.

The celebratory feel of this moment was suddenly interrupted when Jimmy and I were called down to the Governor's office. The prison staff were worried about the hordes of press who were refusing to leave. They wanted me to go out early to face them, which had the effect of making me feel like a lamb being thrown to the wolves. I was beginning to buckle and fold. It was all too much.

In the moment of crisis I managed to find my strength and my voice. I insisted that someone from the prison went down to negotiate some form of press conference. They agreed and Malky went off to do it.

As he did this, my strength failed me. I was wracked with sobs. I couldn't get a grip at all. I knew that Jimmy was feeling the same. He was going through torment as well.

Then Anthony arrived. I had to go and wash my face, to calm myself. Anthony was wonderful. The three of us sat in a triangle with Jimmy in the middle, Anthony and I on either side. He read the well-known passage on love from the bible (Corinthians 13: 4-13).

'Love is patient, love is kind... It always protects, always trusts, always hopes, always perseveres.'

I still find these words very beautiful. When Anthony finished this reading we sat in silence. His white robes, the candles, the reassurance of his presence and strength were all tangible in that moment, as he gave us both a blessing.

After it he held the two of us in a lasting embrace. 'Love knows no fear.' I felt it, deep and unmistakeable. We were *one*. There was only love in that moment, primal and everlasting. This was a sacred and intimate experience of union, shared between the three of us.

★

Afterwards we went downstairs to eat the lunch that Heidi and Margaret had prepared. Some of the other inmates appeared but their presence was tentative. It must have been a strange and probably disconcerting experience for them – after-all, weddings seldom, if ever, happen inside a prison. There was also the issue that attention was yet again centred around Jimmy. It was heartening that despite their possibly ambivalent feelings they wished us well.

There was little enough of the afternoon left as I had to go to the BBC to attend the press conference, which had been organised. Anthony accompanied me in the car. I appreciated having his support as I was mobbed again on arrival. I felt weak and wobbly after breaking down so completely in the morning.

A man called Ken, representing the BBC, escorted me very protectively to the room where it was to be held. When I entered the numbers present, all the cameras, and the glare of the lights overwhelmed me. It was momentarily terrifying. I sat down in the middle chair, while someone attached a mike onto my clothing. I was dressed in Jimmy's red tracksuit top, which felt reassuring. In this way I felt that he was with me at least.

Then the questions started. It was difficult to discuss in pubic the most intimate and deeply personal part of my life which had for so long been kept such a close secret. But my new identity as Mrs. Boyle gave me a new found strength. I tried to be human and vulnerable, as well as resolute in terms of the step we had just taken. Anthony, sitting beside me, was a tremendous support. Somehow I managed to see it through, keeping my composure.

Finally I arrived back at my flat in Wilton Street. Heidi and I sat down to watch the news. The interview with the press came across exceptionally well. I knew that Jimmy would be pleased. It had all gone better than we could have hoped for.

The evening when I visited the Special Unit was for us. I felt an incredible tiredness but also a sense of strength and relief. It was all over now and we'd made it through the day. What a triumph. When I arrived home Phil Davis called round to try to get me to accept his £10,000 offer for exclusive rights on the story of our relationship. This was my first experience of cheque book journalism and I found it a bizarre and disturbing end to an otherwise extraordinary day.

The following morning I woke still feeling overwhelmed by the momentous change in my life. There was a lot to come to terms with. Sleep was much needed. It was all still sinking in, but there was a wonderful childish pleasure in the novelty of being man and wife and in how much we enjoyed and appreciated each other.

Yes, there were many challenges, not least our enforced separation at a time when most couples take off for their honeymoon. Despite this we both felt very confident and sure about the decision we had made. Paradoxically had it not been for these unusual circumstances I would probably not have chosen to get married.

My reason for putting aside my 'women's lib' beliefs in the importance of women retaining their own name when they married, and deciding to take on the name Boyle, was that I wanted to hold my head up high and assert Jimmy's right to freedom and his future together with me. I hoped that our marriage would send a clear message to the prison authorities that he was ready for release, and had earned his right to freedom.

Initially there was an avalanche of greetings and congratulations, which I described as 'a massive burst of collective good wishes and support.' The cards and letters were addressed to Sarah Boyle, Dr S Boyle, Mrs J Boyle... every possible combination. I enjoyed the novelty of all of this. I was happy at this moment to exchange my former name and identity for this new one, as I found myself suddenly attracting an extraordinary amount of attention.

Jimmy and I, having come through so much, were 'just crazily, madly, insanely in love'... our feelings heightened by the circumstances. Also by our determination to make our marriage a success, as a way of proving that all those who opposed it, or who questioned it, were wrong.

8. Early Days of an Unusual Marriage

The headlines in the papers immediately after our wedding were on the whole positive: 'MR AND MRS... AT LAST THEY'RE MAN AND WIFE'... 'THIS IS GOING TO BE A SUCCESSFUL MARRIAGE.'

I was over the moon at the way our wedding was described in the press, as it seemed that our love did shine through. I felt a combination of elation and exhaustion. I decided to take the week off from hospital and called to tell Betty on the switchboard that I wanted to be called by my married name Dr Boyle. This was a last minute but important decision. It was a statement to Gartnavel and the staff and patients there: 'Yes, I am married to Jimmy Boyle. I am Dr Boyle now and you're going to have to get used to it.'

With the benefit of hindsight this was perhaps not the wisest choice given the circumstances, but I was in love at that point and wanted the whole world to know. This is what love does to us, we feel we can take on anything and anyone. The person who sadly experienced much more of the press harassment than me was Margaret. With her husband, Jimmy's youngest brother Harry, being in prison at the time, she was put under tremendous pressure to share the intimate details of our wedding.

To her credit she stayed silent on this. She said that the response of people around her in Castlemilk was very positive. Jimmy's family, in their small flat in the Gorbals, were all delighted. I'd never seen them looking happier. Peggy said that the press was round knocking on her door. Alfie and Freddy were in the Pig (Pig and

Whistle, the pub across the road – their regular haunt) at the time so she was alone. She said that her hair was standing on end and she didn't have her teeth in...no 'effing way would she be letting the bleeding cunts in. Not even if they had walked on top of her!'

The solid support I received from Jimmy's friends and family, as well as my friends and family, helped me to feel confident in facing the challenges I knew would come our way.

At this point I felt a strong sense of our mission – a higher purpose to our marriage. In my diary I wrote: 'We are making a statement about human values of courage, endurance, faith and love. Through this we will reach all sorts of people and achieve great things.' And this has indeed, to some extent, happened. The letters and cards kept coming. They gave me strength to keep trusting in our future, feeling confident that Jimmy would be released. Until that moment came we would continue to grow together. Our love was strong enough to overcome any obstacle, or so it seemed.

Underneath the love, though, was a sense of pressure and a relentless driving force. If I stopped long enough to feel it, there was a mountain of buried pain. The stresses we were both carrying were added to by the choice we had made, but neither of us doubted that we would win through in the end.

Looking back now I can see how testing and difficult our circumstances actually were. The fresh expansiveness of love prevented me from having a more realistic perspective on this at the time. I felt sadness putting up our wedding cards wondering when Jimmy would be able to come to the flat again and see them for himself. Another shadow arrived when I unexpectedly received a call from the switchboard at Gartnavel saying that there had been a truly horrible triple murder in the staff crèche. I felt sickened and appalled hearing about this tragedy and it played on my mind a great deal.

As I have already said, I had reflected on Jimmy's violent past, but I largely dealt with it knowing that this was a product of his former way of life which was now behind him. If I had read *A Sense of Freedom* with the awareness I have now, I quite possibly wouldn't have married him, but I had faith in our future and never at any time felt that this kind of violence would play any part in our lives. I knew his soft and tender heart. He had troubled places inside of him but I didn't probe. I respected his capacity to confront these shadows himself.

What this tragic event at the hospital represented was mindless, savage, brutal, terrifying, out of control violence. Jimmy had an intact and solid core, which had allowed him to emerge from his past. Sadly, we continue to live in a society where violence erupts and results in appalling and unspeakable suffering. The causes of this lie deep within, and we need to grow in our understanding of how to recognise, treat, contain and transform these dark forces.

Protection of the public is essential, but relentlessly punishing the offender only repeats and reinforces this cycle of violence. Here was I married to a man who could be perceived in this same way, but I chose to believe in him, to believe in the possibility of transformation and of healing. This can involve a long process but it is ultimately about choosing to keep faith in the integrity of another human being, and in the capacity of the human spirit to endure and thrive despite all manner of onslaughts.

On the sixth day after our wedding came another heavy blow.

'Jimmy's parole for tomorrow has been cut right down to just two hours and it has been stipulated that he's not to meet me when he's out. I'm still smarting from this piece of bad news.'

This was the beginning of the backlash to all the publicity caused by our wedding. The prison authorities had taken fright and had begun a process of limiting and restricting our access to seeing each other. The question of a staged approach to release for inmates of the Special Unit had been raised but there was no agreement in the Prison's Department about this.

A strong faction wanted inmates to be returned to the traditional prison system to be 'tested' prior to release. This was our first taste of this. The official mantra was that Jimmy was to be treated no differently from any other prisoner.

I thought about Jimmy in his claustrophobic little cell. I was feeling my own aloneness. The winter gales were howling. All I could think about was the wall separating us. I felt desolate and desperate. I drove down to the Lake District for the weekend to see my Mum. Several people have asked over the years how my parents were with my marriage. Despite the challenging circumstances, both of them loved Jimmy from the start and knew that he was the right partner for me.

They had been in touch with each other at the time of our wedding and had agreed, after years of not seeing each other, to meet up. Sadly, I had heard from Dad afterwards that this had been a disaster and left him feeling a complete failure. Mum's side of this, which took quite a bit of extracting, was that she felt cut out of the picture. Dad was quoted in the press saying that he was delighted to welcome Jimmy as his son-in-law. Mum was never given an opportunity to express publicly her support for our marriage.

My father had said on her behalf that she was not unhappy about our marriage. Presumably he was wanting to be careful but she felt hurt that her enthusiastic and committed support was unseen and unacknowledged. There was truth in this.

The rest of my family was also supportive.

Our relationship seemed to have touched those who had similarly deep or meaningful experiences in their own lives.

An unexpected consequence of the challenges of my own life being so publicly exposed was that I now had access to other people sharing experiences, which had touched or tested them in similar ways.

EARLY DAYS OF AN UNUSUAL MARRIAGE

In the first full flush of love I wrote in my diary:

> 'Jimmy means so much to me...the way he gives himself, commits himself, wants me, phones me, appreciates me...the more he gives, the more I light up and respond. I feel so close now that we become almost one in the flesh, as well as the spirit. It's nice being married, it's definite, secure, strong...'

Jimmy, in those early days, had a great capacity to pick up on and show sensitivity to my feelings. He knew when I was feeling low or struggling with something and he would enfold me in his strong arms and hold me as my tears flowed and washed the hurt away. He also had a way of being able to make me laugh with his sense of humour saving the day at moments like this, telling me that I should think of getting him a wet suit and snorkel for his birthday!

Unfortunately this didn't stop me plummeting at times; my energy and mood would dip low, as did my confidence. I had a lot of difficulty managing my relationship with Mum. She would at times say some pretty extreme things; that she didn't think that I cared, or how she may as well be dead or go back to Australia. This was particularly hard for me to hear and made me feel as though I was being a major disappointment as a daughter. I would shrink back into my immature, child-like self and feel hopeless and helpless. Sadly, a lot of our relationship at this time was marked by these times of misunderstanding, and awkwardness.

I started back at work and found lots of congratulatory mail and cards waiting for me. The medical staff presented me with a handsome pair of glass candle sticks. My memory is that many of the hospital staff right through the ranks came to congratulate me, as did many of the patients. At the senior consultant level though there was a stony silence.

There were further setbacks in store for us. Jimmy was informed that his parole was to be further cut back and it was specifically stated again that I was not to meet him when he was out on these visits. I felt really choked when I heard this.

I was still deeply in love but some cracks were starting to surface. He phoned one afternoon excited and happy about his day out. Instead of being pleased for him I felt irritable, upset and almost in tears. I wanted so much to be with him that I was unable to share his joy. At this point in my diary I mentioned what I called my eating problems. These were of course made worse as a result of the stress that I was under. I found his outings outside the prison when I wasn't allowed to see him the ultimate in terms of emotional torture.

Sometimes I enjoyed my hospital work, or certain aspects of it, especially after I was moved onto the acute admissions ward. I was having difficulty concentrating on the books in the library that I was supposed to read to prepare for the membership exams. I felt miserable as the longwinded arcane words swam in front of me. I developed a mental block about the whole academic side of medicine and psychiatry. 'I feel like I'm caught in a vice like grip, not knowing what to do or where to turn.'

I still felt attached to Gartnaval, especially as the thought of cutting myself adrift and not having a job, role or any security was almost unthinkable. 'It would mean taking a big risk and braving a lot to give it up.' I thought of trying to look for something out-with the hospital system in the community. I had a fear that the creative and spontaneous side of me would die the longer I stayed in the professional mould. I came and went with it all knowing that if I didn't do the first set of exams in March the consultants would be on my back, wanting to know why and what my intentions were towards completing the training.

As a junior doctor I was expected to take therapeutic groups with no proper training for this. What I observed was often a very stilted dynamic of drifting formless discussion with apathetic patients listing their symptoms. There were long uncomfortable spells of silence. One of the consultants pursued what he called a 'non-directive' approach. He was a heavy-set man who would plump himself into his chair with a long deep sigh, his eyes half closed, and a miserable look on his face as he sat waiting for one of the patients to speak.

This was certainly not what Carl Rogers, the American psychologist who was the originator of this approach, had intended – qualities of empathy, warmth, and an authentic presence are all required for this approach to work. I will have more to say about this later on. This unenlightened way of offering it only resulted in awkward and embarrassed silences or stilted responses. There was no encouragement or invitation for the patients to do anything else.

Another of the consultants had a more psychotherapeutic approach and I did learn from her. She had visited the Special Unit previously with Maxwell Jones. She was one of the few who I could have deeper conversations with about the group therapy sessions and about the Special Unit and its approach.

*

No mention of my marriage was made in the monthly hospital newsletter, despite the presence of headlines on the front pages of most of the national press. At the same time there was an article with news that one of the clinical psychologists had recently married. Neither was there any mention made of the massacre in the crèche. This for me said it all in terms of the capacity of this respected psychiatric institution for denial and avoidance.

March arrived – Jimmy was hitting a flat spell as well by now. I was getting an inkling of just how much of a daily struggle it was for him too. I was feeling a sense of stagnant malaise, made worse by my bouts of binging and vomiting. It was dreadful having this problem, which is now well recognised and has even been given an official name, Bulimia.

I don't know that this makes it any less distressing as a condition, but perhaps it helps to alleviate some of the deep sense of shame which I struggled with. I can also say that it was a relief to see this condition receiving more recognition and acceptance after Princess Diana courageously shared publicly that she also suffered from it.

In my group work I was exploring new ways of helping people to make contact with each other. This had good results as people started to open up more.

*

Meanwhile, frustrated as we were with the restrictions placed on Jimmy's parole outings, we decided to chance it and meet anyway. Harry had been released from prison and he, Margaret, Jimmy and I sat down together for the first time in a West End restaurant to share a curry together. I had an inkling that this was not a wise thing to do and sure enough the reporters came crashing through the door with their cameras.

'CURRY IN A HURRY FOR JIMMY BOYLE' was the headline in the evening press the following day. We all knew that this breach of his parole would not go down well with the officials in the Prisons' Department who insisted that Jimmy was to be treated no differently than any other prisoner. A few days later we heard that Jimmy's paroles had been stopped altogether pending an enquiry into our meeting. I didn't let myself dwell on it, as for both of our sakes I felt I had to be strong. Jimmy took me by the hand, showing me the time tested way of resolving difficult feelings in situations of confinement by walking with me up and down the yard.

In my work one of the responsibilities that upset me most was having to give patients ECT. This involved having to press a button to send electricity shooting through the brains of patients, sending them into a series of shuddering convulsions. After seeing the film

One Flew Over the Cuckoo's Nest which was showing in cinemas at this time I hated this all the more.

By early March I'd reached an exceptionally low and fragile state, with the many painful burdens of our situation pressing in on me, leaving me feeling isolated and for the most part helpless – up against it with the Prisons' Department. At the same time people in the hospital were raising fears that I was going to be attacked. I took my feelings to Jimmy who continued to be my rock. He would hold me as I went through waves of misery. It was our love that sustained us both through all of this.

These formative experiences helped me to understand the pain of confinement that so many prisoners and their families feel. Although our situation was unusual in many ways, many hearts have been broken and shattered through the impenetrable barrier of the prison wall surrounding the institutions where offenders are incarcerated.

These human warehouses have inflicted untold misery on generations of inmates and their families, and this continues. We have to find a better way. The need to reform the prison system with all of its recurring crises continues to be widely accepted as imperative.

*

I received a call from the *Evening Times* saying that rumours were circulating that I was leaving Glasgow, that I was pregnant and, that I was leaving Gartnavel. The first two of these didn't worry me because there was no truth in them. The latter one did though because I felt suddenly exposed in terms of the uncertainty I was feeling around my career and my future.

People made anonymous calls to the hospital saying that they were watching me and were out to get me. I was never worried about my personal safety, but I did start to feel that it didn't serve the hospital, the medical staff, or possibly my own needs to continue there. There was a blanket wall of silence around a lot of the negative reactions and that made it all the harder to deal with.

Sandra, my one confidant and colleague, tried to persuade me to seek a part time post and to stay on. I appreciated her efforts and support, but the decision was clear for me – I was not going to continue with my membership exams, I needed to leave.

Looking back now I probably should have given this more thought – but at the time I was stressed, exhausted, and overwhelmed by the challenges we were experiencing. I was in no place to make any sensible decision about my career or future. I was aware that I was in a whirlpool. I was being pulled more and more into Jimmy's life. Perhaps I should have resisted this strong current more, but at that time all I could do was try my best to stay afloat in it.

His personality was so strong that it challenged my hollow sense of identity. Who was I apart from being his wife? I can see now that I was lots of things, but having been uprooted so completely in my earlier life I had what I now recognize to be a loss of my inner sense of self. I was on the threshold of contemplating giving up my medical career as well, which only further undermined my self esteem and confidence.

As if all of this wasn't enough, another setback loomed. A shock headline appeared on the front page of the *Glasgow Herald*: 'BOYLE MOVE CAUSES SPLIT,' saying that George Younger, the Secretary of State for Scotland, would apparently like to see Jimmy moved right away to some other prison, away from all the glare of publicity and attention that he was getting in the Special Unit.

I was shattered and devastated to read this news. This was our greatest fear and vulnerability. I immediately phoned Jimmy who told me not to take it seriously. He told me that the thing to do was to get directly through to George Younger's private secretary. Which was what I then tried to do, setting aside my inhibited upbringing in which such an outrageously direct approach would be unthinkable.

Jimmy's capacity for direct action was one of his greatest strengths. He refused to accept that he shouldn't be dealt with in a way that supported his right to a staged release, directly from the Special Unit, keeping me, who was at the centre of his life, strongly and clearly in the picture.

My dad, who in his own way enjoyed this element of challenge, threw himself fully into it, and also phoned George Younger's personal secretary. I don't know whether any of this did any good, but the immediate threat of Jimmy being transferred out of the Special Unit seemed to go away for a while.

The situation continued to test me at every level, and I often found myself failing, feeling worthless and frustrated. I wrote in my diary: 'I think it's the first time in my life I ever wanted something so badly that I couldn't have.' I had led a privileged and sheltered life up until this point – things that I wanted came easily. Now through my marriage to Jimmy I was subject to an outer authority and I was feeling very defeated by it.

Of course I had willingly and with open eyes chosen this situation, so in this sense I didn't feel myself to be a victim, but I was confronted with feelings and reactions in myself which threatened to push me right down at times.

When I lapsed into these kind of states, I would call in on Peggy and Alfie, the one place of refuge which I knew I could always rely on. Peggy would say things like: 'Tell the bastards to hurry up and let him out. We're fed up praying for him!'

Many others of the 'stellar cast' who I met through Jimmy offered support and became long term friends. One of these was Helen Bellany. At this time she was living separately from her husband John (widely recognised as one of Scotland's greatest artists) and was up against all the challenges of being a single parent to her three young children. She had an incredible warmth of presence, also a good understanding of prisons, as at that time she was working as an art therapist in The Scrubs in London. She was a kindred spirit from the first moment we met.

The parole decision was hanging over Jimmy. It was always present in the background, even on the good days. There were plenty of these as the weather became warmer and on visits we were able to sit out in the sun in the yard at the Special Unit. We both felt restless and impatient for an answer. Many prisoners find themselves in this kind of limbo where life becomes reduced to waiting, with no sense of when the next piece of either good or bad news will come.

My moments of deep intimacy with Jimmy sustained me. Life was opening me up to meeting people whose lives had been so different to mine and, although culturally the gap seemed enormous at times, it was both exciting and exhilarating.

Since leaving Australia and arriving in London I had become aware of how class-bound much of British society is, especially when contrasted with Australia where there is a more egalitarian, easy going approach to life. Jimmy had broken free of the constraints of his background and had proved himself to be an articulate and confident spokesperson for the oppressed.

He could relate easily to anyone across the board and that gave him a unique capacity to break through the layers of social conventions which normally separate the different classes. I was trying to find my feet in this new and unfamiliar world and in this Jimmy was my anchor.

This was the cornerstone quality of our relationship, which carried me through, as the afterglow of getting married was encroached on by the gathering uncertainties of this time.

9. Many Rivers to Cross

Jimmy's parole leave resumed. Although I was still not allowed to meet up with him outside the prison walls, I was pleased for him. Having thought he might never be released back into the world again, he now had a sense of his future which sustained him through the uncertainty of this time of waiting.

In my better moments I relaxed into the feeling of strength and contentment which being married gave me. This was the only thing which I had confidence in at that moment. My future remained uncertain. I received a letter from Dr Timbury at Gartnavel asking me to give them notice of my resignation in writing. I did this not realising that I was on the verge of leaving the medical profession for good.

I also received a letter from the Prisons' Department – far from giving any positive outlook or hope for Jimmy's eventual release, it contained eleven separate points, 'putting the record straight'. In their view Jimmy was getting treated with exceptional concessions, being allowed out on regular weekly shopping trips, and that was as far as they were prepared to go. The whole system seemed rigid and intransigent in this respect.

I can see now that it wasn't unreasonable of the authorities to be reminding us of Jimmy's status in the system. He was after all getting a considerably better deal than prisoners in the mainstream system. The point we were wanting to make was that *all* prisoners should be given the opportunity to experience life outside of prison prior to release to ease the process of adjustment afterwards. My own views at that time were understandably enough coloured by the small bubble of self-interest that we were living in.

Lots of people were supporting us and Dad assured me that I needn't worry about the future. This support was invaluable, many don't have it, but we had all we could have wanted for, and more. I asked a friend who had psychic powers if she could predict when Jimmy would be out. She said two years and I was furious. I said that might be so, but I would never accept it. It is interesting to read this now as with the benefit of hindsight, her prediction was accurate. Sometimes it's a good thing not to know what lies ahead.

I found solace in listening to music; the songs of Jimmy Cliffe I remember especially from this time. His soulful voice and lyrics captured the depths of the experience of heartache and separation we were living through, as it closed in on us both.

> 'Many rivers to cross
> But I can't seem to find my way over…'

I would think of Jimmy every night and had so much love for him as I waited.

> **Diary: 2.7.80** 'Bad news…Jimmy's parole has been put back to September. It's a heavy blow…they are stalling, playing for time.'

In my diary I wrote about the stance we were taking:

> 'Something needs to be done, as it's worse than anything to stand still and not have anywhere to put the restless energy. It seems that any attempt to fight and win Jimmy's release on the basis that he is a special case isn't strong enough. I think that the political base of the struggle has to be made wider. It needs to incorporate some sort of statement about the cruelty

of long term sentences, the corrosive effect that surviving years of confinement has on the human spirit even for the strongest of individuals – if release back into the community is the ultimate goal, then surely pre-release training and support has to be an integral part of the parole system. What is the point in squeezing the individual to the point where they crack...or returning them to the community so full of rage that there will be further casualties and a revolving door situation?'

We held onto each other, tight, as the days and weeks dragged by. I wrote about all the ups and downs of this time in my diary.

'Mum phoned, to give her warmest thoughts and share her fury at this very negative approach... 'I wish I could wring their necks!' That's my Mum, when provoked she can explode like a double barrel shot gun with her anger. Anthony (Ross) also phoned to say that he was upset to hear the news. He felt that the authorities were being tough on Jimmy because of all the publicity and were going to long lengths to prove that he wasn't getting any better treatment than the others. He said he would do his best to 'go on shaking the tree'.

Strangely Anthony seemed to be the one person who was in favour of me leaving Gartnavel and getting more involved with community based groups and activities. He said that he could see it leading towards a point where Jimmy and I would be able to work together as a team. In saying this he was giving me back some faith in myself. One of my warmest memories of Anthony is of his enjoyment of challenging Jimmy to arm wrestling – he always liked to claim his superior strength!

*

In July of that year I had an unpleasant shock. The name label

I'd made for the door of my flat had yet again been torn off. This had happened before and it was always a bit freaky as I knew that someone had come all the way up to the top of the stairs and had stood right outside my door to do this. Outside on the street the tyres of my VW beetle had been let down and the words 'KILLER BOYLE' scrawled on the paintwork.

All the publicity of course generated a whole mixed bag of opinion about Jimmy and about our marriage. There were factions who thought he would never change and those who resented his fame and success. Jimmy was very upset about these intimidating actions and it heightened his feelings of powerlessness because he was unable to protect me.

In the confined conditions of our meetings we got to know each other in the depths. This was a gift – often couples can escape into activities, and outer distractions which make it all too possible to avoid really getting to know each other.

My days at the hospital came to an end. There was little that I felt I would miss apart from the patients who I had made personal relationships with. Before I left I had one memorable showdown refusing to give ECT to a patient who was resisting the staff as they tried to force her down on the trolley. They verified with her doctors that she was still to be given ECT (this was her first), after which the pressure on her to accept this intensified. She was wheeled in with about six members of staff around her trying to pacify and placate her. But I refused, saying that I wasn't prepared to press the button on someone who was clearly refusing treatment.

'She's not refusing Dr... she's mad, psychotic, insane.' 'Well,' I said 'I'm still refusing.' Sister looked exasperated as she had to wheel the patient out again. This felt like a small victory. As my (enforced) ECT giving days came to an end it was a rare occasion when I was able to take a stance in opposition to the rest of the staff.

I spent my last night on call and looked forward to being

released from my bleep. I was relieved to be leaving as I knew that I couldn't fit in to the hospital. It was very clear that the institution was not the place for me. Little was said about my departure and in a way this made it more difficult. I said goodbye to the patients and could at least feel a sense of achievement that some in my group had definitely made progress. I had a farewell lunch with Sandra and another colleague, but the only question asked about my future plans was if I was thinking of taking a holiday. A sense of stigma hung over my departure, but by that point I was for the most part beyond caring.

> **Diary: 4.8.80** 'The Parole Board is meeting this week and sources are saying that it seems as though he will be given a date in 1982. Jimmy is worried about how I will take this. What can I say... que sera, sera... we will meet whatever comes and make the best of it. A definite release date would help.'

A couple of days later the news that we had been waiting for was finally communicated. I tried to discern the outcome by looking for the expression on Jimmy's face. It didn't tell me much. He took me up the stairs to his cell and told me that he had heard that he would be given a date for two years' time. A third of the Parole Board had wanted him to serve some of the extra twelve years that he had been given on top of his life sentence for assaults which had taken place in the riots in which he had been involved before coming to the Special Unit.

My first reaction was just wanting to curl up into a tight ball as I felt so much hurt and pain. After a while I was able to cry and felt slightly better. I could see that if I gave in to this it would only make things worse for Jimmy who was doing all that he could to make the best of what was at least good news – this being that he was finally being given a definite release date. Gradually the appreciation of this seeped through us both. A look of real happiness broke over Jimmy's face. There was a new feeling of power and confidence with the dawning vision of a definite time when the door would finally open and he would be set free.

Later that month John MacKenzie, the director of the film *A Sense of Freedom* arrived at my door and took me down to the STV studios in a taxi for a pre-screening viewing. This film was based on Jimmy's life and was made for Scottish Television. The filming of it on the streets of Glasgow had been happening over the past few months. The excitement and the hype around it had been growing, attracting a lot of press attention and predictably more controversy.

The viewing room was like a small cinema with three luxuriously comfortable chairs for us, and a miniature screen. It was quite a moment for me waiting for this first opportunity to see it, with Margaret accompanying me. Seen in such a setting it was a compelling and shattering experience.

Shattering because the film contained so much concentrated raw violence. David Hayman played the part of Jimmy very convincingly and so of course it was difficult for me to keep my emotions in check as I watched it. We both thought that the film was good, but we were concerned that the violence portrayed in it reinforced the image of Jimmy's violent past, without this being balanced by showing more of his transformation in the Special Unit.

The last scene showed him arriving in the Special Unit when he was given the pair of scissors to open a package, which had been sent to him. This was the seminal moment that symbolised change. He responded to this gesture of trust with the understanding that he was being offered his life back again. Although it was well made, I was concerned about the possible negative impact which the film could have on Jimmy's parole situation, and would have preferred its public showing to be delayed for as long as possible.

Part of me wanted to leave this violent past behind, but another part of me knew that Jimmy had to share this in order to show that violence wasn't the way for young people like him caught up in the world of poverty, crime, and street fighting. I knew that it would take courage from me, as well as from Jimmy to stand steady in the face of what could be expected to be an outpouring of public anger in response to the film.

This never happened, which was a relief. I tended to be sheltered for the most part from negative comments about Jimmy's past. The people who suffered most from this were close members of his family who have inevitably taken the brunt of Jimmy's past reputation and life. I was fortunate to be removed from this, representing as I did a world which was a different strand of society – the world which Jimmy would emerge into on his eventual release.

10. Last Days in The Special Unit

At 11.30pm on the *26th August 1980* I had a call from the *Glasgow Herald* to tell me that Jimmy was going to be transferred to Saughton Prison in Edinburgh for training for freedom very soon. Had I heard anything? Had I any comments to make? I felt angry and irritable being phoned up so late at night. It felt terrible that this news had been given to the press before being communicated to us.

The following morning another journalist was at my door at ten minutes before eight. I had nothing to say to her. I went out to buy the *Glasgow Herald*. The headline on the front page was:

BOYLE TO LEAVE BARLINNIE SPECIAL UNIT.

After reading the article I didn't feel too bad as it mentioned Training for Freedom and weekend visits home and said 'within a year, Boyle could be paroled.' Foolishly I let my hopes rise. When I went up to the Unit Jimmy was in a meeting with the Governor. He came out and told me that he had now had it officially confirmed that his release date was to be in 1982, and that he would be transferred to Edinburgh, but we wouldn't know the details until they were decided at a meeting the following week.

Together we tried to focus on the positive, which was that he now had a definite release date. This was a milestone in itself. The community was solidly behind Jimmy and we took strength from this and decided to compose a statement for the press together.

When I left, Jimmy told me to stay strong, but when I got home the reality hit me and I felt terrible.

Two years seemed such a long time to wait, and my spirits fell even further when I began to think of Jimmy being put back into the restricting conditions of the mainstream prison system. Would home visits actually materialise? All I seemed to be able to focus on was fear. What lay ahead felt very uncertain.

The question of how the process of release should be handled for prisoners in the Special Unit had never been adequately addressed when the Working Party put forward their proposal. At the beginning it was looked upon as an experiment, which might influence policy changes towards the treatment and conditions for long term prisoners in the mainstream prison system. Quite what should happen as inmates reached the end of their sentences remained a bit of an anomal. The default response was to pursue the procedures usually adopted which were from a departmental point of view, at any rate, familiar and 'safe'.

The Special Unit had been all about pushing forward the boundaries and instigating a regime, which in lots of ways was out of sync with the rest of the system. Jimmy became a casualty of this mismatch. It really made no sense to expose him (or other inmates) to the degree of re-socialising experience the Special Unit offered and then to slam the door tightly shut again. In a way this was like reaching the final year of school only to be sent back to a primary level class.

Two years felt just impossible to get through. November 19, 1982 seemed like an eternity away. My feelings were made worse by a lot of the press writing in lurid terms about the depressing conditions to which Jimmy would be sent back to. They seemed to be reveling in the fact that he was now at last getting an effective measure of punishment after having had it so easy during his years in the Special Unit. This thirst for vengeance is a depressing phenomenon. It has to be remembered that loss of freedom in itself is a punishment.

When I was at home I felt the empty spaces. The lack of purpose and direction in my work life was starting to take its toll. The prospect of two years ahead with no fixed job to get me out each day was just devastating. How was I going to survive and get through this period? There were other minor setbacks. Both of Jimmy's applications for a day out in Edinburgh, as well as a day out in the country for the two of us were turned down. It was also communicated that the authorities would not allow the film of *A Sense of Freedom* to be shown in the Unit. In my diary I wrote: 'None of this bodes well for what will come next.'

Finally I had a phone call from Jimmy to tell me what was going to happen. There was still a ray of hope that all might yet be well and not as bad as we were expecting. But this was dashed when I heard Jimmy's voice which was harsh and desperate. 'A complete hatchet job.... a travesty of a consultative meeting.' ...the line just cold bloodedly handed out to him was... 'B Hall for 4 weeks, Forth Hall for 3 months, Pentland Hall for 1 month, then C Hall.'

Not that the names meant anything to me, but they had refused to discuss his training for freedom prospects. He was to get no outside visits. My visits were to be restricted to three half-hour visits every two months and all our mail was to be censored. It was just appalling. I felt numb with shock and staggered from the phone. I couldn't control myself and just broke down completely.

Even Peggy had tears in her eyes when I told her, which is the first time I have ever seen this solid rock of a woman show so much emotion. The concern was all for me. 'It's hard on you hen....people like us are used to blows, we get them all our lives – but how are you going to cope?'

Then I drove up to the Unit to see Jimmy. I steeled myself to get through the gate without showing weakness or tears. Malky was ashen-faced and tight-lipped at the news and told me that the staff would be submitting a paper to the Secretary of State.

Jimmy was pacing his cell with a contorted look on his face and on seeing me broke into sobs, wild and deep. It shocked me to see him like this. Perhaps for the first time I realised just how bad it was for him, before he was transferred to the Special Unit, in places like Inverness and Peterhead. Here was this iron girder of a man with an unbreakable spirit, sick and frightened to the core at the prospect of returning to the jungle.

Naked and vulnerable is how he describes himself now, particularly as far as I am concerned. There was the degradation of it all, as well as his physical fears and the torment of being separated from me. I loved him so much and just held him. I knew that nothing would take this love away or degrade or lessen him in my eyes.

We tried to convince each other that our love and our courage would see us through this, but even these words rang hollow that night.

In those days I occasionally took Valium to help me cope with the stresses – this was one of those occasions. I woke with more tears and tried calling the Special Unit, but unusually no one answered. The phone rang and rang and I had a sudden feeling of dread that they had moved Jimmy already. I headed up there and was of course a wet heap of tears when I saw him, but at least he was still there.

We discussed what to do. Taking action helped and there was a lot of support. Some of this came from high up places. One eminent supporter was the Lord Provost of Glasgow, Micheal Kelly. 'He says he's backing Jimmy all the way and that the fight doesn't end when he goes to Saughton Prison. This is just the sort of spirit we need!'

I drove over to Edinburgh to attend a meeting at the Demarco Gallery. Joyce Laing was there and told me that Charles Hills, the Governor of Saughton was at the meeting. Great, I thought, hoping that I would have a chance to get hold of him. There was a smallish gathering of people with Charles Hills sitting on the opposite side of the room. A dialogue started with me, and with others, asking him how he could possibly justify the decision to put Jimmy back into a mainstream prison environment. He cringed and winced, saying that rehabilitation in prisons doesn't just go on in the Special Unit, and that Jimmy was to be treated like any other prisoner.

I was ready to fight like a tiger for my man. We tried everything. I saw Stephanie Wolfe Murray, Jimmy's publisher. She said that she would try speaking to Arnold Kemp (who was deputy editor of the *Scotsman* at that time), and a certain Lady Polwarth who knew George Younger. The strong support line up included Joseph Beuys who visited Jimmy in the Special Unit. He was due to participate in the Edinburgh Festival but said: 'I'm going to have nothing to do with this shit Festival if this is happening to you!'

He said he would make a strong appeal to the whole Edinburgh Festival to rise up in arms about what was happening to Jimmy as an artist. This was all fantastic and encouraging but at the end of the day Jimmy was in the vice-like clutches of the prison system and no amount of protesting or shouting from me, or his many other supporters, was going to change anything.

*

In the midst of this Jimmy was given a day out. It seemed absurd that he was able to be taken for a spell outside on the streets, when he was being told that for the next twelve months he was going to be slammed back into the mainstream prison system, with visits restricted to an hour a month, and no outside paroles. At least it did him the world of good to have a brief taste of freedom. He looked much better after this, his strength restored and I knew that whatever happened he would survive the challenges ahead.

At the start of September the weather turned cold, wet and blustery. Our efforts to rally support continued to have some effect. The Penal Affairs Committee, who were due to visit the Special Unit, tried to have Jimmy's transfer to Saughton postponed until after this had taken place. But it was too late and Jimmy was told that he would be moved the following Monday.

Someone managed to have 'a chat' with George Younger who was basically sympathetic saying that he didn't think the Saughton move was a bad thing for Jimmy as he'd assumed that he'd be able to continue his artistic work and would be well situated for access to the various galleries in Edinburgh. This proved to be completely untrue and shows how out of touch senior politicians can be with the realities on the ground. It was hard to know whether this was a deliberate smokescreen, or simply an extraordinary disconnect.

My final visit to see Jimmy in the Special Unit was of course poignant. I took in everything with heightened perception. It was a very unreal feeling and I had a fear of the unknown ahead. It was hard to conceive what life would be like without my almost daily visits to see Jimmy. I was taken in with Jimmy to see the Governor. We asked him to explain the sudden last minute decision to bring forward Jimmy's date of transfer and of course he couldn't do this. He simply said that he was given the instruction by Mr Alan in the Prisons' Department.

I felt bleak leaving on my own. The cold winter winds were blowing and there was a long, lonely winter ahead, in fact two of them before 1982.

Saturday 6.9.80 – letter from me to Jimmy:

'Hello Darling,

This is almost my last intimate and private letter to you. I've spent the latter part of the evening trying to sort through the mass of papers and packages which has accumulated, yours and mine. With this comes a great sadness for the passing of such a significant and beautiful part of both of our lives. I want you to believe in me, all the time and all the way through... Jimmy I love you with all my heart and soul and will keep faith in the strength and magic of this feeling bringing us permanently together as soon as is humanly possible.'

In my diary I wrote:

'Nothing seems real anymore...but I'm strong and ready for the battle ahead, and so is Jimmy I hope.'

My last visit to the unit was in the early morning. Jimmy was already stripping and packing up the things in his cell. We spent most of the morning doing this, as well as talking to JL and Collie (two of the other inmates), who made cups of coffee. They had a sad and worried look on their faces, showing their feelings of insecurity about the future. Jimmy was brusque, getting things ready. Listening to the talk between him and the other two I could sense a strong element of the old jail culture returning in him.

This came as something of a shock and made me realise how remarkable it was that we'd been able to cross such a huge divide together. It was a busy morning and Jimmy and I didn't have much time to ourselves. There was an air of everything changing, with the process already being underway and the cell looking strange and bare with so little in it. It had been a place which had held so many precious memories for me. I would never forget it.

Other memories from this time include friends phoning through for Jimmy with last minute messages. Robert MacDowell and others from the Demarco Gallery put out a good press statement about the move condemning it, and tried to take out a last minute interdict under the auspices of the European Court to prevent the move. Although this failed it provided an excellent note of humour, which had a lightening effect on us all.

JL and Collie, two of the other inmates, piled up plates of salad and fruit making us a lovely lunch. Jimmy's influence showed, even in this farewell meal. I felt particularly pleased that he had included me in all the pre-departure preparations and farewells, making this as much as possible something that we were going through together. The warmth of the respects paid to him by the staff was incredible. They all paid tribute to the monumental part he'd played in the life of the Special Unit.

Jimmy's departure was a very sad occasion, particularly leaving this way, back to the old prison cells. Bill Florence said that he had never seen him as a prisoner, always as a friend. I said my thanks to all of them as well. They'd been good to us and had given so much. I said a final goodbye to the other inmates. Then with farewells almost completed I walked downstairs. I was OK but Jimmy was not. He was torn apart. I could see how difficult a moment this was for him. I knew that I needed to put on a brave face for the sake of all concerned. I didn't want to walk out of the front gate of Barlinnie in tears. I can hardly remember our parting kiss. It was brief. My last glimpse of Jimmy after he'd said goodbye to me at the gate was of him walking rapidly away. He didn't look back.

*

Endings and the Special Unit

This is a painful subject. The Special Unit had been set up as an experiment and it would have to be said that it succeeded far beyond the scope of the original expectations for it. Unfortunately its success, and the acclaim which it received, posed a genuine threat to the culture maintained by the rest of the system. The argument used to justify Jimmy's transfer out of it was that he needed to 'prove' that he was rehabilitated and that he could 'cope' back in the mainstream prison system again, rather than presumably causing another major riot.

He was also to be treated like all other prisoners. This was a frequent argument used, but it was also maintained that prisoners' release programmes are individually assigned. Of course all the publicity surrounding his book, the film, and our marriage was what they particularly feared, as well as the perception on the part of some members of the public that Jimmy had been given a 'soft ride' and hadn't paid sufficiently for his past notoriety.

All of this came into the picture. At the end of the day it seemed that the authorities lacked the courage to capitalize on the success which they had created, so it was back to 'business as usual' and a tedious and pointless return to the culture of inane and mind - numbing tedium for Jimmy, for a while at least.

I have to mention here the other significant ending at the Special Unit, which was Ken Murray's departure. In the contentious early years when negative publicity brought hostility, he was the public face of this brave and extraordinary experiment.

At an early stage of his long career as a prison officer he was persuaded that there must be better ways to treat violent offenders than through primitive incarceration.

Ken firmly believed in both staff and prisoners being part of a community in which all had a voice in making decisions and setting programmes. His view was that this was liberating not only for offenders, but for prison staff.

In June 1979 Ken had received news that he was being transferred to Low Moss Prison, which was for short term offenders. This was a calculated insult and it hurt him deeply.

Ken, in his own characteristically determined way, went on to prove that the approach which he evolved in the Special Unit, which was internationally acclaimed, could also be introduced successfully with short term offenders. He told me at a later date that he had been able to make a significant difference to the 'revolving door scenario' in this setting, where the measure of success was keeping persistent petty offenders from returning to

1. Enjoying the fells in the Lake District early 1970s after my return to the UK.

2. Jimmy sculpting in the yard of the Special Unit.

3. With Jimmy in the prison yard at the Special Unit.

4. Walk along West End Street in Glasgow on one of Jimmy's Special Escorted leaves. Photo taken by escorting prison officer. Late seventies.

5. With witnesses Margaret Boyle and Heidi Foster on our wedding day in the registry office at Balfron Jan 31, 1980.

6. Wedding day, surrounded by press, Jan 31st 1980. ©mirrorpix.

7. With Margaret Boyle and Heidi Foster in Jimmy's cell relaxing after returning to the prison on our wedding day.

8. Collage from our wedding day with Father Anthony Ross.

9. First taste of freedom - Jimmy's 5 day leave spent in the Scottish Highlands at the start of his Training for Freedom, Nov 1981.

prison.

Ken, along with his long-suffering but staunchly loyal wife Meg, went on to become good and lasting friends. The debt I owe to him is beyond words, because had he not stood firm for what he believed in, this story would never have happened. Sadly, the Special Unit never recovered from these painful endings.

The effects of undermining the positive leadership, like draining a tree of its sap, ultimately led to its demise and subsequent closure in 1994.

11. Stand By Me – Saughton Prison, Edinburgh

After my last visit to the Special Unit and saying goodbye to Jimmy, my first concern was wondering how he would keep his spirits up with this sudden return to a culture he had left so far behind. His soft underbelly had opened up through his time in the Unit, also through our relationship. Now he would have to zip this all up again.

I at least had my freedom, access to friends, walks outside, and the comforts of my Wilton Street flat. The knowledge that Jimmy had none of these heightened my appreciation of them. Initially there was a flood of support from others and I was snowed under with letters and phone calls. We also knew that although this was an abrupt and unwelcome change for us both, there was a definite release date – a time when Jimmy would walk out through the prison gates at the end of it all.

I had thought that I was going to take a steep nose-dive and plummet at this moment, but I didn't. Surprisingly I felt the dark clouds lifting and a tremendous strength and conviction that all would be OK. At least I felt strong, until I went out early the following day to get the papers. I caught sight of a photo showing Jimmy's smiling face from the back seat of the car entering Saughton Prison, and I broke down.

The pain of parting returned full force. In the morning Davy MacCallum and another prison officer, Matt Parks, arrived in their van. We struggled up the stairs with all Jimmy's boxes. Neither of them would accept any payment for this, which was a measure of their good will.

Towards 10 o'clock I took out some photos, Jimmy's watch, and closed my eyes. I sat thinking of him, feeling a sensation of warmth and strength within. I'd whisper his name and tell him that I loved him as I imagined myself in his arms.

We had agreed to think of each other each night at this time – it was my first experience of what I would now call 'distant communication' – learning to tune in and connect through turning within. I kept this up for months on end and know that it helped to feel this inner connection. We also agreed to write to each other every day, and largely kept this up.

The following is taken from Jimmy's first letter to me after his transfer:

8.9.80
'Darling Sarah,
Well, here I am lodged in my new place of residence. The contrast is sharp and startling between here and the Unit. A simple thing like writing to you on prison notepaper is very strange. At the moment I'm pretty bewildered by it all, and feel just like a first offender. I feel anonymous wearing the coarse prison uniform and though there was an impersonal detachment to the reception procedure, the staff and prisoners were friendly. Also in the hall people have been openly warm.

Although only here a few hours, I have pinpointed what I feel will be the major problem for me; the dull and boring routine… One thing for sure these past few hours have brought home to me is just how profound the rebirth has been. I feel a complete stranger in a world that I was once so familiar with…

I hope, like me, you are keeping the lid on your metal box. We'll open them only on those special occasions when we can be together.

Sarah it will be a difficult time for us. Both of us know it, therefore, we'll try to work though it in a positive manner. The main thing is that we'll get there.

Darling Sarah, I'm with you, Your husband, In love, Jimmy x x x PS I've booked a visit for Sunday 28th'

The following day he wrote another letter further describing his new conditions:

9.9.80

'I now have my own pens, sketch book and dictionary but would not like these to be interpreted as concessions as it is ridiculous that such things should be taken away in the first place. One of the things that is concerning me, and came more to the fore as the day progressed, is the rigidity of the regime. All the decision-making is taken away from the prisoner and I can now see at first hand the way the system makes the prisoner dependent on it. What I find ironic is, that undoing all of this was very difficult for me in coming to terms with the Unit.

I'm still undergoing the confusion of the culture shock as it really is severe, much more so than I could have imagined. I feel severely the loss of my creative outlets. It is difficult to explain to the non-creative person what this means. The way it all runs is geared to everyone fitting into the system and not focusing on the needs of the individual. The perfect example is me feeling I've landed on another planet as all that I've previously known, developed and been attuned to now lies a useless mess inside my framework. Let's call it 'Planet Prune' all dried up with contents having been sapped of their best.

There is no doubt that the shock of not being able to see or speak to you is very hard to bear. At the same time I'm keeping the metal box tightly sealed. I'm hoping that you are dealing with yours OK.

I'll say now that my thoughts and core will be focused only on you.

Your husband, In Love, Jimmy x x x' (next to a little hand drawn picture of a light bulb)

These words show the utter discrepancy between the two different approaches. The institutional conditions, into which Jimmy was returned, merely undermined the personal growth the Special Unit regime had encouraged. Jimmy found his own freedom through creating an alternative vivid reality in his head. The metal box was his way of referring to the place inside where he kept his feelings tucked away and hidden. Interesting that it had to be a metal box – showing the degree of protection needed in this harsh external environment to which he had been returned.

And what of me? How was I coping?

It seemed that I adopted another name to share some of my more sensitive feelings with Jimmy, as we were both aware that his letters were getting censored: 'Lucy wants me to tell you that she's braver and tougher in these circumstances than you thought she could be…she's quite a little battler as well, isn't she? She's seeing this as a challenge and meeting it.'

There were moments though when the ongoing pain of separation just broke through.

12.9.80

Diary: 'If you love someone very much, it's a terrible feeling to be parted. Ripped apart, torn apart…I feel this so much today that I'm nearly driven crazy. It's a wild force and energy in me. The cold wintery winds are blowing a gale outside, howling, screaming round the rooftops, and the rain is dashing down just as angrily. This is how I feel inside. I feel violent and closer to screaming than crying.'

What sustained me, as well as Jimmy, was the flow of communication between us – we wrote to each other almost daily. The postal services became like the M8 motorway, keeping the connection between our hearts open as these communications sped to and fro. Mum and Dad also threw themselves into supporting us both as far as they could. Freddie, Alfie, and Pat came up to the flat to help me sort some of Jimmy's things out.

> **13.9.80:** 'Freddie managed to make it up the stairs OK. Coming down was more of a problem for him actually. They just loved it, Jimmy...you should have seen the pleasure and excitement in their faces as they explored every corner and cupboard! Alfie's wee face lit up and he talked far more than he usually does. It was really nice, for me to have them up...they fixed your TV with a coat hanger!
>
> I've put your battered old clock symbolically on the mantelpiece! I've unpacked quite a lot of your things...it's definitely feeling better here than before and suggests that two people live here, rather than me on my own.
>
> Naturally I can't wait to hear from you at Saughton, but I feel strong because I know you'll get a letter through just as soon as you can!'

> **18.9.80:** 'Despite the separation... you are solidly lodged in my core and this is a wonderful feeling. I do all that I can to bring you alive out here... I feel torn apart, of course I do. It is a challenge for both of us to overcome this, and prove that no barriers can ever get between us.'

Feeling into these words now makes me aware of the shadows which would show themselves in the future, when barriers would come between us of a far subtler kind, creeping up on the inside. At that early time, with such a strong focus to maintain, our sights were set on winning through and achieving the goal of Jimmy's freedom.

We had our first visit on October 28 and were reunited at last again in the prison visiting room. Afterwards I wrote:

> 'I felt pretty torn apart and I imagine you did too. I know visits are beautiful, but hellish as well. Anthony (Ross) was struck, as I was, that you were looking rather pale, thin and drawn. No wonder, but it does bring it home to me, the difference from the Unit and how even with your strength it takes it out of you.'

Emotionally this first visit took a lot out of me.

> 'I dip, I spin, I twist, I twirl....I was thinking last night that I've become too stagnant and boring in my thoughts. My creativity seems to have withered and shrivelled since you left. I remember what Mum said about never having picked up the flute after John [my father] left all those years ago... [when she went through her divorce] ...so sad that, but it often happens [and indeed it did happen to me, but much later on] ...I mustn't let this situation do this to me.
>
> I'm still uncertain of what I *ought* to be doing at the moment. I feel like I'm treading time. Mum suggested weekly visits to Edinburgh to acclimatize myself to the place and hunt for somewhere to stay...
>
> With you tonight in my heart, in my soul x x x Sarah'

I was coming round to the idea of moving to Edinburgh, imagining that it might give us more privacy from the press in the future. I was feeling adrift and rudderless with Jimmy no longer being the anchor he had been for me in Glasgow. I explored different options in the sphere of community mental health but had no clear sense of my direction or future. A strong focus was on protesting against Jimmy being placed back into these conditions and campaigning hard for him to be moved onto a Training for Freedom programme (TFF).

H.M. PRISON, Saughton, Edinburgh. November 11 1980

Dear Mrs Boyle,

Thank you for your letter of October 22nd. I think you will realise that there have been certain developments since you wrote and it would have been unwise to anticipate the outcome. For that reason I have not written.

S.E.L's (Special Escorted Leaves – time outside of prison with a prison officer escort.): You will know that the first has been arranged for November 24th. While understanding your concern, I'm pleased that it is not as long a wait as you feared or suggested.

Pre-Release Programme: Your husband has started today a placement at the Wester Hailes Community Workshop. It is 2 days a week from 9am – 5pm. The Workshop is run by a Management Committee of representatives from the Community Associations of Wester Hailes. We have been most fortunate by their generous and responsible attitude to our approach for a placement. I hope others who express a concern for your husband's pre-release programme and future will try to show a similar attitude.

...I hope you will not feel this letter abrupt and short. Over the past few weeks the average daily number in Saughton has been around the 700 mark. I do feel that I and all the staff have used their time and resources to some advantage in your husband's case. Nor am I unaware of his response to the present situation but we also have obligations to all the others in custody.

Yours sincerely, Charles W. Hills – Governor

So, my efforts, as well as the efforts of many others who campaigned vociferously for Jimmy's release, had achieved a positive result. The door was starting to open; this was the beginning of a long and warm relationship with the Wester Hailes Community Workshop. Through the auspices of Lawrence Demarco, a well-known community development worker, and the workshop manager, they had offered Jimmy a placement for his Training for Freedom programme. Finally it seemed that the besieged Governor, as well as the two of us, could breathe a sigh of relief. Things were starting to move in the right direction again.

I received a letter from Jimmy describing his first day out in Wester Hailes. He had unleashed all his pent up energy and was elated at his introduction to the community. It was a vast improvement that he was able to start getting out, but in contrast, my visiting hours were to remain the same, an hour a month. It was an impossible contradiction that he was able to meet and mingle with people in the community, while our times together were still so restricted.

This would have really upset me had not the community found ways to allow us access to each other. This is something I will always treasure, that they were willing to stretch things a bit to allow us some private time to meet.

Also at this time I was able to find and make an offer for a flat in Edinburgh – which to my great relief was accepted. Jimmy was delighted.

This felt like another milestone towards us eventually being able to set up home together. Career wise I felt very much at a crossroads, totally uncertain what direction I should pursue, but I hoped that something would turn up in Edinburgh once I was settled there.

18.12.80: 'My Darling Sarah...Tonight I had a cell search, the first since my arrival here and it was strange to go through this process after eight years. What's so funny is that there's nothing in my cell apart from a bed, small cabinet, chair and chamber pot. This is what I mean when I write about the sharp contrast between my being out in the streets with ultimate trust and having to undergo this. It's really a crazy world where I am – no logic or reason, just rules and authority.'

Jimmy had progressed to a new Hall but although there was slight improvement, for example, he now had access to a gym – it was still a bizarre contrast for him. On his TFF days out he went from being out and about in the community, engaged in his work, walking the streets and trusted to get himself back to the prison, only to head back into the Hall with all its petty rules and restrictions again at the end of the day. None of it made any sense.

21.12.80:'My Darling Jimmy...this is the shortest day of the year, mid-winter, which means that we are now into a new cycle with the days gradually lengthening again. There was also the spectacular new moon last night. I wonder if you were out late enough to see it?

After a visit I generally feel all thrown off balance and find it hard to come down to the normal every day. I thought the prison officers looked very impersonal on today's visit and there were no decorations – no attempt at all to bring any of the Christmas spirit or feeling into this prison it seems. It must be a difficult time for most prisoners and many I guess, like you, will be missing their families.'

For Jimmy Christmas and Boxing Day were predictably devoid of any Christmas feel good factor: 'Christmas Day rings hollow in here as we are all caught in the dilemma of wanting to be with our loved ones and yet trying not to be openly dispirited.'

I spent New Year's Eve alone in my flat, with a candle lit as the midnight bells approached. My thoughts were with Jimmy. The closeness, which I felt brought comfort.

The New Year started with me preparing for my move to Edinburgh. Pat arrived to help me pack for the coming removals. He was a tremendous help and worked pretty well non-stop, dismantling and stowing things carefully and efficiently. In the evening I invited people to a party I called 'Goodbye Glasgow'.

I strung up letters spelling this out across the bare wall. Pat thought I was crazy for doing this. I set out the sculptures, lit two candles, put up our wedding picture and laid out food. It was a gathering of many of those whose friendship and warmth had supported me through my time in this extraordinary city. Betty, Collie's (Hugh Collins) dynamic and feisty mum was one of the first to arrive, bringing with her pizzas, bread, and a bottle of wine. Ken, Meg and Lindsay came, Brian and Joni Wilson, David Godwin from SCCL, Neil Carmicheal and Ruth Wishart.

It was a special group of people who had stood by the two of us through thick and thin. I had met all of them through Jimmy and they were steadfast allies in this strange new world in which I found myself. I had a moment of identity crisis later on that night as the memories of my time in Glasgow whirled through my mind; there was no going back to my former life now, but where was I heading? The only thing that I knew was that Edinburgh was the place where Jimmy and I would be making our future home.

In the aftermath of the move I started to suffer from symptoms of stress. I developed an unpleasant and progressive numbness in my legs, which was disturbing. I felt weepy, depressed and miserable. Jimmy was concerned and managed to get permission from the Workshop to take me to the Casualty Department in the hospital. Here I had myself checked over and was told that it was all OK.

This was a relief but not much comfort when the symptoms

continued. I reached a point of worrying that I might have Multiple Sclerosis. I was undergoing a deep emotional crisis, feeling my confidence ebbing away.

Jimmy suggested visiting a hill he could see from his cell window. I picked him up and we drove there. He told me to get out, and with me staggering, supported by his arm, we climbed the hill together. It was an extraordinary moment. I could feel his energy and strength beside me and when we reached the top *I knew* that I was going to get better. The view was superb – suddenly we had it all at our feet, the city of Edinburgh spread out beneath us with all its familiar landmarks and oceans of space.

This marked something of a turning point. The pressures continued, but I decided to take a three-week holiday to visit friends in Cuba. I took a complete break in my diary-writing during this period and returned with fresh energy. The oppressive weight descended again almost immediately. I wrote about this in my diary:

> 'The never letting- up frustrations of this situation with the authorities pulling the rule book out on Jimmy at every available opportunity, checking up on him all the time and of course double checking to see if he'd seen anything of me. Bastards! I feel all the old anger welling because of the animosity which seems to be directed towards the two of us. A photo which I sent in was defaced and scrawled on, a trivial enough incident but upsetting none the less. How Jimmy survives all this day to day, week to week, is a miracle to me. But its taken its toll and he's become ill with it all. His letters convey a deep sense of loss in how much he's missed me... I can't see things getting much easier in the months to come.'

Two days later though I was on my way to buy wigs. The initiative must have come from Jimmy, who decided that in order to escape the all seeing eye of prison surveillance, we should start wearing a disguise when we met. Looking back on this now, and even at the time, it was hilarious. I bought a black wig for Jimmy, which he wore with a cap on his head, and a blonde wig for myself.

This was the start of our 'Debby and Harry' escapades. I suppose it was our way of rebelling against the absurd and pointless restrictions the system tried to impose on us, and it gave us a few welcome opportunities to escape the pressures of our situation.

I wrote about one of these days in my diary:

> 'Beautiful, beautiful day... perfect blue skies and late afternoon haze as we drove back across the Forth Road Bridge. We both wanted to come home. We did and spent time eating, bathing and making love...It was an all-powerful and intense experience to meet with each other in this way.
>
> The hard part is when inevitably the curtain comes down again and once more Jimmy must go back into the prison. I must settle back to life here without him. Last night he seemed exceptionally vulnerable and upset to be leaving, because we'd had such a beautiful day together.
>
> Once more we talked about having a baby. The practicalities frighten the living daylights out of me...but I know that I have a strong instinct to have a child.
>
> We're going to need to wait for quite a long while yet, probably at least a couple of years. But there's something beautiful in having this idea for the future and it deepens and solidifies the bond between us.'

The blueprint for our future was already being hatched.

28.4.81 'Nobody can know the special way you hold me, but me. Today it was wonderful to be with you. I felt physically never more in love. It was an outreaching of everything in me, to you. I felt wide open to the full limits of our love Even the skies seemed to hold it and to look special because of it.

Like a flame which suddenly stills and looks perfect, our love took this form. I felt inseparable from you, and aroused at every level.

Later the flame flickered and the mirror calm pool became disturbed. I could tell that you'd been swept away by different pressures, from where we were at lunchtime. It's always annoying to lose those peaks of perfection. We want them to last forever. So we eat, and talk, and try to get around it somehow, but there's really no way. You've got to go back and I've got to keep on without you.'

The emotions in us both see-sawed as we continued walking on this edge. At this time I applied and was interviewed for a job with the Scottish Association for Mental health (SAMH). My inclination was to work in the community as I was being introduced to another, wholly new world, with Jimmy's placement at Wester Hailes. SAMH gave me a completely open remit to explore mental health in the community as an action research project.

It was helpful to get this job as it gave me a more coherent role and sense of purpose again. When I spoke to Lawrence Demarco he told me that he'd just been sent a set of statistics showing that Wester Hailes had a very high overdose rate, higher than the older council housing schemes of Craigmillar and Pilton. I used this as a focus to begin my enquiry into why this might be.

It grew into a substantial body of work where I looked at the absence of provision of any social amenities when the scheme in Wester Hailes was originally built. All it was at the beginning was houses, many of them high-rise, and roads connecting the scheme with the city. There was no community centre, shops, cafes, cinemas, sports facilities, parks or meeting places.

The uprooted population swiftly became isolated due to the lack of the amenities needed to provide the glue for the social fabric that sustains people in their lives. It was no wonder so many took overdoses. The medical approach in the hospitals, where diagnosis is focused on individuals, is not designed to pick up on the social dimensions of the problem.

Individuals were blamed when what was happening was actually an indictment of the conditions into which people had been transferred. The buildings might have been new, but in other ways the area was a social desert.

*

The Wester Hailes Community Workshop had grown out of an initiative taken by some members of the community to address the urgent need to create a meeting place where issues could be addressed and responded to. It became a hub for developing a range of different support services. I was especially interested in exploring how, in this setting, groups started forming and constellating around specific areas of interest and need. Many individuals became empowered through this process and learned new skills – here was the therapeutic community model of approach being applied in a community setting.

I experienced a sense of freedom being out and about with a mental health role and remit, without having to wear a white coat. Of course everyone knew and respected Jimmy so this made it easier for people to trust me. With the barriers down, I could get closer, and just be myself. I found working in this way far more satisfying than the hospital. I felt relieved to be out of the medical role, no longer confined to the institutional boundaries.

10.5.81 'Yesterday was Jimmy's birthday. In the afternoon I had a visit to see him. It seemed strange seeing him in his prison uniform. He still appears self-conscious wearing it to see me, as though he's embarrassed by me seeing him in it. Immediately he takes my hands in his. They are soft and warm, but strong as they wrap around mine. We sit close to each other. Before I leave we hold each other and embrace so his whole body is touching mine. Then I walk away feeling more dreamlike than real...'

Indeed – it was overall a dreamlike time, full of surreal contrasts, sunlight, and shadows as the weeks passed by.

12. Freedom Coming

Round about June 1981 I wrote in my diary that there was a possibility of Jimmy being moved onto TFF (Training For Freedom – the last hurdle he had to jump before the gates finally opened for him.) His date of release, Nov 1st 1982, was still a long way off, but it seemed that in response to a vociferous and determined campaign by me and Jimmy's many influential supporters, there was a prospect of him being transferred onto this programme sooner than we had expected.

There were apparently places in the TFF Hostel and there was a rumour that two new people would be moved in there, one of these being Jimmy. In any case things were improving as from now he would be getting out for four whole days each week.

The strain of our compressed times seeing each other and the spells in between was continuing to take its toll. I often found myself feeling exhausted. I was caught up in the momentum of the weekly routine, giving my all to Jimmy and often neglecting myself. The whole situation was out of balance, but I was newly married, young and in love. The driving force underneath was a complete dedication to keeping our relationship strong and alive as the goal of freedom edged closer. Ricky Demarco made a comment describing me as Jimmy's life support system – and in lots of ways I was this, as he also was mine. We clung to each other with an unquenchable thirst for our stolen moments of freedom.

I was confronting aspects of my past which kept surfacing as I found myself unable to break out of patterns of self-abuse which were very upsetting for me. Jimmy tried his best to understand what lay beneath these and he would berate me to have more self-discipline. Much that lay beneath the surface though stemmed from early relationships with my close family.

I made my first venture into therapy to try to explore this: 'I become a pit full of tears, a dark emptiness where I lose all hold of any sense of identity... I cannot move, I cannot speak, I cannot find my way out. I am alone.'

Sharing my hidden vulnerability, which I felt deeply ashamed of, was like taking my pants down and revealing my nakedness. This exploration didn't get far as the therapist had no understanding of the pressures I was dealing with as a consequence of Jimmy's continued confinement. Many people couldn't understand the enormity of what I was dealing with which contributed to my sense of isolation. How could I begin to share the ins and outs of this very different world. It was like a parallel universe, of completely contrasting realities.

There were times when the frustrations would surface in us both and we had to work hard not to take it out on each other. It says a lot about the strength of our relationship at that time, that for the most part we managed this. I was also discovering aspects of the subculture at Wester Hailes. Jimmy was involved in supporting young homeless kids to settle into flats and because I accompanied him often in this work I found myself being taken into this world of young punks.

With their studs and spiked hairdos, they looked scary, and intimidating from the outside, but with Jimmy being the bridge, I was able to make my own relationships with them, gaining access to their world. As the barriers crumbled they shared their stories of poverty, abuse, violence, and abandonment, which had contributed to their feelings of alienation from the world. They roamed around the scheme like pack animals, and were certainly no angels, but many of them had talents, and simply needed a positive element of leadership which Jimmy provided.

When he was out and about Jimmy started to take increasing risks which added to the pressures. I ended up getting angry with him, making the case for more caution. He accepted this and mostly showed a great deal of strength and self-control, dealing with the impossible contrasts he was facing by having to return to the prison, week in and week out. In mid-June I wrote: 'I can see this frustrating situation grinding the two of us down.'

At least I had the focus of my job, which involved me exploring many different groups active in the field of community mental health. I met some wonderful people through this who were dedicated to developing support groups and services in the community. I started to learn some new ways of coping myself which included being introduced to relaxation using a biofeedback box and, for the first time, I became interested in meditation. These were small beginnings, but they sowed seeds for what was to become a very important part of my life later on.

Although I was often seeing Jimmy in clandestine meetings which we arranged during his days out and about in Wester Hailes, we were still having the official monthly visits in the prison. I wrote about one of these:

> 'This is always an unnerving experience. On these occasions I am thrust into the world which Jimmy has to go back to each night. The contrast is extreme. It always affects me. Much as there is pain in this, there is also the pleasure of sitting close to Jimmy and spending the hour locked in the close security of our world together.'

The flat, now the place that we both considered to be *our* home, also held this for us. In my diary there are a few lines written by Jimmy on one of his stolen visits there:

'In the house typing this. Sarah and I sat having a coffee. Now she is away to work and I am sitting here at home, my home, our home. I moved around doing this and that, emptying my clothes from a big box into the drawers, putting up the toilet cabinet, making coffee, reading the papers, having a bath, playing with Cuba (our cat!) It's so good to be sitting here at home doing all these little things that I've never done in such a long time. I'm sitting here loving every moment of just being home.'

I follow on later: 'The glimpse I get of him being at home here with me seems very much more real than its ever seemed

before. Thrown together we go deeper and deeper into each other. This opens up whole new spaces and areas which are always challenging and creative. I learn so much from him.'

And I did at that time, he was full of passion for life and experienced joy in the simplest of things. As he kept pushing at the boundaries more and more, he was like a child suddenly gaining access to a bigger world. We ventured into a pub – a completely normal setting for everybody else, but if the two of us had been discovered sitting together an enormous scandal would have been made out of it, as we were breaking the conditions of his parole.

Jimmy was always willing to take risks, while I was more security conscious. We continued to have to bridge our different realities. A lot of the time my difficulties would surface, but Jimmy had plenty of his own unhealed places as well.

'Tonight his inner wall cracked open and in spasmodic sobs whole chunks of Jimmy's past came spurting out. This is the first time that I've seen him in such a vulnerable state with the floodgates wide open. He went back into the hardship of his early life. The hunger and deprivation which he felt at that age left him very insecure. He mentioned waiting with Harry on the street where they would have to stand for hours before their Ma came home...He felt inadequate because of his torn clothes and having to beg for food.'

All of this was far removed from my own experience. Our two backgrounds couldn't have been more contrasting. The gulf between our lives came especially into focus when his son James Paul visited. Jimmy's two children, James Paul and Tricia were both born when he was in prison. They were looked after by their mother, and her partner, a Glasgow pub owner, John McCue, who became their stepfather.

James Paul was very short sighted and wore glasses. He spoke in a thick Glasgow accent. His mother and stepfather had wanted to send him to Edinburgh to get him away from the Glasgow environment. One day John, acting on this impulse, drove across to Edinburgh, arriving with James Paul at Margaret Boyle's flat. It was hard for Jimmy to suddenly be brought face to face with his past. It was easier for James Paul to relate to Margaret (Boyle), and her twin sons, Chris and Greg, than to either of the two of us.

James was left sitting on the couch in Margaret's flat, dejected, head down, with £20 thrust into his hand as his step father took off. I was aware that the culture gap was enormous and would be deeply challenging for us both as John seemed to be expecting Jimmy to take responsibility for him.

Later I drove James to Wester Hailes hoping that he might say more to me on the way, but he didn't – he kept his head down and only uttered a couple of words. He seemed a strange mixture of vulnerability and shyness, with a stubborn streak of independence. I felt I was groping in the dark trying to get to know this young, isolated boy. He had difficulty with his eyesight and wore glasses with thick lenses, but I felt that there was a lot more than just his short sightedness holding him back.

A meeting was called with Lawrence Demarco (Lothian Regional Council's community worker for the Wester Hailes area), social workers from Glasgow, and Governor Hills. It came across strongly that the Prison authorities were not happy with the idea of Jimmy taking on parental responsibilities for James, nor for him to be given a job at Wester Hailes – so this episode passed with James Paul returning to Glasgow which in many ways was a relief. This situation pulled at me though as I felt the presence of so much pain underneath – which neither of us could do anything about.

Meanwhile our routine continued with me dropping Jimmy off after work, night after night, watching him walking back up the road towards the prison. It never became any easier to deal with this fragmented life. Sometimes though I experienced moments of magic which suddenly broke through, giving a glimpse of something which seemed to transcend the everyday realities.

> 'The sunset up on Calton Hill...The sky stretches like a vast cover above me. I love its luminosity and intensity. Clouds hang silently, voiceless in the stillness. Orange spreads into yellow and blues...oh, I really love these colours. And I really love this view. If only a path stretched from here to the sunset that I could walk along, I'd want to run after the setting sun and chase it down over the horizon. I'd run to get warm, I'd run to get release, I'd run to set myself free...'

The emotional challenges continued and towards the end of August Jimmy's mood plummeted as memories from his time in the cages in Inverness surfaced in him. He had a bad day and found himself pacing up and down in his cell. The experience took him back to the cages, and suddenly he was spilling it all out to me in wracking sobs. He shook and heaved with the shocking memories as he described a terrible assault which was made on him, the details of which I will not include here.

This had a very disturbing impact on me when I first found this section in my diary and still sickens me. We lay close together on the bed, wet with tears and sweat, after he had shared this with me. I felt our closeness and our love offering a counterbalance to all the pain.

> 'How do I feel about Jimmy, knowing that he's been through this trail of terrible violence in his past? This is an important, but difficult question to answer. The squeamish part of me finds it difficult to accept the horror that he's lived through, which could quite easily overwhelm me if I let myself feel it too much. But in amongst it all two things emerge. The courage that he showed and the basic will to live which made him fight, a fight to live, rather than to succumb and die.'

Knowing that Jimmy holds these feelings underneath gives me more understanding of some of the choices which he has made subsequently in his life. This is a subject which I will return to at a later point. The fact that we were able to open up such deep places between us through this last part of his sentence said much about the depths we were able to share together.

I was also confronted with the ugly fact that brutalising environments bring out the worst in people. We have seen this more recently in the horrifying accounts which emerged from the Abu Ghraib prison in Baghdad. That Jimmy was to find himself on the receiving end of these kind of horrors forty years ago in a Scottish Prison, not far away from where I sit writing this account, is perhaps more troubling.

The anniversary of Jimmy's move from the Special Unit to Saughton Prison was approaching. One year on, things were looking increasingly hopeful as there was a definite sense that Jimmy would be moving onto the Training for Freedom Programme proper very soon. We were about to experience the landscape changing again with the prospect of him starting on the final stretch of his pre-release programme, and finally being able to take a five day home leave.

> **16.9.81** 'Its going to be so different. How will it be when we see so much of each other? New problems will confront us. New adjustments will have to be made. I've not slept overnight with anyone for years and neither has Jimmy. So it's going to feel really strange for us both to be sharing the same bed!'

The fact that we were now about to be confronted with these kinds of new experiences showed that at last we were about to enter the final stretch.

13. Release - The Gate Opens

In October Jimmy was finally given a date for his five day leave. The impact of getting definite confirmation of the date was obvious to see in him. He was relieved and delighted.

> **19.10.81** 'We've only a week to go now before Jimmy starts his Training for Freedom. A week today we will be setting off up to Inverness, embarking on our first holiday together. Ready to spend our first night together! We've decided to head up to Inverness to stay in a caravan just outside StrathPfeffer. This was a spur of the moment decision. We don't know what to expect, but we've been told that the caravan is high up on a hillside and has a lovely view.'

I was pleased at the prospect of going back to Inverness again, which was where it had all begun for me, during my days of working at the Royal Northern Infirmary. For Jimmy though the experience of Inverness was very different. I don't think I appreciated then, or subsequently, just how difficult it would be for him to revisit that town with the associations which it had for him of the cages, where he had spent seven dreadful years in solitary confinement.

This special five-day leave was to be our first unbroken time together. I collected Jimmy from the prison at 7am. Neither of us had slept much the night before. For Jimmy it had been his last night in a prison cell. When he returned to the prison his next move would be into the Training for Freedom hostel.

The following is from Jimmy's diary of this time:

> 'Sarah met me at the prison gate. It was a relief to see her. We kissed and then left with the ominous clanging of the prison gate behind us. There was a tremendous feeling of freedom. At home it was great to walk in and out of the house without disguises or feeling apprehensive. It was as it should be, open and natural. Sarah and I were glowing with excitement and pleasure.
>
> Up the long winding roads the scenery was spectacular. Sitting there with Sarah at my side, the prison far behind, and the wonders of the Scottish Highlands all around me I felt quite stunned with pleasure. The clouds parted, and miraculously the day cleared. The skies up here are quite unreal.'

The photographs which I have kept from this time, and the words which I wrote beside them, capture some of the immediacy of this experience. We were both dressed in fleece lined biker jackets – these were more Jimmy's choice than mine, but I let him pursuade me that we needed them. One of the pictures shows me relaxed and smiling, leaning against a fence. Another shows the light shining through underneath dark banks of cloud. A perfect visual symbol of what we were coming through together. There is a picture of Jimmy in the foreground with Loch Ness behind:

> 'How can I possibly explain this experience to anyone after 14 years in prison? Every fibre in me was open and alert to this vast scenery.'

Finally we reached our caravan situated high up on the hillside with a wide and full view of the valley. Again from Jimmy's diary:

> 'It was getting dark though with still enough light for us to see our view from the caravan. Sheep were all around us. We

sit on the side of the hill looking down on the valley with a spattering of cottages and farmhouses. The visual images are overwhelming.

Here we are with each other throughout the day, seeing each other first thing in the morning!!! (My God!!)

It's gonna take time for us to adjust to. Mind you we made the most of it! I asked Sarah if she would mind my getting up early (6.30am) to go for a run? She didn't mind. Sheep could be heard outside the caravan. It had been raining all night but on getting up and going out it was very calm and peaceful. Wearing strong boots and a tracksuit I ran through the countryside.'

There is a picture of Jimmy jumping into the air and another of him standing with both fists raised and a smile of absolute joy on his face. Beside these I have written:

BORN TO RUN AND RUN AND RUN

There are pictures of me in the caravan, struggling with the calor gas cooker. Then three more of us sitting together in front of a small table, with the curtains closed behind us. We are sitting close to each other. On the table top is a candle, a bottle of champagne and plates with bread, cheese and one very red tomato. We are toasting the moment.

From Jimmy's diary:

'This is the ultimate. We've done it! We're together.'

He took nothing for granted:

'It was thrilling to stand in the silent morning and look to the distance without any man-made structure obstructing the view as in prison.'

We drove across to the West Coast and visited Ullapool and Torridon. We were both inspired by nature's ability to create the most powerful theatrical setting in this wild and spectacular landscape where the light was ever changing.

We also visited Glen Affric, which is still one of my favourite places in the Highlands.

Again Jimmy's words:

> 'There are moments in this experience when one runs out of superlatives to say what is necessary to describe it.
>
> There are moments when Sarah and I speak, but lots of the time is spent in silence, in just being with each other.
>
> There is something about opening to the experience of these vast unspoiled landscapes which puts everything else into perspective.'

Predictably, there were also challenges. The nights were strangely difficult. It is easy now to see why this was, but at the time it was quite disturbing and worrying. The feeling was exactly that of sharing a bed with someone who has slept on his own for the past fourteen years. I'm also not accustomed to sleeping close to another body. Emotionally we had both become used to switching off when we couldn't be with each other. Suddenly being thrust together in this overnight situation was such an overwhelming change that it threw up many mixed emotions and revealed stresses which surprised us both.

Jimmy said that he woke up in the morning almost angry to find another body occupying a large part of the space in the cramped caravan bed. I found myself pushing and shoving as well, and restless because it was difficult to get comfortable. For much of the night we slept like two separate people in the same bed. Lovemaking though was all we could have wanted it to be.

We drove back through Glasgow where we visited Peggy, Alfie, and Freddy, surprising them by our sudden appearance. 'Coming, coming, coming... coming, coming, coming.' We heard Peggy's gruff voice as we stood and waited at their door. They were delighted and gave us a warm welcome. Peggy and Alfie were looking old and worn. Freddy's face looked flushed and bloated from too much booze.

There was a lot of pathos for me witnessing Jimmy's reunion with his family. We also called in to see Pat, his brother, who played his out of tune piano for us, in an accomplished way, and with great sensitivity.

It was a mixed experience for Jimmy returning to these streets where he had spent the greater part of his youth and childhood – the times when he wasn't in an approved school, remand centre, or prison. He spoke bitterly in the car about the hardships of poverty and the lack of opportunities for people living in these environments. These scourges still exist today, of course. Poverty continues to be a deeply ingrained reality in these urban districts.

At the end of the five days the reality of having to get used to the prison situation again immediately put us back in the harness. The conditions in the Training for Freedom Hostel were far from luxurious. People emerging from prison are up against it in many ways. Jimmy was fortunate to have all the support that I was able to give him, as well as his own store of creative resources to draw on.

The others in the hostel were working in such places as Dalton's Scrap yard, and the fruit market, where they were open to abuse, through being called 'prisoner' or picked on as they struggled to learn basic skills of survival in the world outside.

I felt stronger and better after our five days. We could be closer together again, and were moving back to the regular contact that we had been able to have in the unit. Jimmy though still had to close off his feelings when he went back into the prison hostel each night. This tortuous, senseless process seemed never ending and made the whole experience of readjustment a very interrupted one. At least we were able to do more things in the evenings, and were also able to spend weekends together.

We made good use of these times – stretching things as far as we could, which was very much Jimmy's way. His licence apparently said that we couldn't go more than five miles outside Edinburgh, but we visited Durham, the Lakes, and the Borders with Jimmy loving it all.

In December we had our first party in the flat. This was a great success. It felt strange to be socialising 'normally' like this but I enjoyed the evening very much. We had a selection of our friends from Wester Hailes and other places – it was a rich mixture. Jimmy had very definite views about alcohol in those days saying that drink merely clouded the mind and that it was always best to absorb experiences with a clear head. The issue of drink only started to come between us at a later stage when he started to indulge more freely.

We put up our first Christmas tree with Jimmy's touch being to replace the traditional fairy at the top of the tree with a pig. Well, I guess pigs can be beautiful too. On his weekend leaves we were able to enjoy getting more used to sleeping together. I liked settling into the snug warmth of Jimmy's body. Jimmy described it as getting used to the shape and curve and rhythm of each other in this very intimate setting.

We looked forward to Christmas, which we would be celebrating together. There were mounting pressures though as wherever we went – meeting family and friends, attending parties - everything centred around Jimmy and I felt somehow left out of this. I can see now that in giving so much of myself to support Jimmy, and trying to model myself on him in so many ways, I was losing touch with my own sense of identity.

Giving up my medical career was a part of this, but there is no way that I could have managed to keep working in a full time job, through this long slow passage to freedom. Issues of self-confidence and my own identity weighed heavily on me and only increased as Jimmy emerged into the world.

31.12.81 'My Darling Sarah... last day of this year taking us into next... *ours*! This New Year is ours. It is the downhill slope to our freedom.

This year we must push together and make ours. There is much, much to do. It will mean hard, demanding work. I know that above all you are a little spitfire who will meet it like me, head on.

Into this year we thrust ourselves – together!
HAPPY NEW YEAR
I love you, your husband, Jimmy xxx'

New Year 1981/82

From my Diary: 'We spent two days preparing for the New Year. On Wednesday we took a long walk in the Pentland Hills. On Thursday, New Year's Eve, we cleaned the house, following the custom in Glasgow where you clean out the old year in order to welcome in the new one. Jimmy has enriched my life through introducing me to these rituals. We lit Heidi's candle, opened a bottle of champagne and toasted our mutual freedom in 1982. In the background were the lights of the Christmas tree and all around us hung rows of cards bringing good wishes from our many friends. It felt wonderful to be together in this beautiful atmosphere, in our home...a year further on than last New Year, and with only a short distance now to go. Then we danced, danced naked in the bedroom. It was fantastic!'

James and Tricia, Jimmy's children, came across to Edinburgh for their first visit together to see us. We picked them up from the station and took them home – but we all struggled. They were like two strangers, arriving from a very different world in Glasgow, one that Jimmy had left behind many years ago. It must have been hard for them getting used to seeing their Da again but they had made the effort to come across and see us and this was of course a start.

In April there is the first mention in my diary of meeting

Sebastian and Evlynn – two young people who were to become our closest friends, and who became co-founders of the project which we established after Jimmy's release, called *The Gateway Exchange*. They both sported spikey punk hairdos and were very creative. Sebastian, like me, came from a wealthy family.

His grandfather, Alec Horsley, was a successful businessman who had founded Northern Foods and was a committed Quaker. He and his wife Susan had corresponded with Jimmy and visited him in the Special Unit. Sebastian had heard about Jimmy and was very much wanting to meet him. Evlynn, his girlfriend, came from Edinburgh. The pair of them had met at art school in London. We hit it off immediately, finding many areas of shared common experience, not the least of these being our shared passion for the creative arts.

We also visited Glasgow, calling in at a drugs project in the Gorbals, then visiting Peggy. She was expecting us and had the table spread with a white cloth. She told us that Alfie had just been taken into hospital. Despite all her complaints about him previously, she was struggling to know how she would cope without him. They had recently celebrated their fiftieth wedding anniversary, fifty years on from celebrating in Peterhead on the morning of their wedding with a boiled egg for breakfast – a luxury in those days. Together they had weathered all the challenges life brought and were not used to being apart.

Peggy brought out a dumpling which she had cooked especially for our visit. 'You'll have to tow it behind your car to get it back to Edinburgh,' said Freddy with a wicked grin, adding, 'Don't take any up to Alfie, it'll kill him!' The humour was ever present in this household. The whole family had gathered, with James and Patricia as well, so it was a very full house and a great experience for us both.

1.6.82 'First of June. Now just five more months to go. Slowly the hour glass of time is running through.'

We had another weekend leave, which we spent driving north to Skye, where, because of drenching rain, we turned around, ending up down at Dunbar the following day. Jimmy was spotted in both places and was pulled up afterwards in the prison for this. He was pushing at the boundaries again, also wanting to run in the Edinburgh marathon which, not surprisingly, was turned down.

> **3.6.82** 'My Darling Sarah – Sitting here in this cell with the sun shining brightly outside I want you to know that you are a tremendous source of strength to me. Marrying you was the most beautiful act I have ever done.
>
> We have less than five months to go till we have reached the first step in our life together. Then it will be a new era. I know that then, as opposed to now, there will be no opaque glass or barred window frames to stop us. We will free each other. I love you with all that I feel and possess at this moment in time. I know that as I develop so too will my life and love for you. The full force of what we share is encapsulated in what I feel sitting here at this moment. I acknowledge this and balance it against the pain of the circumstance – there is no contest. You win every time. You are the sunshine of my life.
>
> Hold this close for it comes from the centre of my existence. I love you. Your husband, Jimmy x x x'

This letter and others written by Jimmy at that time can still rekindle a warm glow in my heart. They are like touchstones, which capture the intensity of Jimmy's love in those days. It has been healing to rediscover them. They remind me of the love that we shared, which was truly alive at that time. It strikes me that had I never embarked on this archaeological dig of my life – these treasures would have remained in dust-covered boxes, and disappeared most probably into a fire or a recycling bin.

Some things are worth keeping and remembering.

*

I spoke at a meeting of the Patients' Association of the Royal Edinburgh Hospital where a new group was being established. I was passionate in my advocacy for psychiatric patients, as much as for prisoners. Both were up against similar problems of stigma, and multiple disadvantages when it came to re-engaging with mainstream society.

I also gave a talk hosted by the Scottish Association of Mental Health to launch my report into Mental Health and the Community. It described my experiences during the year when I had undertaken an action research project looking at some of the causes of mental distress in the community, as well as describing the emergence of many different self-help groups which were offering support at grass roots level.

For me, it represented a shift in my understanding - from simply looking at the problems of individuals to seeing how social conditions contributed to these problems. I was proud of this piece of work when I finally finished my report.

*

Jimmy was about to celebrate a different kind of achievement, one that no doubt doesn't happen often for prisoners on Training for Freedom programmes.

> **23.6.82** - 'His driving test is tomorrow! He was on edge because three different 'screws' had spotted him having his lesson – he was worried about getting pulled in tonight. This puts him under a lot of extra pressure and tension.'

I had been giving Jimmy driving lessons for some time and he successfully managed to pass his test on the second attempt, in September. The first time he was failed for something he has never been pulled up for before, or since in his life, 'undue hesitancy'!

> **30.6.82** 'My Darling Sarah – The wearisome forces of the situation cause me to wilt as the days go by. There is an anguish being held down, being kept wrapped and firmly shut, not allowed to express its full force as we climb through the jungle of this situation, ever watchful, ever alert, it all becomes tiring to the extreme...'

I was tired too, but I didn't give myself permission to feel it as my problems never seemed to have the weight that Jimmy's did. Comparison is unhelpful when it comes to developing a truthful relationship with our own inner worlds. I had yet to learn this.

Our life continued to be full of bizarre contrasts. On another weekend leave we went on a trip to London and took a flight to get there. At the airport we spotted George Younger and his wife. Jimmy homed in on him and directed me to sit as close as possible to them on the plane. The seats we chose were directly behind Mr and Mrs Younger's.

Here was someone who had supreme power over the lives of individuals like Jimmy, who was subject to the sometimes arbitrary whims of the criminal justice system. He recognized us and turned round in his seat to give a greeting. Jimmy and he exchanged comments about the state of the weather in London. At the end of our journey he turned round and shook our hands. It was strangely farcical that we managed to make a connection with him in this way.

In August Jimmy was assigned his social worker, Mike Nagle. Already he was thinking ahead and wanting to make sure that he would have permission to leave the country for a trip overseas when he finally reached the end of his sentence. On the 19th

August, my mother's birthday, Jimmy received his own birthday present – his passport.

Diary: 21.9.82 'Two Daily Mail reporters came round to the door in the afternoon. This is a sign of the pressure which will begin to mount between now and Nov 1st. I have to get myself fit, and in good condition all round for this important time. Just at the moment this last stretch is particularly difficult, as everyone said it would be.'

Sunday 31.10.82 'The day before, still damp, dark, clouded over, giving a real sense of 'the tunnel'. In the morning my spirits were low and I burst into tears at one point. I was beginning to feel that it was all too much, almost as though I was feeling all the strains of the past few months at once – or 'hitting the wall' as they say in marathon terms. In the evening I had to drop Jimmy back at the prison. I watched him walk in the darkness to the prison gate. A small but determined figure, raising his arm in a clenched fist for me once again.

The moment seems unreal. But the relief will be total when I feel it tomorrow.'

Sebastian and Evlynn had arrived from London and were staying overnight, coming as special friends to celebrate and witness Jimmy's release the next day.

Monday 1.11.82 'I woke early. The morning was still wrapped in darkness. I looked out and saw that it was wet. I washed and dressed, feeling excitement stirring warmly within. Everything looked neat and immaculate for Jimmy's homecoming. Now this house and home belongs to us both.'

Sebastian and Evlynn were with me in the car as we drove to

the prison. The streets were dark and deserted although a few coated figures were sleepily making their way to work. When we drove into the prison drive there was a prison officer on duty waiting to meet us. The press were gathered in force on the drive, fifty?... One hundred? I couldn't tell. I stepped out of the car and hesitated. Under the glare of the spotlights I heard voices shouting out questions. How do you feel? I tried to smile and stay calm. 'Wonderful'... But what did they want? How could I say how it really felt under this barrage?

I manoeuvred the car up the drive, then was told to turn back and collect Jimmy at the bottom because he was to walk down the drive towards the press to allow them to get their photos. By the time I had done this and climbed out again Jimmy was already surrounded by the media, cameras, mikes, and lights. This was the moment when he gave his triumphant freedom salute. He was handling the whole thing magnificently and giving confident answers to all the questions. Declaring himself very clearly to be moving into a new future and affirming his commitment to social causes, in particular to youth.

I went over and joined him. We kissed and allowed the nation's cameras to capture this image. We had nothing to hide about the way that we felt about each other, so I took strength from this at least.

Finally we broke free and were able to join Sebastian and Evlynn who were waiting patiently by the side of the drive. Sebastian had a huge magnum of champagne – (which we had asked him to hide) Then all four of us piled into the car and drove off home.

That was it. Jimmy said later that he had passed Charles Hills, the Governor, on his way out of the prison, but he had looked the other way and didn't speak a word. His fifteen-year sentence had ended. The doors had opened and Jimmy took his first few steps out into the early morning and to freedom. His life after prison started in that moment.

*

This was the freedom he had never thought he would reach. There was no pat on the back or good luck wishes from the institution, simply this cold, anonymous early morning opening of the gate. It reminded me of the impersonal nature of the goodbyes which I had experienced when I was working in hospital. The attitudes and procedures of the institution matched the cold austerity of its exterior.

This is the moment where his second book *The Pain of Confinement*, ends. This book was based on the diaries which he kept during the years which he spent in the Special Unit, and includes his pre-release time at Saughton. The final paragraph of the last entry: 1st November '82, is brief and to the point.

> 'I was taken to the gate where I waited for Sarah. These were the longest minutes of all. The gate officer said Mr Hills had called to say he was coming in. I stood on edge. Mr Hills drove in the gate. He didn't look at me. He didn't speak. Sarah arrived. Mr Hills gave the signal and the duty officer opened the gate. I stepped over into Freedom.'

This is how most prisoners end their sentences, ejected from the institution in the cold grey of the early morning, with scant resources to pick up the pieces of their shattered lives. A consequence of this, as I have mentioned previously, is the so-called revolving door phenomena where individuals lacking in skills or support all too quickly fall back on old coping mechanisms and re-offend.

Jimmy's passage was different and in many senses very privileged. We had a home, family, friends, and all the resources we could have wanted to build a future together. He also had years of accumulated institutional experience, which he would carry for the rest of his life – how would this express itself in the years ahead? At that point our focus understandably enough was simply on appreciating the sudden and long awaited change in our circumstances.

We had arranged a special breakfast at home with Sebastian, Evlynn, Jack and Anna MacNeill, staunch friends from the Wester Hailes workshop, and Lawrence. We celebrated the moment with champagne and croissants – what better way to start the day. Later on we had some time for ourselves, which we both very much needed. The image which I had of Jimmy as he lay in my arms was of a new born baby – vulnerable and soft as he re-entered the world.

There was a press conference where Jimmy was asked what, if anything, he was going to miss on leaving prison. His response, which was almost immediate was: 'Well certainly not the porridge!'

In the evening we celebrated with a special Freedom party which I had organised at Calton Studios in Edinburgh. My Mum came to this, Bill and Jane Beech who were also artists and long term friends, Sebastian's grandparents, Alec and Susan from Hull, as well as other friends from Edinburgh, Glasgow and London. Jimmy's family managed to make it from Glasgow – Alfie, Peggy and others, all piling out of the back of his cousin Alex's taxi.

Shaun from the Breadwinner had made a special cake which created a surprise for us all when a little bird thrust itself out of the base and circled noisily above our heads. Frankie Miller (Jimmy's cousin) and others sang, while Jimmy and I put ourselves about happily mixing with the company. There were speeches with much laughter, as everyone came together to celebrate the true spirit of freedom, which rose triumphant at the end of this long and extraordinary passage.

What a night. It was not one to be ever forgotten. The best part of it all was leaving to go home together, then waking up together the following morning. Of course, the memories have faded, but the spirit is there still, lifting me up, whispering to me quietly as I sit listening in the stillness:

'Well done!'

14. *Freedom at Last and the First Baby*

Looking back on it, the change in our lives with Jimmy's release on 1st November 1982, at the end of his fifteen-year sentence was momentous. At the time, the hectic rush of events that followed made stopping to take in the full implications of crossing this threshold impossible.

I know that I was pleased and relieved to reach the end of the prison years – this time of partnering Jimmy through his final four and a half years of confinement had been full of so many pressures, as well as the strains of continued separation. I had a moment on the day of his release when the question: 'Why me?' swept over me as I contemplated the strangeness of having undergone this whole experience.

It was such a rite of passage in my life. I had made this deep and total commitment to marrying without any idea where it was all going to take me. Somebody once said to me that we can only really understand life when we look back at it, at the time it is as if we are lost in the pull of the current, unable to see where it is taking us.

Certainly it was like this for me. There was also a deep tiredness, which must have been present in both of us. The biggest change that I recorded was that we both stopped keeping a diary that first month.

When I did return to mine and to writing about the day of Jimmy's release, we were sitting in a plane on the tarmac of Frankfurt airport waiting to take off on a flight to Kuala Lumpur. Already we were being catapulted into a whole rush of new experiences as, in early December 1982, we left for a holiday together to South East Asia. We were fortunate to have the resources to be able to do this, and after so many years of confinement Jimmy couldn't wait to begin exploring the bigger world. It would possibly have been better to give ourselves a proper Christmas at home first, but his impulse to get away won the day.

As we crossed over the Indian subcontinent the views from the plane window were magnificent. 'The perspective which opens up seeing everything from such a height is incredible. The earth suddenly becomes a vast sphere and we are a tiny speck flying across its surface.' Jimmy of course was experiencing a long haul flight for the first time and was in a state of heightened excitement throughout.

When we landed in Kuala Lumpur we were blitzed by a kaleidoscope of new experiences, which made an enormous sensory impact on Jimmy. He felt adrenaline shooting through his system, with the rush of being exposed to a whole new environment and culture. The winter greys of Scotland were replaced with the throbbing, thronging, vividly coloured, exotic multicultural stream of life that is the way of things in the East. It was both stimulating as well as challenging in its unfamiliarity.

The climate, with its energy sapping heat, mosquitoes and the effects of the sun, brought new challenges; our inexperience resulted in some funny moments. Jimmy's lips got badly sunburned. Trying to be helpful and being a believer in natural remedies, I bought a small jar of watermelon frost from a Chinese herbal street stall and his lips turned green! He got his own back on me when we went for a cheap haircut and he pushed me to have mine first – I emerged in tears with my fringe cut short and straight, like a China doll.

We had applied for a visa to visit Australia where we had planned to spend Christmas with my brother and his family. In the end there was some negative publicity about this locally, with a fear being expressed that allowing Jimmy in would open the floodgates for all sorts of other 'undesirables'.

It seemed that we were up against the same bureaucratic blockages that we had campaigned against at home. The visa was refused. I felt sad that this attempt to introduce Jimmy to the country where I had spent my early life had been thwarted, but we dealt with this and diverted ourselves into making alternative plans.

We headed north to Penang, then on to Chiang Mai for Christmas. Creating our own festivity in a part of the world where this is not part of the local culture was something of a challenge, but the words on Jimmy's card to me sum up the feelings on that day:

> 'My Darling Sarah, I want you to know that my happiness is you. I could ask for no finer gift than to know I am with you. I love you and will never tire of telling you this. Our journey together even at this early stage is magic. We are doing it in style, as we both tend to. Sarah, may you have a very Happy Christmas (if you have a duffer it means I will also!!!)
>
> I love you, Your husband, Jimmy x x x '

By New Year we were back in the south in Phuket, staying in a bungalow beside the beach:

> **31.12.83** 'Darling Sarah – I couldn't be with a better person, in a better place at this special time of year. I am so grateful for all you've done for me over the past year. You more than anyone else have made it an astounding success. This year we make it TOGETHER! One thing that I always keep in mind is that no matter what we come up against we've always got each other. That thought and feeling carried me through so many bad times

in recent years. That, my woman, is the magic of you – I have you. Your Man – in heart, spirit and soul. Jimmy x x x '

There was a local beach celebration at New Year which took the form of a buffet laid out on tables under the palm trees; drumming, dancing, wildness and abandonment... but I felt a bit bewildered by it all and singing Auld Lang Syne at midnight made me feel nostalgic for home. As the New Year began we started to focus on the future and what it held for us both.

The idea which hatched itself was of opening a centre where we could combine our different experiences and talents to support others with backgrounds of prison, mental health problems, or drug and alcohol abuse. The emphasis would be on providing a place where they could be encouraged to tap into their positive qualities and abilities in the community.

I had a few doubts about going into this venture with Jimmy and part of me wondered if I shouldn't backtrack and return to having a safe foothold working as a doctor. The two streams of thought came and went for a while, but the prospect of returning to work within the system felt daunting after what I had come through, and the vision of a centre which could be a creative experience for us both held a lot more appeal.

Two months of travelling in South East Asia, which included our first visit to Bali, had allowed us to relax, and had filled our senses with an exotic overload – we had experienced some of the shadow sides of tourism developing at break-neck speed in this part of the world – the drugs, the prostitution, and the terrible pollution on over congested roads. We had also experienced the breathtaking tranquillity of beautiful beaches, spectacular orange vermillion pink sunsets, and golden temples, all evoking the magic of the East, which has stayed with us both since this time.

*

Edinburgh looked bleak and dreary arriving back, but inside our flat in St Peter's Place there were three large heaps of mail waiting for us, and some provisions left for us by Mum and Margaret, which was very thoughtful of them both. We settled back and enjoyed making the flat look and feel like home once more – simple things, but after what we had been through neither of us took this for granted. Jimmy channelled his physical energy, of which he had lots, in those days, into running and we renewed all our former activities and contacts which had a strong community focus for both of us.

We made one visit back to the Special Unit, making our way through the grim gate and reception area of Barlinnie, which was just as I remembered it. We had to walk through the gauntlet of prison officers who mostly kept their faces mask-like and set, although one or two gave friendly nods. We were called through to take the escorted walk across to the Special Unit and were met by Collie (Hugh Collins) who took us up to his cell.

Malky, the prison officer who had been Jimmy's witness at our wedding, was also waiting for us and gave us a warm greeting. Collie and the other inmates had done their best to keep the place alive after Jimmy's departure, but outside the gardens were looking bare, and although there was still a circle of stones in the yard with some of Collie's sculptures added to it, the place felt static and aged, like something of an empty shell, compared to the hub of activity that it had once been. Jimmy was struck by how small and claustrophobic the Unit felt on his return to it and in particular his cell where he had spent so many nights and days.

Collie brought us up to date with all the recent news and the different vendettas and struggles that had taken place between the small group of prisoners. It felt as though the Prisons' Department was back in complete control, which left the inmates reverting to a more defensive subculture. Collie described apathy and disinterest amongst new inmates whose preoccupations were directed more into drugs, booze, and crime than anything to do with challenging this and looking for new creative outlets.

We were told that Ken Murray was facing another departmental onslaught after remarks he had made on prison reform to a liberal conference were reported in the press. He had been accused of making public statements that could bring the prison service into disrepute. The powers of officialdom seemed to be sticking to a business as usual approach. There was no sign that any of the Special Unit experience was to be utilised by or applied to the rest of the prison system.

This was a time of reconnecting with family and friends, as we started to build the foundations of our lives together. Little by little the centre took physical form and shape. With a wonderful solicitor called Ethel Houston, we created the legal foundation for a Company Limited by Guarantee, which seemed to give us more flexibility than creating a trust fund.

We also gave this fledgling project a name, which was *The Gateway Exchange*.

'Gateway' expressed the passage which Jimmy had stepped through, on his first day of freedom – 'Exchange' was because we wanted to put the emphasis on the positive creative potential which individuals have, rather than focusing on problems, which is where the emphasis tends to lie in most institutions. Our vision was of creating a safe place where anyone, no matter what their background, could come and be encouraged to become part of a dynamic community where their potential and uniqueness would be recognised and welcomed.

It was a dream and a vision founded on Jimmy's experience in prisons, also mine, when I had worked within the psychiatric system. This over-arching sense of mission and purpose strengthened and supported our partnership as we began this new phase.

Our friends Sebastian and Evlynn managed to create an excellent logo for our project. All of this was helping to put flesh on the bones of our vision for *The Gateway Exchange*, the project which was to play such a central part in our lives throughout the 1980s. We managed to find a suitable premises. We had decided what we needed was a shop front with space behind it. This specification led to us discovering a double shop front in Abbeymount which had a large hall behind it, divided by a mezzanine floor. It seemed perfect as it would offer space for an office, a café, and workshop behind.

This space had previously been owned by a rather eccentric millionaire publisher – the front windows displayed books on Mary Queen of Scots and the history of Scotland, while the back had been used to store paperback pornographic books. Apparently this business had been doing a thriving trade, mailing these publications to individuals all over the globe. We had a good laugh about this. After some negotiation our offer for purchasing the property was accepted – we were delighted.

In notes from the catalogue from one of our earliest exhibitions, called 'New Beginnings' Jimmy writes his own account of our vision for *The Gateway Exchange*, which I will include here because it makes the link between his experience of discovering his creativity in the Special Unit and this new phase in our lives into which we were launching; we hoped to offer these same opportunities to others, especially those who had never been able to discover their unique potential, or see themselves in a positive light.

'It was Christmas '82. Sarah and I lying on a sunny beach in Thailand discussed and thought about our future. Blissful though the surroundings were, reality for us was on the streets in our own country. It was here that the idea was conceived.

Our search for a building was successful: we named it *the Gateway Exchange*. We believe in sharing. People coming through the gate should be able to share and exchange their qualities as well as their weaknesses as they are natural aspects of the human condition.

Meanwhile youngsters in dead-end streets roam in packs or sit in squalid isolation, with no future, nothing to do, nowhere to go. Drugs and more drugs. Drink and more drink. Prison and more prison. Poverty and worse. Things aren't getting any better. Sympathetic noises are made by influential people. Words don't ease the misery.

As an artist I want to change the world radically through creative action. It is not enough for me to create objects to be stared at. I want to continue doing this but more important I want to develop skills as a social sculptor; to help mould and shape a more equal society. The faces of those drugged kids, the pinched features of the despairing adults haunt me.

Six months into getting the building ready has seen some of them come in and connect. Already the place has a life of its own. It's like a new born baby. All of us play a part in it. Actions speak louder than words!

I will always remember that period when I discovered my own creativity. It was as though a dam had burst inside me. Some years later this powerful feeling is still there. In those days I was considered an 'exception to the rule' but never at any time did I believe it. And now, working in the Gateway I gain a great deal of satisfaction from seeing untrained though very talented young people begin to realise their potential in much the same way as I did.'

As the Gateway was beginning its life, my own creativity took expression through changes happening in my body. In August, shortly before Mum's birthday, I had a positive result from a pregnancy test. When I shared this news with Jimmy he was absolutely delighted.

In his excitement I heard him telling friends that 'Sarah and I are pregnant', and although he clearly couldn't share the physical part, he wanted to be as fully involved as possible with me in the whole process. (He had been in prison when his other two children, James and Tricia, had been born). When I had the scan a couple of months later it was an amazing experience to see on the screen the outline of the miniature embryo within me taking form; a head, a backbone, a clawed hand, a tiny fluttering heart.

I was very moved; what a miracle to be actually able to see this little being, who is now my thirty-year-old daughter Suzi, at such an early stage. Although I felt nauseous at the beginning, for the most part I kept well throughout this pregnancy, feeling a deep happiness within myself.

These developments dominated this first year in 1983. On 5th November we held a party at our home to celebrate the first anniversary of Jimmy's freedom. It was a small gathering but all the friends who came had played an important part in our lives. One important departure this year was Peggy, who surprised all of us by dying before Alfie. He missed her terribly after fifty two years of marriage but he was brave in dealing with his loss.

My last memory of Peggy is of visiting her in hospital where she lay with a £10 note tucked under her drip line, which fed into a vein in her wrist. She wasn't going to take a chance of anyone stealing it from her in her state of incapacity.

18.3.84
BORN FREE....Baby will bring joy to Boyles

This was the headline of a Sunday Mail exclusive which made this announcement along with a picture of Jimmy embracing me from behind with his hands holding my enlarged belly. The birth of our baby daughter Suzannah Angela was about to take place in ten days' time.

She was born in Elsie Ingles Hospital, a hospital dedicated to obstetrics and a unique institution in Edinburgh. Elsie Ingles was an innovative Scottish doctor with a philanthropic vision who originally established this maternity hospital for poor women. With it being my first pregnancy I remember a feeling of nervous anticipation.

Jimmy was very supportive. His presence throughout was more important than anything else to me. Finally, just as somebody said that the head was coming into view, I was aware of him dropping forward onto the bed, then slipping sideways onto the floor. It took me a couple of moments to realize that he'd fainted. A nurse helped him back onto his feet.

We joked about it – Jimmy who'd witnessed so much violence in his life, was floored by the sight of his daughter arriving into the world. Fortunately, the cooler air outside revived him and when another contraction started he came rushing back in. He was back in time to welcome her – an amazing moment which created a peak of happiness and fulfilment in my life that I doubt will ever be equalled.

Birth is a miracle each time and a mystery. I remember wondering about this new little person who would be entering our lives, speculating on how it would be when we suddenly found ourselves face to face. I had been 'in love' with Jimmy but this was different, perhaps even deeper, more primal, and very extraordinary. It was an experience of being opened to a completely new dimension in myself. My identity changed at that moment when I became for the first time, a mother.

Suzi arrived at a point when we were fully immersed in the early life of the Gateway. It was a time when we had put the call out for anyone who was willing to come and join us in this venture – it was all hands on deck and full steam ahead.

PART THREE

EMERGENCE OF THE NEW

15. Launching the Gateway Exchange

On the last page of *The Pain of Confinement* which was published in 1984, Jimmy writes:

'With freedom Sarah and I will have an opportunity to work at our marriage and relationship. Another aspect to be attended to once the 'media circus' is over will be my exploring the pain of my confinement. Locked inside me is a tremendous amount of pain which I've had to hold in over the years. It will take many years for me to untie the knots inside. In Sarah I couldn't have a better partner to share this with.'

Sadly, this never happened, at least not to the depth that might have made a substantial difference. Most of us have an innate tendency to avoid pain and this is why there is often a resistance to opening up old wounds. It can feel like being invited to step into a fire and which of us wants to get burned by the flames – avoidance seems easier and comes disguised in a variety of different coping strategies.

One of the ways in which unhealed pain can express itself is in a kind of unstoppable momentum on the surface of life, which can of course be productive and creative, but it can also conceal deeper aspects which are never given the chance to emerge.

At this early time, there was *no time* to sit down and reflect on what we had come through. Jimmy turned forty this year and we teased him about his age and grey hairs. His signs of ageing though were minimal compared to Dad who suffered blindness in his left eye due to a blood clot lodged in the retinal artery. He had the part time support of his companion Ingrid, but he spent at least half of the week on his own which must have been very challenging as he suffered this crisis. I wrote in my diary: 'Old age, seen in this light, is like a physical prison.'

Alfie suffered another collapse and was taken into hospital, but insisted on being taken back home. The reason for this was that he felt if he was admitted to a geriatric ward he probably wouldn't get out again, which was very likely. Both he and my Dad suffered the trials and challenges of ageing with good humour and dignity.

Although I felt for them, our focus was on the increasing demands of the Gateway, as well as on the all-consuming experience of caring for Suzi in these early months. With these two 'newborns' on our hands we hardly had a minute to ourselves. Despite this our relationship was strong at this time.

Work with the Gateway was progressing. In the early stages this took the form of working to clean out, paint, and refurbish the building. We painted the front office red and black – colours which expressed our determination to establish ourselves as a centre of radicalism and free thinking. I remember one of our neighbours, a kind elderly woman, bringing us cups of tea when I was pregnant and we were painting the outside windows through a spell of cold weather.

Experiences like this lifted our spirits during long arduous hours of physical work. Others came along after hearing about us through word of mouth, attracted by the prospect of being part of something new, with Jimmy's reputation and natural leadership ability having a lot to do with this.

Recognising that the creative impulse is present in everyone, and in all life, we wanted to establish a place where creativity could be taken out of the established art world. In notes from a catalogue for one of the earliest exhibitions, *New Beginnings,* which we held in this new space, there are words written by Jimmy which describe the underlying impetus which gave rise to this project.

WHAT IS ART?

What is art? This is a question which has been raised and tossed around the cliquish art world for many years and is one that has never been adequately answered. Perhaps one of the reasons for this is that art has become a currency related to wealth and success. In real terms it has alienated itself from its origins – the creative process. In recognising this we are attempting to bring it back to its roots.

In coming together to make a collective statement about these roots we found the common thread lay in each of us being trapped in a lifestyle that we are unhappy with. This led to the creation of the 'Gateway Exchange'.

It all began with a shell of the building and a core of people with lots of enthusiasm. These people came from all walks of life, some from disadvantaged backgrounds, others from privileged ones. No one expected to be, or was, paid for the hard work being done. What it was and still is, is a melting pot of human experience that generated an atmosphere of integrity which attracted others.

We learned from that particular period that creativity lies in us all. We argued, discussed and debated all aspects of the building from the colour scheme to the structure and building a fire escape. In doing so what we have done is to redefine the whole concept of art. So, for us, they are an art form in their own right.

Many of the people involved were considered 'write offs' – individuals who the system has labelled as failures, but within the Gateway their skills were recognised and encouraged. This doesn't mean that it has been easy, but what it does point out is that if the system invests in people and provides opportunities, their potential will emerge.

This exhibition – New Beginnings – is a breakthrough in all that we have achieved. These sculptures, paintings and collages have all been produced by self-trained people. In saying this we want them to be an inspiration and encouragement to others. This is our art!'

While we experienced many moments of elation at the progress we were making, it seemed at times as though the work was never ending. Jimmy was under considerable pressure, worrying about coordinating the work properly and trying to keep the costs to a minimum, and trying to ensure that the correct standards were strictly met and maintained.

We had fantastic support, without which we could not have made the progress that we did. In all of this we saw the potential which people of different backgrounds and paths in life had. Angi, a young woman from Wester Hailes produced cooked lunches off portable stoves. Sebastian arrived from London with a van load of sculptures and paintings. Ben (Conroy), and others we know from Wester Hailes and other places, joined our team in those early days.

The emphasis was on working together to create a premises that we could all feel part of and be proud of. We had a stream of visitors from all walks of life – journalists, social workers, ex-prisoners, prisoners' wives, ex-junkies, ex-prostitutes; the word seemed to being going out that something special was happening.

The following is taken from the introduction of our first annual report: *Gateway Exchange One*.

'The moving force behind each initiative has been the enthusiasm of the individuals who have thrown themselves into the heave and thrust of everyday life in the Gateway. The building opens at 9am. Each morning starts with the ritual of cleaning. This completed, the dynamic shifts to centre around any number of possible jobs – from the heavy physical, to working in the kitchen, answering correspondence, being the sympathetic voice on the end of the telephone, hanging an exhibition or doing creative work. The day isn't structured although we have certain fixed events – e.g. the weekly meetings after lunch on Fridays. The routine is generally flexible according to the different tasks to hand. The doors close at 6pm, but often the work goes on until later, or other groups arrive to make use of the space for evening meetings or rehearsals.'

My descriptions of what was happening in the Gateway in my diary are interspersed with updates on Suzi (who we called Suzannah in those early days.) 'Suzannah is smiling a lot these days – a dazzling smile when it comes. I'm still getting used to the fact that she's responding to us and coming alive as a little person. I really love her in these moments, we all do.' She was often in the midst of us as we were working and was a natural focus for everyone's attention. I never wanted to be a 'stay at home' mum, so this interweaving of our lives suited me perfectly.

Jimmy's book launch for *The Pain of Confinement* was held on 24th May 1984, at the *Gateway Exchange*. Everyone had worked extremely hard to get the premises ready for this important social event. The evening itself was a great success and the reviews overall quite complementary. It raised a few niggles though for different people, Ben Conroy being one of these. It was probably especially difficult for him as he had shared the times in the Special Unit with Jimmy and was sensitive about the way he felt he came across.

Ben, to me, has always been one of the other, less publicly known, success stories of the Special Unit, and perhaps Jimmy could have acknowledged him more for this. Sebastian and Evlynn felt disappointed that their early morning presence at the prison gate to greet Jimmy on his day of liberation wasn't acknowledged.

We all, it seemed, were sensitive about how we were individually portrayed in this story. I felt that he could have said more about me as a person and the unfolding story of our relationship. This book though, was written right at the end of Jimmy's passage back out into the world – he wrote much of it in a small, cramped space in our new flat, so perhaps some of its contents suffered as a result of his hurry to be finished and done with this whole interminably long, pain-filled time of confinement. This would be understandable.

As if we didn't have enough on our hands, we moved that Summer, buying a flat which was right next door to the *Gateway Exchange,* in Abbeymount. We realized that living above the shop might have its challenges, but as the Gateway was consuming so much of our lives we felt overall that living close by would help to simplify matters. My focus, when I found time to write in my diary, was on the fulfilment and happiness which I was experiencing through becoming a mother.

At the same time my identity questions continued to hover in the background. A lot of the focus from the outside was on Jimmy and although we did some interviews together I often found it difficult to assert myself. I wrote the question in my diary: 'What am I doing with my life? What am I good at and what do I want to do?' The stresses which I thought we had left behind us had now arrived back into our lives, taking a different form:

> **Diary: 5.7.84** 'Jimmy says we're always racing against time – how true! We move house in two days time, go on holiday at the end of the week, have Sebastian and Evlynn's wedding on Iona, and have the Gateway to look after as well – all that and caring for a three-month old baby is no mean feat. At times I feel it and no wonder.'

Every day we found ourselves busier at the Gateway with increasing numbers of people streaming into the place and the workforce becoming larger. We also had visits from community groups who made their way across from Glasgow. Heroin was starting to flood into the housing schemes at this time. The rising tide of drug addiction, especially amongst young people, was provoking parents and people in some of the communities worst affected to set up projects to help provide support for those affected by these problems. They looked on us as a source of expertise in terms of how to go about establishing these fledgling services.

There was also the creative work now starting to take place in the studio spaces created at the back of the Gateway. The area underneath the main hall was transformed into a sculpture workshop, which we called The Underworld. I wrote in my diary,

> 'The pace is hectic, but the progress is exciting and the place is now really beginning to shape up and look as if we're nearing completion.'
>
> **Diary 14.7.84:** Written on Iona... 'Sebastian and Evlynn's wedding day – we are here on this beautiful island, an oasis of peace after the hectic turmoil of the past few weeks. The rush and the hurry have been essential in order to meet the deadlines of the work at the Gateway, also to manage the upheaval of moving house – and the flurry of last minute things to do before leaving on holiday – but our nerves have been stretched. I said to Jimmy 'never again do I want to attempt to do so much in such a short space of time' – it's crazy to put so much pressure on.'

Fortunately, we had three whole weeks to unwind and relax. After our short stay on Iona, we headed for France, but stopped in at Glasgow on the way to visit Alfie who had collapsed again and was in hospital. He was on a geriatric ward where most of the patients were bedridden.

> 'Alfie was demonstrating his determination not to succumb by sitting in a chair at his bedside, his hair neatly groomed and dressed in his dressing gown. Clearly his end is close but he was not ready to accept it. He shed tears on seeing us but he was overjoyed to see Suzi again. She had a pensive concerned look on her face for most of the visit – she seems to be a child who intuitively senses the mood of the occasion.'

Alfie died while we were away on holiday. I wrote:

> 'A man who was worth far more than the life he was able to lead. We will both miss him very much.'

As we headed south we called in on Mum in the Lake District and had a memorable meal with Peter and Glenna MacDougal (Peter wrote the script for the film *A Sense of Freedom*) in London – it was strange for me to suddenly find myself sitting at a dinner table with Billy Connolly and other well-known people, but I count myself as fortunate to have had these moments in the course of my life, which has been so full of contrasts. We were also able to call in and introduce Suzi to Dad. I have some touching pictures from this visit. He was delighted with her and sat beaming with love, while she lay on his knee gazing up at him.

Our holiday in France proved fateful in ways, which I couldn't possibly have foreseen at the time. We spent our first night at Epernay, which lies at the centre of the district where champagne is made. This was the beginning of what proved to be a long love affair which Jimmy had with champagne – later on when his affections for this drink started to come between us, I would remember this first visit as the moment when it all started.

We drove south through the Alps and on down to a small place near the Riviera coast called *Pont du Loup* (Loup means wolf and I could perhaps have taken this as some kind of a warning). We were on our way to visit a man who had many years previously been a property manager for my grandfather. He had written offering us a place to stay, after reading the publicity about our marriage and Jimmy's release. It felt like a tempting offer so we accepted.

It turned out that he lived in a palatial villa with extensive garden surrounds – it was all very elegant and lavish, but it felt strangely empty to me. Jimmy hit it off well almost from the start with Edward. It was the kind of relationship which I had observed him having with Alec Horsley, Sebastian's father. It was very much a man-to-man friendship. Jimmy represented qualities that the older men admired and respected, possibly because he acted out their own more repressed emotions and spirit.

The formality of the meals and the luxurious decor of the house reminded me a little of Matson Ground, my grandparents' house, but I felt intimidated by the scale of it all. It was not the relaxing holiday stay that I had anticipated and looked forward to.

Edward had a multitude of grudges, which he shared with Jimmy. He was lonely, disillusioned with life, and embittered with the establishment, which was why he was living in 'exile' in the south of France. A friendship became established between them which bizarrely, like the champagne, resulted in unfortunate long term consequences in my life, which I could not have anticipated at the time, but possibly sensed. I felt excluded and took refuge, taking walks around the garden with Suzi.

Early cracks were appearing in what I had thought was our rock solid partnership. Jimmy accused me of over-riding him when we made decisions. Quite possibly I did at times, as I can also be strong willed – but he was starting to express an underlying tension around a theme not discussed much between us, but an important one, this being that of the material difference in our backgrounds and circumstances.

My ownership of wealth made him feel uncomfortable. It did me too, which is why from the start I had said that everything that was mine was his. I trusted him completely and wanted him to feel that we shared everything equally between us. To me this was the best and simplest way. He contributed in lots of other ways to our partnership and I felt that the bedrock of our relationship was this deep sense of trust and respect.

I hoped and believed that this foundation would hold steady and would allow us to build a life which could benefit and be an inspiration to others. We shared everything and decided together to invest our own funds into the Gateway to buy the premises and launch the project.

The tensions swiftly passed. Most of the rest of the holiday was pleasant enough, although we returned home exhausted from all the driving. It hadn't been a restful holiday that was for sure.

A week or so after we arrived home we were caught up in the turmoil of working at whirlwind pace to prepare for the opening of the Gateway. Floors had to be varnished, 150 chairs had to be painted, food and drink had to be ordered, along with posters and T-shirts which we would be putting up for sale. Jimmy's creative mind devised a stunt for the opening which consisted of Billy Connolly, who was going to do the honours for us, being presented with welding equipment and being asked to break his way into a painted casket – which would then open to reveal a powerful bronze cast logo for the front gates that he and Sebastian had made.

The team of helpers, many of whom had relapses, disputes, visits from the police or other such crises happening in their lives, held up remarkably well. Everything looked clean and gleaming with newness for the opening. The exhibitions were all beautifully hung and the upstairs looked stunning with the varnished floor, chairs all set out and the shrouded chest and welding equipment waiting to surprise Billy.

The opening night was a big extravaganza, much in the same style as other events we had done, attended by a good mixture of different folk. Billy was definitely the star of the show and of course brought his unique brand of Scottish humour to the occasion, as well as introducing a more serious note as he linked what we were doing to the striking miners and CND, predicting that knocks would come our way on the basis of being successful. The evening flowed very smoothly and there was genuine pleasure all round that we had asked Billy to do this for us – he certainly came up with the goods.

Unfortunately, later on that night the flow of alcohol started to produce unwelcome effects as various people went over the score and some became very drunk. It all felt a bit like a ship heaving and rolling on the ocean dangerously close to taking in water.

I wrote in my diary again about the pressures:

> 'I go back to when I first married Jimmy – sure enough he didn't promise me an easy time (it won't be a smooth ride he said) – and it certainly hasn't been. The pressure of the last few weeks has almost been too much – but its been a matter of once having passed a certain point, there being no possibility of turning back. I've felt the strains physically, mentally and emotionally – and yet I have discovered within myself a strength and resilience which has weathered it all.'

There was hardly a breathing space before the Edinburgh Festival was on us. With our space newly prepared we were earning some much needed funds by operating as a venue.

Various theatre groups gave powerful performances, which attracted good audiences and generated a strong response through the controversial issues which they raised. One of these was *Mea Culpa* which was about Myra Hindley.

I noted that the overall direction and progress of the place was pretty sound, but we encountered some serious teething problems. One of these, which provoked a mad rush and panic in the first week, was that we needed to get a second emergency fire-exit constructed in order to comply with building control regulations.

Fortunately, a flash of creative thinking, combined with hard and skilful work, resolved this problem. A fire-escape was located in a disused distillery. This was then stripped out and fitted to the back of the theatre which we had recently created. Our core team, Sebastian, Jimmy, and Mick worked tirelessly and resourcefully to achieve this miracle.

There were areas which we needed to tighten up on. People had started abusing access to the phone, a small amount of money disappeared from the cash box in the café, and a cassette recorder belonging to one of the visiting theatre companies also disappeared. We created a management committee, which consisted of individuals who had accepted additional responsibility for overseeing the day to day smooth running of the centre. When problems like these arose we put the emphasis on learning from our mistakes by talking things through.

Jimmy and I were having to get by without nearly enough time for each other, which at times led to irritation and sharp words. Sometimes I thought back nostalgically to the Unit days when we were courting – there was no time for such romantic indulgences now.

Overall though we were building up a strong team of people regularly involved in the centre. The weekly meetings provided opportunities for sitting down together as a group to discuss and review our progress. We wanted to create a model that was based on open communication and honest sharing, including interpersonal issues along with the work agenda.

Suzi was growing fast. She required a lot from us both, but we loved her to the point of distraction and she was very much at the centre of our lives. All of the milestones through her first year were a source of joy to us both. With the pressure off a bit after the Festival we were finally able to be more affectionate with each other again.

On November 1, we celebrated Jimmy's second anniversary of freedom. I wrote: 'We have packed so much into two years that it's unbelievable!' We celebrated with a bonfire and fireworks at the Gateway. The team put so much enthusiasm into building up a large pile of wood, that when it was set alight we came perilously close to setting fire to our precious building. Fortunately, the leaping flames and blaze subsided just in time. This image symbolised the momentum and energy in Jimmy following his release. He had such an enthusiasm for everything that we were doing that he was hard to keep up with at times.

There was a shadow side to this which was experienced by others as well as me. Sebastian often felt overshadowed, and tensions surfaced from time to time in the Gateway as a result of people feeling left out. As we neared the end of the year Jimmy and I had a really bad row – our worst so far. (Not bad I guess given all that we had come through.)

This particular one arose out of his plans to make what I thought was a crazy trip with Sebastian –The Lakes, Preston, Hull, and then Edinburgh again. All this in a day and a half, on the back of a trip to London, with television people coming to the Gateway and a play on at the end of the week. I put my foot down. This was bitterly resented by Jimmy although he accepted it in the end. The raw nerves were a sign that we were running on a thin margin at that time.

One aspect of his adjustment back to the world that I noticed quite early on was that he had little understanding of distance and time. He would plan a trip without any realistic awareness of how long it could take to get to places.

He would get carried away by his enthusiasm to fit everything in – interviews, talks, appearances at conferences – and ended up exhausted. Just as with a storm, a good row, once it's passed, can help to clear the air. Fortunately, this is what happened on this occasion.

We spent Christmas at a farm cottage that we had bought in the Lakes close to where Mum lived. This place, which was called Low Lindeth, was set in a very quiet spot, surrounded by trees and the low rolling hills of the fells. It was a haven for us for a number of years. We spent a delightful Christmas with Suzi rolling around on the floor, relaxing in front of a blazing fire. It was her first Christmas and a magical time as it snowed on Boxing Day which created a winter wonderland all around us.

16. Another New Arrival – Feeling the Pressure

I seem to have lost all diaries through the years 1985 and 1986. It almost feels a relief not to have to relive every moment of what proved to be two very full, demanding, challenging, rewarding and creative years for us. We were accompanied through these years by Sebastian and Evlynn Horsley, who became co-directors of the *Gateway Exchange* with us. They worked full time, for no payment, creating the extraordinary artistic backrop, which was what made the place so special and unique. The *Gateway Exchange* defied all conventional attempts to typecast or label it.

As a place it was an expression of a new approach to rehabilitation that went beyond anything that was happening in the social services at that time. It was always a hive of activity, of connections, meetings, gatherings, of individuals and their stories, and of collective effort to run this place independently of established grants.

It was an early attempt at social enterprise – brave, controversial, idealistic and groundbreaking. It was also anarchic at times, lacking in clear focus, all consuming of our energies, and ultimately unsustainable, but we hadn't quite reached the point of recognising this.

Attempting to run the centre on a voluntary basis resulted in a small number of people, and especially the four of us as co-directors, carrying the bulk of the workload. Some of the newer arrivals who came along and used the facilities started to have a disproportionate say at the weekly meetings, expressing views that were not grounded in a realistic understanding of the place.

We eventually had to restrict participation at the weekly meetings to those who were regularly committed and involved. Openness and transparency were important and we always tried to honour this, but we had to begin establishing some boundaries. I remember these weekly meetings as dynamic, challenging, frustrating, honest, and beyond all *real*. We sometimes confronted difficult issues, for example, when one of our members underwent a sex change. This brought up diverging responses in the group, not all of them understanding or complimentary – but feelings were aired and eventually this person's new identity was accepted.

We had children coming into the centre and one young boy, Lee, was especially direct – he simply asked straight out 'Why is X... dressed as a woman?' Without waiting for an answer he gave a cheeky grin and called her Angi-man!

As well as developing different creative departments, we were also active in tackling social issues. We were aware that the prison authorities didn't seem remotely interested in why a person had landed inside or what happened to them on release. Often the problems would rebound on the communities the offenders came from. It was clear that the penal service needed to provide more than mere containment.

The recidivism statistics told the tale. We were looking for a change in approach within the prison system that addressed some of these problems and particularly advocated an increase in dialogue with community representatives. We felt this especially strongly in relation to the rising tide of drug use in prisons.

The lessons that emerged from the Special Unit experience suggested that changing the conditions and approach could help the individual to break free of cycles of offending, and re-offending, which were causing such misery. We did what we could in our limited contact with prisoners to encourage them to be creative and to express their feelings through the written word. We produced, among many other productions, a small booklet called *Poetry from Prison*. Quoting from the introduction to this:

> 'We believe that creativity provides the key for individuals to survive and overcome the crushing effects of confinement. This is why we encourage prisoners to communicate and to send us creative work. We feel that this positive side of imprisonment should be given greater recognition and priority. If at the end of the day a person is to emerge from prison a better and wiser human being, he or she must be helped to find new resources for coping again outside. Creativity offers a way forward which is constructive rather than destructive.'

We also organised public meetings in response to the worrying number of suicides taking place in the Glenochil Complex for Young Offenders (situated in Tullibody, near Stirling). We connected with those who we called 'the human face of the system' and were in touch with prison staff, who were often up against it from their colleagues. Like us, they questioned further punishing the individual, when there was an urgent need for improvement in attitudes and conditions throughout the prison system.

We campaigned on the drugs issue. We had a lot of contact with the parents of drug users as well as with ex-addicts. We gave out a clear message that *The Gateway Exchange* was a drugs-free area and emphasised that the individual needed to take the first step by expressing a willingness to come off. We supported the work being done by rehabilitation centres that were active in Scotland at that time and preferred to advocate withdrawal as opposed to the prescribing of long term maintenance scripts.

As this became the prevailing statutory response we found ourselves somewhat out on a limb in this respect. We did however establish excellent links with the Calton Athletic Support Group from Glasgow, who were an inspiring example of energy and commitment. They succeeded in getting a number of young people off drugs through creating a local football team and encouraging their members to run marathons. Started by an ex-drug user, Davey Bryce, they had considerable success in this difficult area.

Mental health – heavy drinking, lack of confidence, depression, anxiety and panic attacks, sexual abuse, relationship break-ups, bereavements – we saw all of these problems and more. We had an open door approach, but we did insist on people arriving in a sufficiently clear-headed state to discuss their difficulties. We offered a listening ear and acceptance, as we encouraged people to become part of the team.

We did not offer any formal counselling at the beginning, although this was established later on. In the prison system we recognised how conditions created mental stress and, with no adequate outlet, often resulted in outbreaks of violence or suicide attempts. We felt that this whole area suffered from serious neglect.

Reading through our first report and taking extracts from it, I am almost overwhelmed by how much we did take on in those early days. Looking at it from a distance now, what we did was extraordinary for that time. For a short while we were able to function as some kind of beacon for those who felt alienated from the mainstream or who were seeking to address these kinds of problems in their own communities. I feel proud of what we achieved even though the realities of trying to tackle so much meant that we ended up finding ourselves over stretched and under-resourced.

Meanwhile another important personal event was about to take over our lives.

> **Diary: 13.4.87** 'New stirrings...Kydd Jay Boyle is about to enter the world.'

The previous August, midway through the Festival, I suddenly recognised, unfamiliar changes in my body which told me, before I had it confirmed with a test, that I was pregnant again. I remember the day because I had gone out and had bought a sculpture called 'Baby Walker' by a well-known Edinburgh sculptress called Edith Simon.

It was also the day when news came through that Dad had died. I remember being very upset when I heard this, but had to push my feelings aside as we had so much on our hands with the Festival in full swing. We were again trying to boost our finances by operating a full schedule of theatre performances in what was, by then, called the Mandela Theatre.

*

The loss of my Dad might have affected me more had I not experienced the early annihilating loss of him in my childhood, when he disappeared out of my life. Although I was able to reconnect with him as an adult, and renewed some of the closeness which I had always felt with him, he was in other ways largely on the periphery of my life.

Strangely enough I felt the loss of him more intensely a year later when, on the anniversary of his death, I found myself feeling 'bloody awful'. I felt myself wanting to cry all day, and finally in the evening I ended up in tears. It was only when I sat down to write about this that I realised the sadness stemmed from his death on August 15 the previous year.

He had his faults, but he was a man of integrity and courage, capable of great kindness and he loved me as deeply as I loved him. I realised one year on that I missed him terribly and I felt a deep regret that he had died on his own at home, collapsing when he went to the toilet. This was not the end I would have wished for him.

Life fortunately, on another dimension, transcends the purely physical and has an endless capacity to renew itself. I'm sure he would have been delighted had he known, that the day when he was released from his physical body, I realised that I was pregnant again. He would have been even more tickled had he known that this time I was to have a baby boy.

> **Diary: 24.4.87** – 'Baby due today...but still nothing. I'm feeling tired and weary, it's like an anti-climax after all the build-up in excitement.'

The calm before the storm. My labour started in the middle of that night with a sudden strong contraction. The Elsie Inglis Hospital was just down the hill from where we lived so we didn't have far to go. Jimmy sprang into action and supported me all the way through my very short labour. This time he didn't faint. Kydd Boyle arrived at 4.45 am on the April 25.

Afterwards we looked at each other in fond disbelief. We were sitting beside the window looking out on the hazy early morning mist and the pastel colours of the sky behind the silhouette of Arthur's Seat. We had just experienced this whole miraculous process again. Here was another new life entering our family and world. This time the process had happened in a mere hour and three quarters which left us feeling delighted and stunned.

His name, which had been given to him by Evlynn, strongly supported by Jimmy, was an unusual choice which evoked a funny reaction from the staff who didn't know quite how to take it – but he's come to suit it and we all love him with it. Kydd was not an immediate feeder, as Suzi was, and because of this and a slightly low temperature he was taken from me and placed in an incubator in the special care baby unit.

Fortunately, he was able to be brought upstairs to be welcomed by a keen crowd of admirers – Jimmy, Suzi, Sebastian, Evlynn, and Anna (who was to become like a member of the family as she looked after both Suzi and Kydd for years.) Suzi's first comment as she peered cautiously through the perspex sides of his cot was: 'he's tiny.' Then, feeling braver, she gently stroked the side of his head. 'Soft.' Later she gave him his first kisses and sat cutely with him on her knee.

That evening Jimmy came for a quieter visit and it was lovely to watch him walking up and down proudly holding Kydd, our son, to his chest. I phoned my mum to share the news. She commented favourably on his name: 'Is it an abbreviation of Kenneth?' she asked. I found out later that Jimmy had spelled the name out for her, saying 'K' for Kenneth. Poor mum, yet again she was having to make a rapid adjustment to another unconventional choice we'd made.

My stay in hospital was short because I'd woken the next morning hearing loud cries which I knew were Kydd's. When I climbed out of bed and looked into the side room where he had been left, I found him tightly swaddled up with his cot placed right beside a radiator. He was looking bright red in the face like a boiled tomato. The staff had clearly overdone it in their enthusiasm to bring his temperature up.

I rescued him and phoned Jimmy saying that we wanted to get home.

It was an exceptionally lovely weekend, with brilliant sunshine that the whole country was basking in. Jimmy arrived in a Rolls Royce to collect me so Kydd and I were taken home in style. Where had the Rolls Royce come from? Sometime previously Angi, one of our core team, who was minding the phone in the Gateway office had taken a call – she announced to Jimmy that someone was on the line asking if he wanted a Rolls Royce.

I can't remember the details but it seems that this was a wealthy rock star who wanted to offload some of his assets for tax purposes. Would Jimmy refuse an offer like this? Certainly not. He, Sebastian, and most of the team in the Gateway were over the moon about this unexpected gift to us. It was blue, gleaming, substantial – an undeniably handsome car in every conceivable sense, and I cringed from the start.

It was in these moments that the parting of the ways between Jimmy and I was beginning. The Rolls Royce clashed completely with my image of what I felt we were about. We were working to help the underprivileged, the disadvantaged, the fringe-dwellers of society. A Rolls Royce belongs in another strata – a strata associated with wealth, largesse, consumption and excess. Although, and quite possibly because I come from a privileged background, I carry a reverse kind of relationship with excessive displays of wealth. I don't like them.

I decided that for the most part I would regard the Rolls Royce as his and that I wouldn't ride in it. If I expressed my unease I was mercilessly teased and told that I had too many hang ups. On this particular occasion, bringing Kydd home from hospital for the first time, I decided to override my self-imposed ban on riding in this vehicle. Nothing was going to diminish my joy on this particular day.

I was re-experiencing the intense feelings which had been awakened in me when Suzi was born.

> 'I'd forgotten these. The tiny body, soft skin, sweet milky baby smell and the overall perfection of Kydd's new born physical form. It's just stunning. Maternal love must be one of the deepest and strongest instincts. I spend all morning feeding, cleaning, massaging and fondling Kydd, taking great pleasure in looking after all his little needs in this intimate way.'

I had wondered how I would manage with a second baby – would I find in myself enough love for both of my children? The answer to this question was a most definite – Yes, absolutely.

★

By the summer of 1987 we were running into mounting problems. The model of the Gateway Exchange which we had established, while it produced some remarkable successes, hadn't relieved the pressure on the four of us at all. This had increased with the growth of the place and the natural demands made by newcomers on our experience. There was also an increase in administration work. The constant pressure of trying to cover so many different areas, and generally finding ourselves short-handed, resulted in exhaustion.

The fact that we had achieved so much with an entirely inexperienced workforce, many of whom had to overcome personal problems to take part, was amazing and due in a large measure to the very strong spirit of the place.

We tried to find creative ways around some of these problems, one of these being an idea to rent out the café. The space itself was depressing so although we had been resistant to applying for local authority funding, because of Jimmy's background, we decided to pursue a new line of approach and seek a £25,000 grant for these renovations.

Jimmy was the one who was delegated with this task. He met with two local counsellors, having what turned out to be a boozy lunch with them, but at least came back with the promise of support pretty well secured. It seems that this was the way in which this kind of business was done in those days. It had been good to steer clear of this up until this time, but our continued survival necessitated a turning towards statutory sources of support, so this is what we did.

We also had to look at ways of trying to relieve the burden of responsibility for the running of the Gateway, which rested heavily on the four of us. We had a management meeting where we discussed staff salaries and wage payments – we had been reluctant to employ people at the beginning because we wanted to put the focus onto other kinds of exchanges, especially the benefit that we all experienced from being part of the dynamic community and creative drive of the Gateway.

However, our earlier stance, while admirable, meant that inevitably people came and went, while the burden of keeping the centre open each day and running consistently depended on us.

While we were grappling with these kinds of problems in the centre, at home the pressures expressed themselves in a different way. Kydd's arrival provoked some naughty behaviour from Suzi. She at times resented his presence and all the attention he received, and at one point suggested that we could give him back.

She needed extra patience and understanding while she adjusted to his presence. She was affectionate with Kydd but had no respect for his small size or new-born vulnerability. She prodded, poked, and hugged him like a grizzly bear tormenting its victim. I would become cross with her. She would then start to cry.

Her tantrums brought explosions of rage and frustration which were exhausting to withstand. Having two children was definitely a heavier load – even though I had assistance from some wonderful childminders, the best and most longlasting of whom was Anna. Anna had come into our lives through another good friend at that time, Joanna Blythman, who worked for the Scottish Council for Civil Liberties. She introduced us to Anna who was a young secretary with clear blue eyes, a delightful warm smile and a natural gift with children.

Kydd was filling out and becoming much more alert. I have delightful pictures of him, dressed in a navy striped baby-grow, with a white cap on his head looking thoughtful and wise. Sitting in his baby rocker with his tiny fingers resting on his cheek, he did look like a wise old soul as he stared intently at us.

Wisdom was what we very much needed at that moment. We had difficult choices to make. Our attention was overtaken, though, by Kydd developing a very high temperature. I had to take him into hospital where he had to have a lumbar puncture and be given intravenous antibiotics through a needle inserted into one of his tiny hand veins. All of this was very stressful, and he was responsible for my longest ever stay in hospital, which was five days in all. Fortunately, he recovered well after this.

Renovations were carried out on the café space in the Gateway. The walls were transformed from a depressing grey colour to white, creating a light and airy area with a proper servery, tables and a well-lit exhibition space around the sides. It changed the look and feel of the place substantially.

We had to employ staff to run it, but the Festival was approaching and we hoped that we could break-even through this time. We had an exciting programme of events, but after the Festival we hit another crunch time when we had to look at where we were going, and what we were doing. How could we balance striving to be successful commercially while at the same time supporting people with difficult issues and problems? It wasn't going to be easy.

> **Diary: Monday 31 August:** 'We talk a lot about the future of the Gateway. Jimmy has promised never again to work as hard as he's worked this Festival – through to the early hours each night and all through to the early morning on the weekends. This year we have to try to make the Gateway stand on its own feet. The aim is to generate some income through the café and theatre. We need to try to earn sufficient finance to employ staff to run these areas and to provide more structured workshops in different creative activities.'

While my focus was on the Gateway and on the children, Jimmy, along with Sebastian, had started to develop a new commercial line, which was importing and selling champagne.

> **Diary: 10.9.87** 'Jimmy has just come back from Fife where

he and Sebastian have been today – driving around in the Rolls Royce selling champagne. I don't like to nag but nonetheless find this champagne lifestyle difficult to live with at times. '

In the process of starting the champagne importing business (which was kept beneath the VAT threshold) Jimmy's image started to change. The casual clothes and tracksuits that I was used to him wearing were increasingly replaced with suits when he was going out. Looking back the changes were gradual, but it was clear that Jimmy was increasingly cultivating a new image of himself. It seemed that he was reliving some of his lost youth as he took great pleasure in making these trips with Sebastian.

A piece appeared in the Sunday Mail at this time with the headline: CHAMPAGNE JIMMY BOYLE. Sebastian had apparently enthused to the *Sunday Mail* reporter about the champagne business, including details of holiday trips to France to sample wines and touring in the Rolls Royce. I felt upset by this unwelcome publicity, which contrasted uncomfortably with the rest of our work in the Gateway that was based on using the creative arts to challenge the status quo and raise important social issues.

The appearance of the article provoked a serious discussion about our present commitments and overall direction. I wrote:

'I'm on a bandwagon that I'd like to get off – certainly as far as the WashHouse, (which was a new acquisition), the champagne and the Rolls are concerned. Yet there's no turning back either, its all progressed too far. On a brighter note, we all played a game of 'Peepo' with Kydd tonight and he lapsed into hearty chuckles. What a lovely sound. There's no doubt the children are our strength and joy in life – and Kydd's laughter proves to be a good antidote for this morning's bad press.'

I was starting to resent the amount of time and energy Jimmy was putting into the Gateway and the property next door that we had acquired, called the WashHouse. This second property was at one point used to establish a bronze casting foundry where Jimmy, Sebastian and others worked on creating a public sculpture commissioned by Sebastian's grandfather in Hull, called *Imprisoned Mankind*. This was a powerful piece – a larger than life-size seated figure with a bowed head.

The figure sits in the middle of a cluster of four steel bars. It was intended to symbolise imprisoned minds. It was similar in its conception to the iconic small sculpture called *Solitary* that Jimmy had made in the early days in the Special Unit and which was so powerfully expressive of his lost years.

Making the sculpture, which had to be cut into twenty-five pieces for the casting process, was a marathon achievement on which Jimmy, Sebastian, and an inexperienced but willing team worked. The WashHouse was also used as a Fringe venue and as a band rehearsal area; there was no shortage of good ideas – just a shortage of time and energy to follow through with them all.

Our problems were put on one side when there was a rooftop protest with hostage-taking at Peterhead prison, followed by a similar incident at Perth Prison. Given our reputation, it wasn't surprising that, with the prison system being in crisis, a lot of the press contacted the Gateway for comments. Jimmy was frantically busy responding to media enquiries, as well as completing recommendations for a report that we produced on this crisis. We were often active in terms of corresponding with prisoners and responding to prison issues.

As the pressures in our own lives mounted it seemed that they threatened to undermine the progress that we had made on so many different fronts. When Jimmy was first released he had been so positive, and so inspiring – what had happened?

Someone had said to me at the time that it would be interesting to see how he changed once he started encountering life outside again. Now I was seeing some changes that disturbed me. Fortunately there was still plenty of the loving, positive Jimmy to help reassure me that we would find a way through these difficulties.

17. *Funding Crisis and Change of Direction*

November 1987 brought a dawning realisation that we were in trouble. We had applied for additional funds to support us with some of our running costs, and had been hopeful of getting these, but we were then told that because of a government clawback there were no funds available.

> **Diary 19.11.87** 'The phone call is all very casual in tone and polite. It takes place amongst the usual carry on of the Gateway front office – but underneath there is an ominous feel to it all. I feel sick in the pit of my stomach. We'd been banking heavily on getting this £15,000 – without it we are in serious trouble financially. Today I look at the café books and discover that the balance has dropped by about £6,000 since mid-September. In other words, we're making a loss of £3,000 a month. With £3,000 remaining in the account we've only got enough to take us through until Christmas.'

> **Diary: 26.11.87** 'It's hard for us to think of losing the Gateway – I keep wanting to hang onto bits of it, e.g. the Theatre, the Café, but unless we think of a different way of running it, we won't be able to because the costs are too high.'

We celebrated the end of the year in the Gateway by having a Christmas meal together and presented the regular participants with a small bonus payment of £50, which they so much deserved.

It felt like the last Christmas, which is what it proved to be. Jimmy and I were able to take a Christmas break in the Lakes and I wrote: 'I think of it as one of the nicest Christmases I can remember.' These occasions when we could finally stop were so welcome and so necessary.

There was a real pleasure in the four of us being together after such a busy and stressful year. Sebastian and Evlynn joined us and when the weather turned bad, we hunkered down, watched films, made meals and had some well-earned rest.

It was a flat start to the New Year as the café had closed and the morale of the place seemed to be at an all-time low. The January blues had caught up with us. The overall situation remained the same with closure being imminent unless new funds materialised. Jimmy and I celebrated our eighth wedding anniversary, again in the Lakes, where we spent many happy times. These were times when we could enjoy the children, with their love, laughter and playful innocence filling our days. 'Mummy I love you for ever and ever and *ever*' said Suzi. Kydd had become her true love and she was very affectionate with him, taking him for short walks. He was tolerant of the tumbles and survived these well.

In the Gateway we worked with many young kids who Jimmy had initially met when he was involved in the homeless flats project in Wester Hailes. We had seen these kids through different crises through the years and some of them became regular participants in the Gateway, as well as close friends. One of these was a young man called Graham Tant. Graham was one of the many unemployed young people from this scheme who had ended up injecting heroin in the 1980s.

The other addicts were often family members or those who belonged to relatively close-knit groups of friends. Because they knew each other well, they thought it was fine to share needles. Tragically this led to a situation where these conditions, which were replicated in the other large housing schemes in Edinburgh, allowed for the rapid spread of HIV, the virus responsible for AIDS.

I can't remember when I first heard of this strange and apparently deadly virus. It was probably through accounts in the newspapers that started to appear, which then led to me reading Randy Shilts's bestselling book *And the Band Played On – Politics, People and the AIDS Epidemic* which was a masterpiece of investigative journalism reporting on how AIDS was able to spread unchecked through the early 1980s. At first it seemed that this silent, deadly epidemic was happening a long way away from us, amongst the gay community in the States. As the epidemic gathered momentum we held a powerful workshop at the Gateway called the AIDS Mastery.

This was led by Sally Fisher and Gaye Baynes, two formidable women, who had been involved in creating these workshops; they were initially devised by the acting community in New York to support friends who were struck down with this life threatening illness. The AIDS Mastery was a response directed at empowering those affected by the symptoms, stigma, and fear surrounded this condition in the early days as it spread like wildfire through these communities - either through sexual contact, or through sharing contaminated needles.

Reality struck home to us that it was on our own doorstep when Graham went for an HIV test and it turned out that he was positive. We were all devastated and at a loss to know how we could or should respond. It was all the more upsetting as Graham was playing the lead role in a Gateway Exchange Theatre production. He starred in two plays which we put on – *The Hardman* where he played the part of Jimmy (this was very challenging for him but he excelled in this role) and *Gotcha!,* another hard-hitting play.

Despite this upsetting news, he gave strong performances in these demanding roles and received excellent reviews. His young son, Lee, attended every night and knew all the lines off by heart.

I didn't record the names, numbers or unfolding time scale, but during this period more and more young people came and shared with us that they were HIV positive. The implications for them were extremely serious. From having led their lives feeling that they had a future in front of them, overnight they found themselves infected with a life-threatening illness. They often looked well when initially diagnosed, but symptoms invariably overcame them – weight loss, pallor, pneumonia and sometimes skin lesions.

Worst of all was the stigma surrounding HIV infection in the early days. In the hospitals they would be isolated in screened off rooms, hospital staff would only go near them wearing gowns and face masks.

They were on the receiving end of some virulent public abuse from those who interpreted infection with the virus as some kind of punishment from God for their wayward lifestyle. Some members of the public wanted them to be sent off to remote islands. Fear and panic dominated the response in the early days, leaving these brave young people to face a cruelly shortened lifespan with the minimum of support.

We had quite a few of them visiting us in the Gateway. Beyond taking sensible precautions with hygiene, our initial response was to do what we could to normalise things as much as possible and not give in to the fear. We went on a search for information and made contact with some of the front line London groups. We had little idea what we were facing at the beginning.

Tragically, we were at the start of a time when a devastating number of young people died from this condition, with all the implications that this raised in terms of bereavement on an unprecedented scale amongst their social groups. Children with HIV positive parents found themselves orphaned at a tragically young age.

The scale of this unfolding tragedy is best illustrated through what happened to Graham and his family, who we knew closely. Graham had two brothers with the names Malcolm (Minger) and

Micheal (Slimey). Having shared needles they all became infected around the same time. All three of them died within a few years. Graham left behind his young son, Lee. I remember Graham at one point saying to me that it was as though they were all standing in a bus queue, not knowing which one of them would go first. We faced many other equally harrowing situations through being witnesses to this time.

As always there were gifts and opportunities to be found in facing this inconceivable crisis. One of these was the emergence of a number of front-line support services, all of which operated initially out-with the mainstream services. Almost all those who became infected came from backgrounds where they had acquired the virus through sharing contaminated needles.

The gay community was equally devastated as the virus was transmitted through sexual contact. The people who stepped up to offer support services were often their friends, lovers, and family members. We found ourselves in close contact with these groups, doing all that we could to assist them.

*

As our problems of trying to find funds to cover the running costs and maintenance of the Gateway mounted, we found an unexpected way to transform our difficulties. The building which had seemed to offer so much creative scope and potential at the beginning, had started to feel like an albatross round our necks. Here were all these new groups needing space to work – we had the space, but lacked a clear focus because of the spread of our work, and as a result of this we were struggling to raise the funds we needed.

We returned from a holiday in the summer to find morale at a low ebb. Those who had kept the centre running felt isolated and unsupported – negativity, pettiness and bitching seemed to have taken over, which wasn't surprising, given that at that point we were facing the almost certain prospect of having to close the Gateway. Then came a moment when Evlynn mentioned that the idea of an AIDS Resource Centre had come up at a working together day for AIDS, held by the Lothian Region.

Why didn't we offer our building to provide support and accommodation for these new groups? Our idea was to approach both social work and the health board to offer the use of our building for these purposes.

Suddenly, after everything looking bleak and hopeless we were putting forward an exciting new vision and getting positive responses.

It was tentative at the beginning, like any new venture. Jimmy, Sebastian and Evlynn had all expressed a desire to move on from the Gateway. Jimmy, at least, provided backup in many essential areas and Evlynn continued to be involved in the *Fighting Back!* series of workshops that we had started together – these were based on the work of the AIDS Mastery and focused on empowering people through offering opportunities for creative self-expression.

I found it hard to let go of the Gateway and found myself becoming excited about the potential for us to transform and evolve into an AIDS Resource Centre for the city. It seemed that our legacy might continue in the form of a new and much needed facility for the HIV community.

The Festival ended with the theatre group in tears after the last performance in the programme. The theatre, which had hosted so many extraordinary performances and events, had certainly lived up to the name which we gave it: The Mandela Theatre. One of the last plays performed there was to commemorate Elsie Inglis, a local doctor who had died in 1917, whose inspiring life had been honoured by naming the hospital, where both Suzi and Kydd had been born, after her.

Sadly the Health Board announced plans to close this hospital. Our theatre group decided to mark this occasion by putting on a production about her life, hoping that this might make the authorities think twice before following through with these plans and depriving our community of a much appreciated local hospital. It didn't succeed in this respect, but it was an outstanding production.

Evlynn also shed a few tears as the gallery she had created and played such a leading role in, finally closed. Our final exhibition was called *And Nobody Wants to Know*. This showed a series of haunting pastel images of AIDS sufferers by an American artist, Diana Constance. It was a fitting exhibition with which to close, given that it expressed powerfully the human tragedy that had by now overtaken Edinburgh - which led to it being called in the press the AIDS capital of Scotland.

For all of us this was a difficult time. We had given so much to making the Gateway the unique and special place that it was for five years. Many people in all sorts of different capacities had come through our doors. Many individuals had blossomed as a result of crossing the threshold and becoming part of the vibrant energy of the place. They expressed the uniqueness of their personalities, backgrounds and life experience in a multitude of different ways – through painting, sculpture, pottery, photography, videos, writing, poetry, theatre productions, dance, and movement. They also helped us to staff the centre, build the theatre, dark room, video suite, pottery, foundry, band rehearsal area and tackle an amazing array of different jobs. Many discovered previously hidden talents, throwing themselves into the ongoing unpredictable life and work of the centre in impressive and courageous ways.

We also had our failures, especially, sadly, in relation to our work with ex-prisoners. Quoting from our last annual report:

> 'We must put our cards on the table... our work with ex-prisoners has not been very successful at all. Actually working with individuals on release is a very demanding, sometimes

disheartening experience. We have dealt with all types of offenders including the so called 'evil trouble makers' but what we have found to be the common denominator is that they are all institutionalized to an extent which is frightening. They find it difficult to cope with the Gateway, and the choices and responsibilities we make available to them. Typical traits have been an inability to open up to the group, to be 'ducking and diving' on the quiet, resorting to violence to communicate and generally to be unable to trust anybody around them, including us.'

It was sad that in some instances we had to ask people to leave the Gateway to protect ourselves and others. We also had to recognise that some weren't ready to cope with the type of demands we were placing on them. Many of these individuals seemed to be heading back into the institution they had recently emerged from. We did not have the resources to work in a more structured way with them, nor did we, have the expertise to know how to help resolve their complex difficulties.

What we were experiencing was how the conditions that existed in most prisons tended to only reinforce these problems, so that the individual on release would return to the community even more damaged.

Taken from our annual report:

'We continue to argue for meaningful regimes in our prisons, for educational and social programmes, for prisoners to be able to see their families as we do on the outside instead of having their visits limited to nine hours a year, for a proper complaints procedure to look into grievances, for the community to have meaningful links with the prison and for support programmes to help individuals cope with the prospects of release. We believe that loss of liberty is punishment enough and that rehabilitation and a regime which encourages individuals to understand their behaviour, is the way forward.'

My own personal response to these difficulties was that I felt a strong calling to have a deeper understanding of the psychological problems that gave rise to repeating cycles of offending and self-destructive behaviour. This quest for answers and ways of working, which could help some of the more damaged people who came to see us, provided me with a strong incentive to seek further training when I moved on from the Gateway.

In September I wrote:

'Today I feel as though we have broken through. The heaving and the pushing has worked – the boulder is moving. The whole climate seems to have changed and suddenly the Gateway is being seen in a glowing light.'

We had our first steering committee meeting and the nucleus of a new entity was formed. We worked in close contact with groups such as Frontliners, Body Positive, Scottish AIDS Monitor and Positive Help. All of these front line services were in support of the idea of our facilities being adapted for use by these groups and the HIV community.

As we were putting these proposals together for a first funding application one of the individuals concerned experienced his lover's discharge from hospital with the knowledge that there was nothing more that they could do for him. The meeting ended with him in tears as he shared this painful news. This situation brought the reality home to the rest of us. It was clear that we couldn't delay.

Jimmy went off in search of funds and again attended a 'liquid lunch' with counsellors, but returned with an apparent commitment to give £50,000 to set this project in motion. I was uncomfortable about this less than healthy wheeling and dealing with the local authority, but we felt that our vision was thoroughly deserving of their support.

5.10.88 Headline from the Evening News:
Abbeyhill Site for Victims: AIDS DAY CENTRE PLAN

'Edinburgh's Gateway Exchange, which opened five years ago, looks likely to be the city's first day centre for carriers of the AIDS virus.'

Afterwards in my diary I wrote:

> 'From the ashes, the public announcement of the emergence of the new AIDS Resource Centre proposal. News is leaked from Lothian Regional Council where the future of the Gateway Exchange is prominent on the agenda of the Social Work Committee meeting. We are caught off guard and unprepared, but now there is no turning back.
>
> With this announcement a whole new identity is established – such is the power of the press. On the same day, we heard the news that S's partner had died. His death came far sooner than anyone had expected. The HIV community is devastated. This death strikes at the heart of everyone's fears. It seems that this is a turning point for us all.'

Things moved ahead with unprecedented speed. Another grant was approved which gave money for capital costs. Fearing that things would be taken completely out of our hands Jimmy and I agreed that we should try to raise trust fund money to appoint a coordinator to take the new proposals forward. I can remember at this time a slightly schizophrenic feeling as I was involved on one

FUNDING CRISIS AND CHANGE OF DIRECTION

side of the office with the closing down of the Gateway Exchange, while on the other side of the office I had a desk where I was working on this new project. I would literally run from one to the other as different calls came in.

> **Diary 2.11.88** 'Yesterday we celebrated Jimmy's 6th anniversary of Freedom. The years have sped by. One issue starting to raise itself is when and how we should tell Suzi a bit about Jimmy's past. We both feel that this should be before she starts school next year. Yesterday when she asked why it was Jimmy's special day we just said that it was his 'happy day' – a good enough description for now I suppose.
>
> We had another visit to the Special Unit. The Unit after a difficult few years with serious problems stemming from inmate apathy, drug and drink abuse, is now surfacing again. There is a good group of inmates keen to do all that they can to make the place work. It was good to sense some of the old atmosphere being recreated again by a new group of people.
>
> Prior to this visit, on the weekend, Jimmy complained of having bad dreams – when he is back inside prison again, fearing losing everything. This aspect of his prison sentence still hasn't disappeared.'

This was a reminder of the stresses and strains that Jimmy was carrying underneath. Although he appeared to have made such a good adaptation back into society, his prison experiences had left him with traumatic after-effects. He increasingly wanted and needed time to return to his own creative work. His years of working for the Gateway had consumed almost all of his energies.

> **Diary 5.11.88** 'The end of the Gateway – going out after five years with a bang! We have a Guy Fawkes night party for everyone who has been part of the Gateway during recent years.

> Many old faces show up – Margaret Dougan, Anne Dobie and Lisa, John Hood, Lyndsay John, Graham, Minger, Debbie, Lee to name just a few.'

I wish we could have appreciated and named all those who stood by us through these years. It was an emotional night which passed off smoothly with the crackle of flames from the bonfire. At least we could celebrate that our hard work and many achievements were transforming into something new.

On the Sunday of that weekend we held our last AGM – this was a small meeting where we tidied up the official business and where Sebastian and Evlynn handed in their directorships. I honour them both here for all that they gave – without their loyalty, love and enthusiasm we could not have survived these years as well as we did. They were exceptionally talented and crazy enough to stick with us through all the highs and lows, as we travelled on the Gateway Exchange rollercoaster together. It had been quite a ride, but now it was time to make a fresh start which we were all looking forward to in the New Year.

We were being launched into another transition. It was the end of an important early phase in our lives together. Various strands of this time continue. The building that housed the Gateway Exchange was leased to the Lothian Regional Council for a peppercorn rent for twenty years. In part this was to repay the public funds we had been given to renovate the café. In part, gifting the building was our contribution to support the HIV community and respond to this unprecedented crisis.

*

The AIDS Resource Centre was given the name SOLAS. Having considered different names to express the idea of light, support, and providing a safe place – and finding most of the ones in the English language already taken by other centres that were forming at this time, we started to explore the Gaelic language. SOLAS, which suggests the radiant light and warmth of the sun, felt very right at this dark time. A couple of years later the name was changed to Waverley Care. This organization continues and is this year celebrating its twenty-fifth anniversary.

The garages and the Wash House were sold. The remaining funds from the Gateway Exchange were put into a trust fund to benefit other community groups. It has been through different incarnations in terms of its administration, but continues to this day under the umbrella of Foundation Scotland – an innovative and professionally run organisation, which manages funds that are used to support community projects and initiatives throughout Scotland.

That our project and funds should have become part of these much larger, stronger and sustainable bodies has felt an appropriate way of honouring the legacy of the Gateway Exchange and all the seeds that were sown through this time.

*

Sadly, Sebastian and Evlynn's marriage ended shortly after this time. In 1990 they both headed back to London. Evlynn returned to St Martin's Art College where she took a degree in Sculpture. She went on to create an innovative couture design company called Precious McBane. Tragically. her life ended in 2003, when she died suddenly from a brain aneurism at the age of forty-three.

I had a strange premonition before she left Edinburgh that our friendship was coming to an end. It didn't make sense at the time as she was only moving to London, but we hardly saw her after that, and then came the awful, unexpected news of her early death.

Sebastian also died young, in 2010, but his death at the age of forty-seven was self-inflicted. He died of a heroin overdose. Despite his active participation with us during the years of creating and running the Gateway Exchange, he became a narcotics addict after his move back to London. He ardently pursued fame, cultivating an image of himself as a 'dandy' and 'artist', engaging in prolific sexual exploits and bizarre rituals.

He published his own book called *Dandy of the Underworld*, which he described as an 'unauthorized autobiography'. In this he claimed to have had an affair with Jimmy in the early 1980s. It was upsetting to read about this because I know that it was untrue. The Sebastian I remember was so much more worthy of appreciating than the distorted image of himself to which he so obsessively dedicated his final years.

18. A Move to the Suburbs

The 1980s were drawing to a close. Jimmy had been able to return to his fitness, writing, lecturing, media appearances, meetings, and conferences. These included making a visit to Long Lartin Prison, and lecturing at the London Art College. In many ways, without the Gateway to constrain him, he was experiencing a new sense of freedom, which he was enjoying.

In terms of my own life I continued to be involved with taking SOLAS forward in the early days, but I became clearer as time went on that it was time for me to step back into my career. The Gateway experience had taken me far from where I had started off in medicine and I had no feeling of wanting to return to working in hospitals or clinics, so I decided that I would focus on training in counselling and psychotherapy.

We sold our flat in Abbeymount, along with the Wash House, and bought a large house on the outskirts of Edinburgh, in Colinton, a suburb overlooking the Pentland Hills. Jimmy had been keen to have more outdoor space, and in particular a place where he could sculpt again. He was very excited when he found this house, which had a lot of character and a beautiful garden.

It was also quite secluded and had excellent access to Colinton Dell, which provided a woodland path for his early morning runs. He played the leading role in locating this new home for us. I appreciated that it was an unusual and spacious house, but I also experienced a lot of anxiety about its expense, and up-market image, which for me were in conflict with my social conscience and middle-class guilt.

Jimmy, having come from a very different background to me, had none of these qualms. The poverty of his early years meant that he found it an exciting new adventure to take ownership of such a grand home himself. His mother had been a cleaner and used to work for people who owned large houses like this in Glasgow. My needs were different to his. I had lived in flats ever since leaving home in Australia and had less lavish tastes. I had also never lived in the suburbs before and found this a completely different experience to living closer to the city centre.

I tried to suppress my feelings but suffered from anxiety around this move, which resulted in sleepless nights. Our differences were once again starting to surface, but for the sake of keeping the peace I went along with it, trusting that my hang-ups would settle.

On the second page of a diary beginning in 1989 there is a picture of Jimmy and me standing together in the sun with the green fields of Glynebourne behind us. We were in the south of England staying with Bill Beech (who was head of the art department in Brighton University) and his wife Jane, artists who had worked with the inmates in the Special Unit and who were long term friends of ours. They lived in Lewes, and were introducing us to the Brighton Festival.

We look relaxed and happy – Jimmy is standing up against me with his arm around my shoulders. This was a happy time in our lives together. Without the pressure of the Gateway we had space and time for new experiences. At home, life started to have a more domestic feel to it. Jimmy was becoming a good cook and was enjoying extending his knowledge in this direction.

We moved into East Muirend House in early June, a move which felt like a retreat from the busy life that we had been living to the seclusion of this new home in the suburbs. Jimmy revelled in it and was especially pleased with the wine cellar, which he had painted right away. I had reservations and so, as I discovered, did

Mum – but in the middle of the summer with the rhododendrons in the garden in bloom it looked beautiful. I did what I could to set my doubts on one side and make the best of it.

People came over to visit us and we were all able to enjoy this perfect setting in the warm weather – it was a promising and sunny start. The children loved the space and freedom, with Kydd strutting around outside, wielding the garden hose like a miniature John Wayne and taking great delight in soaking anyone rash enough to come up to him. Suzi started attending the local primary school in Bonaly and we settled into a new routine. I started seeing one or two clients for counselling in a separate space at the top of the house.

This was a small beginning. I was helped and encouraged in making this transition by a friend of mine, Jo Burns, who was a Person Centred counsellor. It was at this time in my life that I became inspired by the approach of Carl Rogers, who was one of the most influential American psychologists and psychotherapists of his time. His legacy had given rise to the Person Centred Approach. Sadly, as he died in 1987, he came just too late into my awareness for me to meet him personally, but it was his approach that I felt most drawn to when I decided to seek training to become a counsellor and psychotherapist.

What especially attracted me was that he addressed the power dynamic in the therapeutic relationship. My early experiences in the medical profession and in psychiatry had made me question the belief that the doctor, or therapist knows what is best for the patient/client. Carl Rogers's belief was that the task of the therapist/counselor was to offer an authentic therapeutic relationship within which the person seeking help could come to a deeper understanding of themselves, and learn to trust their own resources for healing and growth.

In other words his approach was based on the empowerment of the person seeking help, rather than boosting the therapist with an inflated sense of her own intelligence or power over this individual. I had some experience of this in other therapeutic approaches, and certainly amongst psychiatrists in the hospital setting, and found it potentially dangerous.

I had always believed in encouraging the inner light and potential that I saw in each person. This was the approach we had pursued so passionately in the Gateway. I was now keen to take this to a deeper level in my work with individuals. The following quote from a leading Person Centred Counsellor, Brian Thorne, describes in essence what this approach involves.

> 'Rogers believed that a human being deserves the deepest respect for what he or she is no matter how worthless or inadequate he or she may FEEL. He also believed that it was the therapist's task to seek to understand as accurately as possible the client's inner world and to be without façade... or the comfort of the protective cloak of professional authority.'
>
> (Carl Rogers by Brian Thorne – p 45)

Having spent the past few years taking off my white coat, it was natural that I should feel a resonance with this approach. I was drawn to discover more about it from those who had experience of this training and who offered me qualities of acceptance, warmth and respect, which I valued. It is curious to recognise that this new influence arrived into my life as I approached the threshold of forty. Each decade has for me been like a new chapter taking me into another phase of my life.

Jimmy organised a special meal to celebrate my fortieth birthday at a restaurant in St Mary's Street in Edinburgh. He made this occasion memorable for me and in this way helped to make me aware that it was a significant milestone.

Another experience that was important for me that year, 1990, was attending a workshop with Elizabeth Kubler Ross, in Carberry

Towers in Musselburgh. Elizabeth Kubler Ross was a remarkable and courageous doctor, originally from Switzerland, who was internationally acclaimed as one of the world's leading authorities on death and dying.

My friend Madge Bray told me about this workshop and suggested that I should attend it. This workshop with the title, *Life, Death and Transition* was an opportunity to meet Elizabeth in person, as well as to explore the issues of death and dying, which had become so much part of our lives through the unfolding of the AIDS epidemic.

Although I had experienced the AIDS Mastery, which was a very powerful workshop, this seven-day workshop was an even stronger catalyst; it launched me into a time of personal healing and inner growth, which became the main focus of this decade. I see forty as a time when awareness begins to turn gradually towards exploring who we are as a person, as opposed to simply being focused on externals in life – work, home, relationship, children.

At that time I didn't have a high regard of myself – I saw Jimmy as the one who had strength, brilliance, and unbounded talent. When the spotlight was on him, my own light seemed to disappear. I could at times find myself falling into black holes inside myself, when my confidence would drain away and I would lose all sense of my own worth or identity.

I enjoyed being a mother, but I could use my children to hide behind and had moments when I would find it hard to feel my own worth as an individual with needs of my own. I attended this workshop believing that I would learn more about how to be of help to others. What I didn't expect was that it was to have such a dramatic impact on my own life.

*

The workshop was held in a large room in a stately looking building that stands in extensive parkland on the outskirts of

Edinburgh. The size of the group was an initial shock as the room was filled with about one hundred people. The other shock was that we were all invited to sing. I had explored other forms of creativity over the years but hadn't sung since my school days and felt very self-conscious about the sound of my voice. Singing was Elizabeth's way of taking people into a place of making deeper contact with themselves. I was about to encounter locked away emotions and a soft vulnerable core which I was unaware of at that time.

The main focus of the workshop was on what was called 'externalising' our emotions. In other words we were encouraged to open up and express feelings that are normally suppressed, hidden behind the face we present to the world. People were encouraged to share their stories – many of these were heartrending. The work took place on mattresses, which provided a safe space to let go, with a facilitator alongside.

As they got into their 'stuff' people started ripping up phone directories, and beating them with rubber hoses as they let out strong torrents of emotion. In the normal world there would have been a mass attempt to stop any of this happening, to tape the wounds and to stem the flow of feeling to protect the vulnerable. Here none of this was allowed, emotions were given full reign, carers were told firmly not to look after others, Kleenex were in plentiful supply.

I had wondered whether I would sit through the workshop unable to access my deeper emotions, but a comment from a man working on one of the mattresses about how he had left his children without saying goodbye turned out to be my trigger. Suddenly I felt the rage and pain of my father leaving me without coming to say goodbye, and that was it...I was on my knees on one of the mattresses howling out my long repressed anguish.

My facilitator was a beautiful blonde Irish woman, called Phyllida, who had a guitar and sang with the voice of an angel.

In her role as facilitator she encouraged me to express the hurt and pain that I had felt as a nine-year-old. It was a deeply cathartic experience that surprised me as I hadn't realised that I was holding onto so much.

Elizabeth watched us all from the back of the room, an elderly woman with a piercing gaze. She was small in stature, casually dressed and unexpectedly ordinary looking in her appearance. She didn't look at all like someone who could take a whole roomful of people into the cauldron of their long-repressed emotions. She was straight-forward and astute in her observations and was an extraordinary pioneer in terms of her work with the dying. Elisabeth encouraged patients to share their stories and in doing so did much to break down the taboo around talking about death, insisting that we could learn most from those who were closest to it.

Phyllida has since become a close friend, soul sister and companion through the years. I also met Nick Price who has become another lifelong friend, and Nan Mulder who has inspired me with her beautiful paintings. Shortly after the workshop ended Nan and I were involved in supporting another participant who died from cancer. This experience was testing and sad, especially as she had a partner and two young children, but the message of the workshop was that freedom comes through learning to let go with love.

*

When I went along to this workshop I had imagined that my own life was secure in the context of my marriage to Jimmy and love for him and the children. My drawings told a different story, which was one of cracks emerging. At the time this meant little to me, but this turned out to be quite accurate in terms of what lay ahead.

Jimmy almost certainly could have benefitted from participating in this workshop, and it might have been a catalyst for his own healing. It was not a culture that he was at all familiar with though. He decided that it was not for him, and stayed at home to look after the children. The following year Elisabeth and her team were invited to give a workshop in Saughton Prison, which felt like a real breakthrough – this kind of work in prisons could be truly transformative.

The life I was now leading was very different from the all-consuming Gateway years. I had more space and time, but I was restless inside myself. Jimmy was finding his way back into his sculpture and was enjoying his new-found sense of freedom. Suzi and Kydd were becoming more confident and, symbolic of their growth, were delighted with themselves when they managed to ride their newly acquired bikes without stabilisers.

As mentioned at the end of the previous chapter, when the Gateway Exchange closed, we created a trust fund and were able to make grants to continue helping a wide range of different self-help and community projects. This helped us to create a better balance in our lives. We were still able to make a contribution to the social issues we felt passionate about, but our energies were no longer consumed to the degree that they inevitably were when we were running the Gateway.

We invited two other Trustees to join us – Rodney Stares (Director of Foundation for Community Leadership and a personal friend) and Barbara Orton (a talented film-maker and dedicated community activist). Together we supported a wide variety of inspiring projects over the years through the running of this trust.

Mum had suggested that we should employ someone to help us run the trust fund when we set it up. This proved to be an excellent way to keep things moving ahead smoothly. The person who stepped into this role was Anna, who was already like a member of the family, as for years she had helped look after Suzi and Kydd. She now became even more of a key person in our lives as she took on the role of being PA to Jimmy as well as administering the Gateway Exchange Trust.

Despite these new developments, an unsettled feeling remained with me. Ever since Jimmy had been released from prison people had been suggesting that we leave Scotland and start a new life elsewhere. He was always keen to do this. I was the more conservative one and less sure in this respect. We also now had the children and their schooling to consider. None of these factors needed to have stopped us from making a move, but we ended up staying. Suzi, who was seven at the time, was the clearest of all of us as she said forcefully: 'If you two leave Scotland, I'm staying!'

Sometimes it can be helpful to start looking more deeply within ourselves, rather than changing the outer circumstances. This was where I felt I needed to go. I started having personal therapy in September 1991. It took me weeks of contemplating this before I found the courage to lift the phone. When I eventually did, it was much easier that I had expected. The Person Centred counsellor who I saw was warm, respectful, and skilled at drawing things out of me. I found it a little unnerving talking about myself, but I knew that I needed help with issues relating to my childhood and parents' divorce. It was time to share some of this.

Allowing someone to 'see' me in such sensitive places was challenging. My secretiveness was deeply ingrained. I found it hard to step out from behind my inner wall and show myself. Feelings surfaced which had been long buried, but the acceptance I felt was healing and helped me to feel stronger inside myself. Embarking on becoming a counsellor myself I knew that I needed to have deeper access to my own inner resources. I also needed to be able to be real and transparent in the relationship and this meant that I had to know myself.

My greatest fear was always that the inner stream would dry up and that I would end up discovering that I was empty – merely a vacuum, a hollow black hole in my deepest core. This seems strange now but at that time I had moments when this was how I felt. The support of having someone else alongside meant that I was able to face and experience these feelings, as well as the long buried hurts that gave rise to them.

Eventually I was able to discover the natural, joyful, playful, spontaneous, loving essence, which was who I was underneath it all. Gradually I learned to trust that my core was intact and by looking within I could have access to a wealth of inner resources.

*

It was particularly important for me to begin discovering this deeper faith as we were experiencing a number of people close to us dying. Elizabeth's message was that every experience has a lesson for us and that living fully is possible even in the face of death. The worst enemy is fear. The greatest friend is hope. Her words were a great support when we were confronted with the reality of death and dying through the continuing ravages of AIDS.

Sometimes this left us at a loss to know how to respond. A couple of months previously we had visited Malcolm Tant (Graham's brother) in City Hospital. He was very ill with pneumonia and had lost a lot of weight. He had also lost his normally quick sense of humour. His breaths were shallow and pathetic. Seeing him looking so depleted was very shocking – we felt utterly helpless at this tragedy unfolding before our eyes. We had only recently attended his wedding to his beautiful young partner Debbie.

A very short time after this last hospital visit we attended his funeral. This was held in Milestone House, the hospice which had been created for respite and terminal care for those with HIV. The community involved in offering these support services did all that they could to acknowledge the individual in all their uniqueness. Funerals were individually designed and personal. Malcolm was buried wearing his team's football strip. Despite the sadness there was an outpouring of love from his family and friends, which

10. Breakfast at home on the morning of Jimmy's release - Nov 1st 1982 with friends Sebastian Horsley, Evlynn Smith, Anna McNeill and Sarah Noble.

1. Cover of Gateway Exchange One. Annual report.

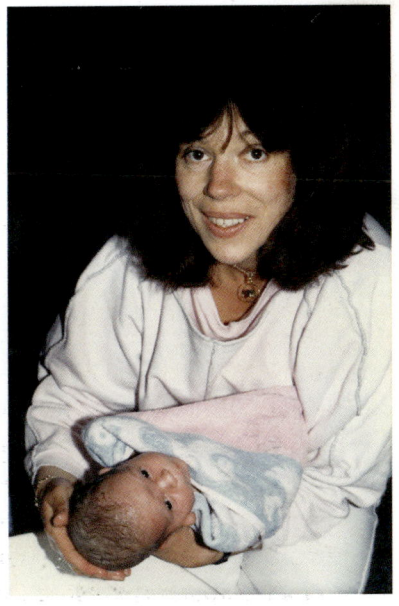

12. Holding newborn Kydd April 1987

13. Jimmy holding newborn Suzi - Peace, baby, peace, March 1984.

14. With our beautiful baby daughter Suzi, March 1984.

15. Family breakfast at Abbeymount 1987

16. Work underway at 21A - visiting to check on progress with the family in 1993.

17. The family with Anna at 21A 1994.

18. Helping Mum across the threshold of 21A for her remarkable late in life move back to Australia 2003.

19. Celebrating the 100th (Suzi's 30th, Jimmy's 70th Birthday) in Antibes, France, June 2014. Our first family photograph together for 15 years.

brought dignity and meaning to his all too short life.

Another death at this time was that of 'Big Jimmy' who had been one of our team of regulars in the Gateway. He was one of the many who had wandered in off the street and who found a sense of belonging through becoming part of our core team. He was a big burly man, often with a powerful body odour, who had been brought up in children's homes.

His education was limited and he was physically dis-coordinated. He described being punished when he was young because he was unable to tie his shoelaces. His emotions were turbulent and often childlike. He could be enthusiastic and willing, but could sometimes be obstinate and aggressive in his outbursts.

Despite this, he stuck with us, and we stuck with him. He was especially appreciative of Suzi and Kydd when they were brought into the centre, and in response to them he showed his affectionate, playful nature. At heart he was a gentle giant. He died suddenly and unexpectedly of a massive heart attack, shortly after we finally closed the centre. His passing was especially poignant as it marked the end of this time in our lives.

19. *Spiritual Emergence*

I found a Christmas card from Jimmy inside a diary he gave me for my forty-first Birthday.

> 'To my Darling Sarah, Another year... so fast. But all through it I loved you with all the strength and freshness of years gone by. Thanks for being you. I love you, Jimmy x x x'

Jimmy was always very good at writing wonderful cards and messages to me over the years, and I'm glad that I've kept so many of them. Despite these affectionate words, underneath cracks were appearing.

1991 began with Jimmy leaving for a three-week trip to Australia. He was tense before his departure, partly worrying about a talk he was scheduled to give and partly with pre-flight anxiety. It was to be our longest time apart, and perhaps symbolised that a time of increasing separation was beginning – although I was fortunately unaware of this at the time.

While he was away, Suzi started at a new school. Things hadn't worked out at the local school so we ended up moving her to one of Edinburgh's private schools. This had not been a choice I had wanted to make, but I knew that finding the right school for her was important. She came out beaming after her first day and settled in well. She still has friends from this school so despite my difficulties with elitism and privilege, in hindsight I can see that she has benefited.

My social conscience again had to be over-ridden. I had an image of a waterfall at this time and it seemed that life was taking me over some kind of an edge. This was what was about to happen, but not in a way which I could have anticipated or expected.

Strains were starting to show themselves in my relationship with Jimmy. We were starting to lose each other and were spending less time together. When we eventually managed to speak about this he admitted that he had been having visions of us separating ; he spoke about the inner tensions of having come from having nothing, to having everything in such a short time.

I exacerbated the tensions by coming back from one of my therapy sessions and talking about how ill at ease I still felt in the house. Jimmy was, not surprisingly, upset about this as he had invested so much of his time and energy in making improvements and loved feeling at home in this space. In his characteristic way though, once he had accepted that my feelings weren't going to change, he set about contacting estate agents and began a search for properties in a more central location.

By this time I had started on a training course with Person Centred Therapy Britain, to support me in my new career as a counsellor. This course came with a health warning that it could result in difficulties for couples. It was a long training which involved attending six five-day residential modules over two and a half years. These modules alternated between Stirling University and a centre close to Norwich in East Anglia.

I gave little thought to this at the beginning because I believed that our relationship was strong enough to withstand the challenges that this intensified experience of personal growth would bring. I proved wrong in this respect. The course and what happened on it was to fundamentally change me in ways which eventually broke us apart.

There are pictures from this time in the early 1990s, when we were living in East Muirend House, which make it look as though we still have it made as a couple. At this stage there was still a lot of love between us. There was a lot of potential in our marriage, but it was also starting to need attention. With another house move being imminent this wasn't going to happen.

*

Jimmy, on one of his early morning runs discovered a property in Inverleith that seemed to have potential. This was a property that had seen better days, having originally been the extension to the grand house next door. It had been taken over as a Bed and Breakfast, which had subsequently become a neglected wreck, but it had a spacious plot of land behind and was right in the heart of Inverleith, next to the Botanical Gardens. It was advertised as 'an opportunity – not for the fainthearted' – but the location, as well as the space which it offered, made it perfect for us.

As we stood at the back, looking up at the crumbling edifice of the original house, I remember feeling an extraordinary peace. I also spotted two dead but well preserved red admiral butterflies; these seemed like good omens. Hard to explain in any rational way, making a decision on the basis of signs such as these, but from an intuitive place inside, it all felt right.

Jimmy, as ever up for a challenge, threw himself with enthusiasm into the process of selling East Muirend House, then buying and renovating this new one. With spare land at the back there was an opportunity to build separate premises to create an office for the Gateway Exchange Trust, and counselling rooms for me. Underneath would be garages and at the back of these a sculpture studio for Jimmy. The basement of the house could be converted to make a granny flat for Mum, who was by now making it clear that she would be happy to accept our invitation for her to come and live with us.

This was largely Jimmy's suggestion. It was one that was a challenge for me, but with Mum becoming more frail it seemed inevitable that this should happen. This was the year she celebrated her eightieth Birthday and we had our last visit from my brother James, his wife Jo and their children Charles, Nick, and Clare.

At the start of the following year we had a phone call from James to let us know that he and Jo were going to get divorced. This news was like a sledgehammer blow as it came right out of the blue and brought back memories of my parents' divorce. I found it difficult to see this same pattern repeating itself.

Sebastian and Evlynn had separated, now James and Jo's marriage was coming to an end. Meanwhile Jimmy and I were sometimes close and sometimes a long way apart. Relationships it seemed were a testing ground for many of us. I hoped that Jimmy and I would have the maturity and commitment to continue to grow in our marriage, and that the new insights and skills that I was acquiring would support this.

At that time, through my participation in the Person Centred training, I was discovering more of myself. In this community of people I was able to begin letting down some of my strongly held defenses and open the places inside which had long remained closed off. I was not alone in having an external persona, which often masked and disguised what I was feeling inside. It was challenging to access and express the more authentic and sensitive aspects of myself - especially in a large group.

The warmth and support I received helped me to begin accepting myself more. I could also see how judgements, impressions and projections that I formed towards other people dissolved in this setting. As the masks fell away, intimacy deepened.

*

Another aspect of myself beginning to surface was my spirituality. Spirituality is experiencing a sense of connection to something bigger than ourselves, and typically involves a search for meaning in life. I was not someone who thought of myself as religious. Nor was I comfortable with the word God, which felt overly masculine and patriarchal. My Father was an atheist, despite his father being a church parson. He reached his later years not believing in anything beyond this world.

My Mother tried introducing us to church in my childhood and later on in my teens, but she herself found the language and format of traditional religion unhelpful, so her attempts to take us into the fold were half-hearted and short term in nature. I was confirmed in my early teens, but God remained a distant and remote figure. The Methodist church services I attended for a while were stultifying.

In my early teens I decided to stop going to church, preferring to spend my time outdoors and at the beach. My spiritual yearnings and impulses went underground for many years. They surfaced in my twenties through my interest in yoga and eastern philosophies, which was awakened by books given to me by Mum who read extensively. My experience of visiting India to do an elective, as part of my medical training, felt like a spiritual awakening, with everything seeming very vivid and intense when I was there.

On a second visit I attended a vipassana meditation retreat which led to some very powerful inner experiences – but feeling a long way from home and disturbed by the intensity of these I shut them away and resumed the life which I had been previously leading which felt safe at that time.

Jimmy was very open to his spirituality when I first met him, but his early experiences in Catholic approved schools had thoroughly alienated him from religion. On his release spiritual matters played almost no part in our lives. Jimmy would always light a candle to remember his mother if he went into a church, but in other ways he made clear his dislike of anything which smacked of religion.

On the counselling course there were others interested in spirituality, and it was a topic we discussed and explored. Like sexuality, it felt edgy but important to open up these aspects. I had also joined an early morning meditation group that met during these course gatherings. I initially saw this group as quite a strange looking bunch, sitting together in what looked like a lifeless and boring silence. I was surprised to discover when I did eventually join them, and started to participate in these sessions, that the silence was rich and nourishing. This was a complete revelation to me.

These influences possibly prepared me in some kind of way for a very profound experience I had in one of our large group community meetings. This experience may be difficult for other people to understand, but I have chosen to describe it because it affected me so deeply. I was exploring how I was in relation to the men in the group and had spoken about a comment that was made to me by Brian Thorne, one of the male trainers, which had shut me down.

I had Brian on a bit of a pedestal as he had a long and distinguished career in the Person Centred Therapy and was very articulate. He was also a deeply spiritual man with roots in the Anglican Church. His responses often touched me as he had an extraordinary capacity to relate in sensitive and perceptive ways to people's hidden depths. I wanted to feel close to him but I was not finding it easy. I was therefore taken completely by surprise when Brian looked at me very intensely and said that if only I knew everything that he felt about me, even before the course started. He then went on to share his deep admiration and love for me.

As he did this, the room changed and everything in it was irradiated as if by an exceptionally bright light. The group continued on. It seemed that no-one else had experienced this, but Brian's expression of feeling had been so strong, like a laser, that I was left literally reeling from it.

The light that I had experienced, which illuminated everything, was like a bolt of electricity or the full radiant energy of the sun suddenly being shone onto me. I was left with a deep glow, feeling virtually speechless. Its power continued on afterwards and I had a sense of reeling backwards, finding it difficult to absorb the fullness of what was offered in that moment.

This experience catapulted me into a process of intense spiritual opening which was both wonderful and also incredibly challenging. It was beyond the parameters of anything I had experienced previously. I was aware of a flood of very powerful feelings. I drew a whole series of images as I felt waves of intensity breaking over me. Eventually I found a quotation from William Blake that resonated:

'We are put on this earth a little space that we may learn to bear the beams of love.'

These words wouldn't have made sense to me before, but now they had a whole added dimension of meaning. I felt as though I had been blessed with a beam of love, which had, in an extraordinary way, blown my normal personality apart. I was unexpectedly birthed into a time of intense inner experience. I had no map or compass for this. I simply knew that what was happening was different and left me with an awakened passion for spiritual exploration as I allowed myself to be guided by inner promptings.

I felt privileged but also confused by what had happened. I wrote Brian a note sharing some of this experience with him, asking for an explanation and a meeting with him. I was curious about what his experience had been as well.

The following is from my diary:

> 'What he had to offer was a supportive presence. He said he felt as though something had passed through him and he too had been struck by the power of it. What was it that happened, I still ask myself? The glow that I have been feeling, the excitement in the pit of my stomach, the currents running down to my belly, is still with me. When I stop still I can feel it. And yet there is also

a reassuring sense of calm and ease when I am with Brian and a return to the ordinary.'

What had happened to me I now know was an experience of 'Spiritual Emergence'. This term refers to the awakening of the spiritual potential within an individual. There is in life a natural process of growth towards a deeper, more connected and expanded way of being that usually occurs slowly and is gently integrated. When this process occurs rapidly or becomes very intense it can seem disruptive and out of context with everyday life, precipitating a personal crisis which is referred to as Spiritual Emergency. I have now read books on this subject, but at the time I had no knowledge or understanding of this.

Brian was able to give me some spiritual advice that I found helpful to anchor myself through times of turbulence in my inner process, but he didn't give me any further insight. What he shared with me were some words from Julian of Norwich.

'Our soul sits in God in true rest, and our soul stands in God in sure strength, and our soul is naturally rooted in God in endless love.'

I found these words, as I sat and contemplated them, gave me a feeling of deep comfort. I was not alone. I was rooted, secure and held, as we all are, in a boundless field of love. I'd never had this awareness or experience before.

Mother Julian was a mystic who lived in the fourteenth century and had profound spiritual and religious visions and experiences that she wrote about in a work called *Revelations of Divine Love*.

These were so controversial for that time (it would have been deemed to be heresy by the church) that they remained buried for five hundred years. It was only in the twentieth century that the importance of her work in both literary and spiritual terms was recognised. Brian was involved in writing a book about her when I had this experience. This feels significant, but of course there is an ultimate mystery about all of this.

What I do know is that this experience resulted in a completely new understanding for me of my relationship with the dimension I call the Divine. The revelation that God is Mother as much as Father, and ultimately a source of vast, boundless and all-encompassing love, present in the whole of creation, literally transformed me. It is not easy to describe such a deep experience. It was not a change in beliefs or concepts, more a deeply embedded knowledge that I was bathed and supported in a stream of pure, unconditional love, in a way I previously had not thought possible.

I still have difficulty with the word God, because this dimension is so vast, nameless and oceanic that it feels uncomfortable, to say the least, to attach a name to it. But if I imagined my soul surrounded and bathed by this vast and boundless source of *love* it brought me comfort.

These feelings remained active and alive in me, but apart from corresponding with Brian, I spoke to no one about what had happened. Why was this? Brian wrote some words to me in a personal letter that made me feel very special. I didn't want to expose such sensitive feelings. Although I didn't find Brian physically attractive at all, there was a sexual charge that came with this experience. The way that I understand this is that as the currents of awakened spiritual energy powered their way through me, every aspect of my being sprung to life. This was nothing to do with physical contact as these boundaries were always respected. I felt shameful and confused about these feelings.

As a result I resorted to secrecy. I didn't share the experience with anybody – fellow students, trainers, my supervisor, nor most significantly, with Jimmy. I feared that he would rubbish everything as I knew he had antagonistic views about religion, while Brian was a devout Christian.

When Jimmy used the word 'God', which he did frequently, it was as an expression of his annoyance and frustration. Because of this I maintained a silence about this experience. My choice to remain silent, while understandable, is something I regret as it unfortunately resulted in a widening gulf between us.

Otherwise it was reassuring to arrive back home. Suzi came to me first, full of warm hugs and excitement, showing me her birthday gifts (I had been away for her birthday and had felt guilty about this). Then as we were watching the video Jimmy had taken on her birthday morning, Kydd came and clambered like a limpet on my back. He clung to me, finding his own natural way to restore the connection between us. Finally, I sat close to Jimmy as I shared some parts of the week with him. I discovered that the sense of spiritual union I was experiencing hadn't diminished my other relationships – it had enhanced them.

I decided to begin a regular practice of meditation in the early morning. This seemed the best way to remain open and sensitive. In some senses the spiritual laser blast I had received was like an ongoing atomic explosion...far from it resolving in a few days, it became a process that continued to unfold within me. My challenge was how to integrate the new aliveness and brilliance I experienced in my core, and yet stay grounded in ordinary life as well. This was to be an ongoing balancing act as life continued. I felt in need of a road map, but there was none available.

*

Meanwhile there were touching and funny moments as Suzi and Kydd became accustomed to me meditating each morning. They were both curious and respectful about this; they would wander in and sit beside me, but soon became bored and would wander off again. As children do, they became used to me sitting quietly with my eyes closed and soon regarded it as part of the normal pattern of our lives.

When I was with Jimmy there were times when it seemed we were going on completely different paths, but other times when family life brought us close again. We spoke at one point about the lack of close intimacy in his life.

Tactically I used this as an opportunity to introduce the suggestion of counselling as a way of exploring this. He was resistant to this idea, saying that he didn't see the need for it. I felt conscious of the differences emerging between us because I was trying to open myself at deeper levels, which was the opposite of what he wanted to do. I was clearly on my own in terms of where these intense new inner experiences were taking me.

Fortunately there were still some memorable times we were able to share together. One of these was an opportunity to hear the Dalai Lama give a public talk at Samye Ling, a Tibetan Buddhist Centre in Scotland. To my surprise, we were privileged to be given front row seats for this special occasion. His theme was peace, but what was more impressive than anything he said was his quality of centred stillness, as well as his radiant and lovely smile.

Jimmy said that his smile looked as though it had been made in heaven. This was something on which we could both fully agree. Shortly after this I had an opportunity to visit and be properly introduced to Samye Ling, which was the first Tibetan Buddhist centre established in the West. This centre was to provide a refuge for me later on when I really needed it.

Another moment of intimacy came when Jimmy told me that he had heard from friends that Anthony Ross had suffered a stroke and was in a coma. We were asked to think of him. Jimmy wanted me to put my arms all the way around him, the way we held each other when Anthony had put his arms around us both and blessed us on our wedding day. It felt as though Anthony was still forging strong bonds of love around us.

Despite the wear and tear evident in our marriage, the invisible force field was still there holding us together. This experience gave me a sense of coming back home. After Anthony died we attended his funeral, which brought back memories of his warm and generous spirit. He was described in the sermon as a mobile priory. He invited anyone and everyone into his space and gave generously of himself, offering the same quality of unconditional loving to all.

His belief in the 1940s was that what was needed to save the world was some kind of spiritual revolution. He was both a man ahead of his time as well as a man of his time. It was a gift in my life to have met him, and as my own journey deepened I could appreciate even more his qualities of presence and vision.

He was like a human lighthouse, beaming love to everyone, especially those who found themselves on the fringes – the outcasts of society.

PART FOUR

IN SEARCH OF SELF

20. The Challenges of Emergence

Others we knew were confronting far more serious crises, which helped to put the stresses of my own continuing process of emergence into perspective. This was brought home to me when we visited Graham, who had ended up in Milestone, the HIV/AIDS Hospice. He had by now lost a great deal of weight and had the shrunken, wasted look of a terminal AIDS patient. We could never have imagined that he and others, young people who had been so full of life when we first met them, would end up looking this way.

We sat with him as he reviewed the past thirteen years that we had known him. Jimmy's first memory was of meeting Graham, his partner Angi, and their one year old son Lee, at home in a flat in Wester Hailes. At this time all that they had was a new video sitting on bare floorboards, otherwise there was absolutely no furniture. This summed up their priorities and bore witness to the fact that they were financially broke.

Graham had started using drugs and had been taking what he called 'smack' for three months before he found out that it was heroin. Jimmy had begged him not to take this, but Graham thought that he knew better. Now he regretted all his mistakes – the tragedy of his present condition was that it was ultimately preventable. This was a poignant visit, which I wrote about afterwards in my diary:

'He remembered the acclaim he got for his performances

in Gotcha and the Nutcracker Suite – how nervous he had felt about playing Jimmy's part and how he almost couldn't stop himself from laughing as he raised the TV set above his head in a gesture of extreme anger and frustration – and saw a man watching almost fall out of his wheelchair!

Now here he is with his life almost spent and there's so much he's missed out on – but he still has the spirit he used to have. He asked how long we were going to be away on our holidays and when I said 3 weeks, he said: 'I'll hang on, nae bother.'

What really matters to him is still being alive on Lee's birthday – he turns 14 this year. It'll probably be the last one they will share together. I'm in tears as we drive home. He's the last of the three brothers to die and it'll mark the end of a phase in our lives too when he goes.'

Jimmy and I, with the children, headed off on a summer holiday to the USA, but an unpleasant surprise was in store for us when we landed. We'd had a wonderful flight, having been upgraded to first class - which allowed us to spread out in luxury. Looking down from our window seats we had an amazingly clear view of Greenland, which was apparently very unusual as it is normally obscured by clouds.

On arrival we were held back at immigration after Jimmy had ticked the section on the back of the visa waiver card asking about previous criminal convictions. Steely-faced immigration officials went off to check on their computers and returned to confirm his negative entry status. We were both stunned at the news that he would need to be immediately deported back to Britain. Suzi, Kydd and I were free to go but it was devastating leaving him, knowing that he was going to be flying back to London.

This whole experience was resolved a few days later by a decision to spend our holiday time in Antigua rather than America, with Jimmy determining that he would not have similar problems there. It was a costly episode and very stressful for Jimmy, who missed out on seeing his brother Tommy in the US and was left feeling the weight of his past pursuing him.

Fortunately Suzi and Kydd dealt with this episode well and the sun and serenity of Antigua helped us all to recover. Back at home, a picture was taken of the four of us for an article about this experience which appeared in the *Guardian* – it is a picture that, for me, sums up the worst of that time. I look dreadful in it, somehow separate and alone, standing behind Jimmy, as he sits with Kydd squeezed into his side and Suzi with her arm wrapped protectively around him.

> From my diary: 'Living together apart – we live together, but we lead such separate lives – why? This separateness scares me.'

The sense of aloneness increased as my intense inner journey continued and the spaces between Jimmy and I became more obvious. I felt deeply unhappy about this, and my expression in this photograph somehow captures it all.

*

As we had expected Graham died that Autumn. On our last visit he was lying in bed, breathing irregularly, with his eyes closed. He looked more peaceful than I had ever seen him. It was as if he could at last be free of the stubborn and difficult aspects of his personality. It was painful saying goodbye. His two brothers, Micheal and Malcolm, had died on the October 5 and 9 respectively over the past two years. He was the last of the three of them to reach this point of departure, also in the month of October.

He'd been like a cat with nine lives but he'd used all of them up. He lived life defying the odds, which were stacked against him from the start. As with so many others he died before his time, maintaining his dignity and humour as he bore the onslaught of his illness, and right to the end kept his strong and brave spirit.

*

Autumn was for us a time of endings and new beginnings as we put East Muirend House up for sale and Jimmy became involved in overseeing building works on our new home in Inverleith. The previous month I had attended another residential at Stirling University. Unfortunately the surge of spiritual energy and excitement from seeing Brian Thorne again contributed to me having a stressful time during the week. I recovered, but when I returned home my ongoing challenge was trying to find a way to integrate the spiritual experiences.

I would have moments of heightened perception when I was in the middle of doing quite ordinary things. I found myself open and receptive to dimensions that were finer, vaster, subtler than those which we normally attribute to the everyday, and felt crazy at times, flooded by these altered realities.

The continuing feeling of being accompanied by a loving presence was reassuring though. I also often had the strange experience of being guided by an animal presence – the blue heron. I wrote about this in my diary:

> 'The heron which first came to me in a dream, now seems to be appearing in my life at significant moments, when the inner and the outer are in particularly close alignment.'

These were what I called 'special moments' – they felt like reminders that I was not alone on this journey.

That Autumn I began to keep a spiritual diary as a way of accompanying myself on this journey into new realms of consciousness. I was tentative about this at the beginning but it helped to write about what I was experiencing, along with anything that touched me or gave me further insights along the way. This journal was a rich source of inspiration and helped to strengthen and empower my inner life.

*

It can't have been easy for Jimmy being alongside me as I came through this time of emergence. I have a drawing where I show him standing with his foot resting on a block of stone, holding a string, which symbolises how I was saw myself – a figure floating in mid-air, a brightly coloured butterfly woman who has her arms outstretched to the sky – above us both is a large and very bright sun.

I have shown Jimmy smiling looking up at me, but it wasn't all comfortable or easy as I found myself wrestling with questions about how to reconcile the different parts of my life. In lots of ways Jimmy was the one dealing with the practical aspects of our lives, keeping me grounded as I came through this time. But I would become irritated with his drinking, which seemed to sabotage moments when we might have connected more deeply with each other. It felt a paradox that I could feel so much love inside and feel my oneness with the rest of humanity and the universe, but I couldn't express it to Jimmy, the person I was closest to.

As the end of the year approached he was carrying plenty of his own stress; he was involved with endless meetings with the builders and with Ben Tindall, our architect, trying to ensure that the contractors would meet their deadlines. Our move was scheduled for just before Christmas. Mum was also due to arrive at this time and was to move into her new self-contained basement flat, which created an additional sense of pressure.

We finally moved in on December 23 with the builders, electricians, joiners, window cleaners, carpet layers, and our removers all somehow managing to work around each other. To add to the chaos, Jo and the children, Charles, Nick, and Clare, arrived in the middle of it all. It was a last minute dash for everyone but in the end, despite the upheaval, it all went smoothly. Outside the snow started to fall and we were treated to a very special white Christmas.

There were family tensions to deal with but not ours on this occasion. My mother had a phone call from my brother just before Christmas to tell her that he was planning to get married to Samina, a colleague whom he knew from the University in Perth. This was all a bit too sudden for me, coming so soon after the news of his separation from Jo. It seemed to me that having been married with a family for all these years, he was now planning to excise her out of his life in the manner of a surgeon removing an unwanted part.

Being at such a distance from my brother clearly didn't help and the news activated my childhood experience and all its associated upset. Jo dealt with the situation courageously and with dignity and was particularly helpful in the aftermath of our move.

We took a break over New Year, spending it in Paris with our friends Bill and Jane and their children Tom, Sam, and Lucy. The good humour and fun we shared helped to dispel all the stress, so the year ended on a good note, which was a relief.

Suzi decided that she too was going to keep a diary and she hunted all over Paris for one she liked. It was interesting to hear her say that she thought that writing in her diary could help her with her feelings. She'd been annoyed with Clare over something, had written this down, and immediately felt better afterwards. It seems that this tradition of writing is continuing in the family.

When we returned James was visiting and Mum was keen for me to talk with him. I felt very tense and we both seemed to be avoiding each other. When we did finally sit down I hurt him by saying that I would not be attending his wedding. Shortly after I said this he got up and left. Any mature emotional communication felt impossible. Mum was trying her best to keep the peace between us. James resented Jo coming for Christmas and felt that

I was being very unsupportive of him. I was annoyed at him for coming at such a difficult time, without any acknowledgement of this. The anger swirled around in both of us with everything unresolved.

Apart from these tensions, we all settled well into the house and living closer to the centre of Edinburgh made some things, especially the morning school runs, much easier. Mum seemed in good spirits, although getting used to city life in her eighties, was a daunting prospect. She was enjoying the closer contact with all of us, and I found myself feeling more relaxed about her presence than I had expected.

Then it was Spring: time for Suzi to celebrate her tenth birthday. I reached the end of a big piece of work for the course, my self-assessment, which needed to be handed in on the final residential module. The other development of importance in our lives was that the Mews – a separate building with garages, Jimmy's studio, an office for the Gateway Exchange Trust and counselling rooms was completed. Anna, our wonderful Secretary and PA, moved into the new office on March 1 that year. I was looking forward to having a self-contained work-space separate from the house and Jimmy was excited about being able to begin sculpting again in the studio.

*

While Jimmy took the children on a visit to France and EuroDisney, I set off for my final residential week; this took place at Hawkstone Hall, a residential centre in Shropshire. On my way there I wrote that I did not want to end up on a rollercoaster, as I had on the previous residential in Stirling. Unfortunately, my emergence process was not going to stay nicely contained and integrated.

For the first part of the week I had a feeling of holding onto something big which I couldn't express or articulate. It then started to break through. It was related to the intense feelings for Brian which I'd been carrying all year and which left me feeling vulnerable and confused. The reliance I placed on his support and ongoing letters had created an unhealthy emotional entanglement with him. Keeping this secret resulted in me feeling isolated and separate from my fellow classmates. With the benefit of hindsight it would have helped if I could have spoken to one of the other trainers about what had happened, but by this time the awakened Kundalini was stirring dangerously and I was starting to lose my grip on outer reality.

The experience of disintegration and fragmentation that had happened in Stirling started all over again, along with powerful currents of heat and energy flowing in my core. My feelings for Brian and my love for Jimmy felt entangled – I wanted to extricate myself from this impossible confusion and celebrate the strong , clear heart within me.

By this point the inner fire of vibrating spiritual energy had a seemingly unstoppable momentum. I wasn't able to shut it off. I found myself glowing like a light bulb, and unable to function in any normal way. I had to retreat to my room where I had experiences of bliss, alternating with disintegration, rivers of tears, shakes, shivers, and spasms. I felt I had no skin – my flesh felt raw and exposed and even slight sounds caused my core to hurt. Underneath from the depths, something huge, immense and unspeakably powerful was slowly rising, and suddenly I made the connection. Of course, out of the depths of our soul, there reaches a point where we begin to sense some kind of direct connection and communication with the Source.

*

Unable to stop this process, I allowed myself to slide deeper into these depths – out beyond my mind – suddenly letting go into something calm and vast. I surrendered completely, allowing myself to expand into the all-embracing light, but I had fears that I would never manage to find a way back. People came and went through this time, including Brian who did his best to support me in this extraordinary process. I wanted to rejoin the group but he told me that my mind was fevered as it surely was. I needed safety and boundaries so I remained in my room.

Then the worst fragmentation began as I reached a place of complete desolation and abandonment.

I knew that I was losing it and realised that in this state I would be unable to take my diploma. I felt a lot of fear about my inability to cope and how I would manage to get myself home, also about *who* would be arriving home. For the first time in my life I felt on the edge of needing to be admitted to a psychiatric hospital.

What saved me was the presence of one of my classmates, Fiona. She appeared suddenly beside my bed and with loving eyes accompanied me through the final, most awful stretches without flinching. She kept hold of my hand and gently began to work on my body, massaging my aching muscles and joints, moving the energy through me, holding steady as I descended into the depths of anguish; soothing me, loving me, and stroking my energy back up as it started to stream through me again. We laughed together at the craziness, and ended up in what felt like a strange dance together. She was completely with me in it all. This deep connection literally saved me.

She left and shortly afterwards another classmate, Mark, appeared. He sat calmly beside me, holding me with a kind and steady gaze. He emanated peace and stillness. He was willing to go with me at a very slow pace, which was all that I could manage. We took a walk together through the grounds - visiting the chapel on the way - where I shed more tears. He then brought me back to my room.

The following morning I was able to attend the meditation group and I spent time in the garden in front of a beautiful statue of Mary. Gazing up into her face I had the most extraordinary experience of something direct being transmitted, similar to what I had experienced at Ditchingham. This resulted in what felt like a super-fast experience of integration. It was unexpected and defied all logic, but I was beyond trying to explain anything by this point and was simply relieved that I felt well enough to attend the final ceremony and receive my Diploma.

This experience taught me the importance of deep surrender. I was learning to trust the process all the way to the gateways of the soul and beyond. This has been invaluable when I have been in situations where I have needed to support others undergoing deep processes. It certainly wasn't the way that I had intended to graduate at the end of the course, but I was grateful to manage to take my diploma with the others in the end, by a hair's breadth.

I still needed to get home. I was clearly not ready to leave that day, and planned to remain for an extra night. It was unnerving at first when everyone else left as I was still in a state of heightened sensitivity – open to every aspect of the natural world around me. What concerned me was how I was going to manage to cope with the outside world again.

I was as sensitive as a newborn infant at that point and having to travel the three hundred miles home alone on the train was difficult. I travelled home with my Diploma, which I was naturally pleased to have received, but the words on the paper felt meaningless in terms of what I had just found myself passaging through.

*

The next challenge was going to be meeting up with Jimmy and the children again. I knew that I would need to go slowly, slowly, slowly, but how would they be with me in this fragile state? When I arrived at the station there was a long taxi queue but to my surprise Jimmy drew up in the car, with Suzi and Kydd with him. Suzi and Kydd were full of smiles and clearly delighted to see me again, and excited to tell me about their time away. Jimmy felt tense. Not surprisingly he was tired after their holiday and visit to EuroDisney.

He understood my need to take everything slowly when I explained this to him. I felt so fragile, only just managing to hold everything together. Jimmy suggested taking my things straight up to the bedroom when I got home. Suzi had a warm bath prepared with bath oils. We chatted, then I slid into bed. Jimmy offered to sleep upstairs to give me space. Suzi brought my tea up and scrambled eggs she'd made herself on toast, with basil leaves on top. Then I heard a bit about their holiday experiences through the week – the hotel in Rheims, EuroDisney and time with the Beeches. A little was all I could manage but it was lovely to be back with them again.

My process started up again in the middle of the night, but I was able to let it go; I simply couldn't do it anymore. I woke up feeling tired – but appreciating the tiredness as it was a natural feeling after all the streaming energy that had become exhausting. After lunch I had a chance to speak to Jimmy. When one of the trainers had called to let him know that I would be a day late arriving home, he hadn't been told anything about how I was. Jimmy said that in the state that I was in I shouldn't have been allowed to travel home on my own. He felt angry about this. Also that no one had given him any advice about how he could help me. His partner's perspective was important.

It certainly seems to me now that when people go into extreme states it is important to ensure proper care. I had come perilously close to completely fragmenting and losing my inner core. I felt closer to him than I had for a while as we spoke. He said he was aware of me not being 'me' at the moment, and so were the children. He suggested me going away for a few days, possibly to Samye Ling, to let this whole experience settle. This was disconcerting, but he was being truthful.

I wasn't sure at first, having just arrived back to the comforts of home. Later on though, when I tried to tell the children what had happened using drawings, it upset them - especially Suzi who was in tears afterwards. It was the wrong thing to have done. I should have checked with Jimmy first. It was too much for them. My trust in myself was very low at that point. Jimmy was right, I was trying to move back into my life at home too quickly. He phoned my friend Thom McCarthy at Samye Ling and arranged to drive me down there.

Why Samye Ling? I think that this was because Jimmy sensed that I had a spiritual connection with this centre and hoped that with their understanding and experience they could help me. We spoke a bit in the car on the way down – I wanted him to understand, but it was really too late in the process, the worst of the damage had been done.

Although his response and support were fantastic in terms of taking care of me in my fragile emotional and physical state, what he didn't say at the time was that my emotional entanglement with Brian had left him feeling hurt and betrayed. This was understandable.

*

Spiritual Emergence (or Kundalini Awakening) is a concept which few understood when I was having this experience. Afterwards I very much hoped that it would be possible for me to meet with my trainers to share with them what had happened. Sadly this wasn't possible; the course had ended and they all had other responsibilities.

Even now, all these years later, it is still not easy to write about or share this episode. There is also a risk of some people thinking I must be completely crazy. I have described it because these kind of experiences, if understood and supported in the right way, can be openings to a deeper reality and truth. It can be lonely, though,

THE CHALLENGES OF EMERGENCE

if there is no-one close at hand to offer guidance and support. Having fallen into this turbulent river of emergence, with the deep shifts it brought about in my core, I was on my own travelling downstream. There were no maps or guidebooks, but through grace I seemed to find exactly the right support when I needed it.

21. The Stormy Search

The time at Samye Ling was very healing. This is a well-known Tibetan Buddhist Centre in the Scottish Borders. Dominated by the colourful and exotically decorated temple, it has a rich and interesting history.

I had first discovered the centre once when I was driving back from the Lakes, and had decided to vary the journey by taking a different route passing through Langholm. I had spotted the golden temple roofs and out of curiosity, having heard good things about the place, turned in to have a look for myself.

I was welcomed by Thom McCarthy, a long-term member of this community, an effusive ex-New Yorker and Vietnam veteran, who gave me a guided tour and general introduction. Thom opened my eyes to see beyond the ramshackle building-site appearance of some of the complex, explaining what each aspect represented and the vision lying behind it all.

Since its beginnings Samye Ling has been a place of destination for numerous spiritual seekers, progressing from the early somewhat anarchic hippy days to become a respected centre offering access to Tibetan Buddhist teachings as well as offering retreats.

The complex is situated alongside a river running through the valley. The temple is aligned with a special point of confluence where a smaller river joins the larger one at right angles. In Tibetan Buddhist terms this is supposed to be very auspicious. The atmosphere throughout is peaceful, saturated as it is by the meditations and prayers, which take place daily.

Thom said, as he showed me around, 'If a knotted up snake is left alone, it will untangle itself'. I have always been grateful for the clarity and simplicity of this advice. What I needed was a good rest. I could immediately feel myself benefitting from the peace and soon found myself settling. I enjoyed walking slowly alongside the river, sitting in various places around the grounds and meditating in the temple. Time in nature was healing for me – and quite naturally I started to feel better.

I had an interview with Lama Yeshe. Lama Yeshe is the Abbott of Samye Ling, and brother of Akong Rinpoche, the original founder. He has an air of authority about him, born of his innate qualities of optimism, faith, and strong dedication to the Buddhist path. Having spent twelve years on retreat in intensive meditation, his entire life is an expression of wisdom and devotion. He manages to combine this with tremendous joy. This is expressed in his smile, which shines from his whole being like a sun.

I was anxious before my interview, but I found him easy to speak to. He was wise, but also had a light touch and playful sense of humour. After I had told him my story, he said that I wasn't mature enough to have been able to digest the experience I had with Brian. I had held onto it too much and had formed a strong attachment, causing problems. He likened the experience to me having been given a teaspoon with half honey, half poison – this was exactly how it had felt. He said that when the Kundalini awakens it is like disturbing a sleeping poisonous snake. It has no way of seeking satisfaction and can only do harm, becoming self-destructive.

I had dreams of encountering a huge serpent at one point and can relate to this image. He suggested that I visualize a transparent light and work on de-solidifying this experience. The Buddhist practice is all about doing everything for the benefit of others, not for self- advancement or gain. I clearly had a long way to go, but I was grateful for the advice he gave me.

I was also grateful to Ani Lhamo, his assistant and senior nun. Ani Lhamo, who is originally from the Highlands, and speaks with a soft Scottish lilt, gave me some simple and useful instructions in meditation. There was no pressure or expectation that I should become a Buddhist, simply an attitude of openness and willingness to share what was of use to me – meeting me very much where I was, at an early stage on the path.

*

Jimmy came to collect me. On the way back in the car I could sense how confusing this was for him. He was struggling to understand the changes and the extremes he was experiencing in me. I wanted to be 'normal' again, but I knew that full integration and recovery was still some way off. Little did I know how long it would take for this process of spiritual emergence to settle into a more integrated place inside of me – the truth was that I would never be who I was before – I couldn't undo what had happened.

What I had experienced had fundamentally changed my orientation to life. While I had appreciated my time away, I also wanted to be back in the heart of my family – I never had any doubts about that.

Suzi asked me if what had happened to me had happened to others on the course. I told her that it was only me, feeling how impossible it was for her to understand. She had been very worried about me and in fact was sick on the night when I went off down to Samye Ling. It was hard for me to hear this but I hoped that family life could now resume as normal again.

The Mews was looking good and it was time to begin engaging with my work again, but I needed to take things slowly. In a way this was a gift, although it didn't always feel like that at the time. I had to be careful not to take on too much, or over expose myself to outside pressures. It was a time of having to let go, let go, let go. This wasn't easy, as it was so different from the way I had previously been in my life, always wanting to race on ahead.

In my diary I wrote:

> 'My newly emerging self has a very different make up –it feels softer, gentler, slower, deeper, more reflective and seems filled with some unspeakable, unquenchable longing.'

I was surprised at the slow pace of my recovery but, helpfully at this point, a friend loaned me a book called *The Stormy Search for the Self*, co authored by the two well known transpersonal psychologists, Christina and Stanislav Grof. This gave a fully documented picture of spiritual emergence, and included accounts by others. Finally, I was able to see what I had experienced being validated and described in print.

Two weeks after Kydd's 7th birthday it was Jimmy's 50th. This was a memorable moment in his life and given everything that he had come through to reach this milestone, I decided to honour him by commissioning a portrait by John Bellany. John was delighted to have him sit for this, as they shared an excellent rapport.

Jimmy was proud and happy with the finished painting, which joined another John Bellany work in our front room. John, who in common with Jimmy, enjoyed large spaces (our front room, having been the ballroom extension to the house next door was big enough for Kydd to use as an indoor football pitch!) promptly renamed this now elegant looking room the Bellany suite.

Jimmy's fiftieth birthday in 1994 coincided with Nelson Mandela being elected president of South Africa, following the first free elections in the country for 350 years. Desmond Tutu captured the spirit of the occasion when he proclaimed: 'This is a day of celebration for all of us, black and white. This is a day of liberation.' This was the time when the spirit of celebration spread around the world and we shared in the collective feeling of witnessing an extraordinary moment in history.

*

Together with Suzi and Kydd we made a trip across to Glasgow so that Jimmy could share with all of us some of his past memories. It was a wide gulf between the crowded tenement lined streets in the Gorbals where he had grown up, now replaced by anonymous and impersonal looking high rise tower blocks, and the spacious tree lined Edinburgh street where we were living. Although the hardships of the poverty which he experienced in his youngest years were real and contributed in many ways to his early choices which led him into a life of crime and violence, he always appreciated the wit, the crack and the colourful characters he had known, coming from this background.

This time of happiness and celebration was short lived. An early morning phone call a few days later from his brother Tommy, brought the sudden and heartbreaking news that his son James Paul had been murdered in a location close to the area we had been visiting. Jimmy headed off to Glasgow straight away. I found myself at home reflecting on this tragedy. He had been hunted down by his partner's ex-lover, recently released from prison, and stabbed with a knife.

Suzi helped me to make the tea. Kydd tried to find something happy to talk about. There were a lot of phone calls and it helped to be able to speak to others. There is a picture in my journal of a sun covered over with a black sphere. Underneath I have written: 'James's sudden death has cast a shadow, a very deep one.'

There was a lot of love and concern from others, but it was a difficult time, especially for Jimmy. We had continued to hope over the years that James would manage to emerge from his drug addiction and would be able to move on in his life. Sadly, it was to end with him as a grey-faced figure in a coffin. There was an outpouring of grief amongst his family.

For his mother Margaret it must have been an unspeakable loss. Also for his sister Tricia – her face was distraught and my heart broke for her. Jimmy and other male members of the family carried his coffin out of the house for the last time. The funeral service was simply and movingly conducted by Father Gerry who spoke about the importance of rituals in our life. It was a solemn occasion as we gathered in the chapel to pay tribute to James's departing spirit. The incense, music, and words of intonation evoked a dignity I imagine he had seldom, if ever, experienced in his all too short life.

After all of this Jimmy was keen to get away somewhere warm for a holiday. I was seemingly resisting this, which resulted in Suzi and Jimmy starting a 'Down Under Pressure Group'. I appreciated the way in which Jimmy would use humour to break down my blocks and resistances. He was having recurring dreams of prison and even started to talk about possibly seeing someone about this. In the end he went off on a short holiday to the south of France and this seemed to help him.

He has always sought the sun and the warmth as a way to deal with the uncomfortable feelings that pursue him. This strategy is understandable but it leaves the deeper places underneath unattended. This whole tragedy of James's death should have made us stop and take some time out to be with it. The fact that we didn't, I felt sad about.

Glasgow was starting to feel to Jimmy like a can of worms. His response was to turn back to his creativity and writing to deal with his pain. This was his time-tested way of dealing with life's most difficult experiences.

Christmas was stressful for me that year – I was in conflict over my inner needs for some kind of spiritual nourishment, contrasting with Jimmy and the children's more straightforward enjoyment of presents, good food and TV. Our slow inner drifting apart was continuing.

Family life continued and with the sun lovers in the majority, we took a holiday after Christmas to Miami, The Caymans, Cuba and Jamaica. It was a tonic to have so much light and warmth in the middle of the winter. This helped curb our restlessness and life settled down into a routine again.

On our anniversary Jimmy gave me a card with two velvet hearts on it and spoke of a journey that had never been easy, but steady: 'my heart beats its strong sound and I am here ever and true.' For all our difficulties he was still a steady pillar standing next to me in life, but where were we heading?

The sense of our diverging directions was expressed in the different choices we both made for breaks, which we took early on that year. Jimmy went away for ten days in March heading to London and then south of France. When he was away I wrote:

> 'I miss his humour, his energy, and his positive spirit. He has a more relaxed approach to life than me and when there are difficulties, he knows how to sort things out – quickly!'

I found it hard at times with him not being around and felt like a half deflated balloon. I was starting to get to know a place inside me where I felt very alone.

I had a three day retreat at Samye Ling. This helped me again as I was able to receive some basic teachings on the fundamentals of the spiritual path. I also had an experience of feeling quite blissful – a feeling that arose in me naturally and felt like having my batteries wired up to the mains again. I was able to experience a deep state of inner peace and calm which was clearly what I needed.

Jimmy sensed this too, and was perhaps more aware than I was that I would need to continue this search, even though he was neither willing nor able to accompany me on it.

'Jimmy spoke today of understanding that I'm on some kind of a journey, understanding that there's a restlessness in me, a searching and a need for something other than what he and the children can give me. I know this and this truth disturbs me, frightens me...'

Later on in this diary I have written about:

'...the silence of the wide gulf which exists at the moment between me and Jimmy. Is this noticeable to others? In the quiet of the evening I become aware of the fear I feel at this yawning chasm. Is it bridgeable?'

I wrote down a sentence from the book *Women Who Run With The Wolves*, which summed up the dilemma I was struggling with:

'Compliance causes a shocking realization...that is, to be ourselves causes us to be exiled by many others, yet to comply with what others want causes us to be exiled from ourselves.'

'I want to be in communion with Jimmy as myself – not as an exiled, unhappy, disconnected self. But for him to accompany me would mean change in him too....and if he doesn't want to, what are the choices for me? I feel pretty stuck with all of this at the moment so I am doing nothing.'

Time spent with friends helped to paper over the cracks, but I would all too easily feel overwhelmed and would end up retreating into myself. These were old patterns that would leave me feeling powerless, voiceless, and miserable. I was able to disguise these places in myself, but it felt at times as though I was leading a double life.

On the surface our wonderful extrovert friends, Madge and

the Beeches joined us in the Lakes, which helped Jimmy and the children as the atmosphere was full of laughter, and hilarity as we said our final goodbyes to Low Lindeth. This lovely cottage with its peaceful surrounds had been our home in the Lake District for the past ten years. With Mum now living with us in Edinburgh it made no sense to keep this as a holiday home. We decided to look for somewhere in a warmer climate which would allow us to begin a new phase.

In the summer we attended Anna's wedding. It was lovely to see her looking self-assured and happy as she stood alongside her handsome six foot tall husband, celebrating with family and friends. In contrast, as I wrote in my diary:

> 'Somewhere along the way Jimmy and I seem to have lost our joy in each other. Our relationship works well on the surface but at a deeper level we both recognize now that we have serious problems. We don't flow, don't communicate, don't engage in an intimate way. A lot of the time we travel along together like two estranged souls.'

Admitting this left me feeling heavy and sad. It was clear that we had drifted apart and were both feeling stuck. For the first time we were seriously considering the possibility of having some couples counselling.

This felt like a risky step but I hoped that it might help us to find a way past this impasse. Other pressures continued though which meant that despite both of us feeling that something needed to happen, months went by with neither of us doing anything about this.

Jimmy received a phone call from Tricia expressing her resentment that we hadn't done more to support her and accusing him of not caring about James's death. Her call hurt him deeply in a place where he felt powerless to respond because of the guilt he felt anyway in relation to their childhood. It was a toxic situation, which remained unresolved.

The other challenges came from my family as our first meeting with James and his new wife Samina had ended pretty disastrously. He reacted when Jo and her new partner planned to visit us, and continued to show little understanding in terms of all that we were trying to do for mum. Families! At times it seems that these closest relationships are the hardest of all to deal with – underneath of course lie unhealed wounds which few of us dare to take the time or trouble to confront.

I had never been good at expressing my anger, but at least I now had some spaces in my life when I could just let go and *explode*! These tended to be in my therapy sessions and with friends whom I had met on the Elizabeth Kubler Ross workshops where we would thrash out our anger on mattresses. This helped as I was trying to set my inner self free, having for most of my life felt stifled and repressed. Underneath I wanted to *rage, scream, kick, bite, stamp my feet, make a mess and not be nice at all!!!*

It wasn't comfortable to discover that I contained all these infantile, primitive, powerful, venomous feelings – but there's a certain kind of energy which comes from saying 'Yes' to them. Perhaps it would have helped if Jimmy and I had found a safe way to have a full blown row, but my habit of niceness meant that I deflected most of my negative feelings onto myself. This of course merely compounded the stuckness. Instead of the anger I would find myself collapsing in tears.

Jimmy directed a lot of his energies and feelings into a book he was writing at this time called *Hero of the Underworld*. He had started this work when he was in the Special Unit and there were some brilliant ideas in it. It was about a group of characters spurned and rejected by society, seeking refuge in the sewers and creating a whole alternative society. This manuscript preoccupied him and went through different incarnations as he was determined to finish and publish it.

Some of what he wrote was so brutal and horrible that I felt it shouldn't be published. This became a contentious issue between us. His feelings of rage went way beyond mine because of what he had been subjected to in his nightmarish years of solitary confinement and beatings. I understood this, but I was worried about the effect on his public image if he did manage to get this manuscript into print.

That November 1, was the thirteenth anniversary of Jimmy's release from prison. We probably wouldn't have remembered the date, if a friend hadn't sent us a card, as this former life now felt so long ago. We weren't doing anything special but went out shopping for some furniture for the house and by chance bumped into Ben Conroy who was chatting to a friend at the back of an antiques shop we found ourselves visiting. This chance meeting felt significant because of the link between them going back to the times of confinement which they had shared together. Synchronicity is extraordinary at times.

At the start of December I had my final session with Christina, the therapist I had been seeing for the past year. Her support had helped me to keep in touch with my deep process and the ongoing task of letting go of Brian. I had moved on and felt free of the past. I'd had to passage through places of unending sadness, tears and aloneness. It had been unnerving at times, like shooting the rapids, but I'd survived it.

I'd also found myself in the wastelands feeling despair at the loss of my creative flow. These as I have come to know are all stages on the journey towards finally meeting the person we are underneath – that mysterious centre which we call the Self.

22. Moving Ever Further Apart

The following year was 1996 and we celebrated our sixteenth Wedding Anniversary. Jimmy's words to me were a reminder of his continuing love and appreciation – life might have been pulling us in different directions on the surface but his feelings were genuine and he continued to express himself in ways that would touch me. He said that at the beginning I was a light in the darkness for him, and that I still am.

My mood see-sawed up and down as I tried to see the positives in our marriage, while continuing to feel the increasing sense of separation. What was essential for my well-being was the connection which I felt with the innermost thread of meaning in my life. This would be strengthened whenever I visited places like Samye Ling. Other close friends, who had their own experiences of relationships ending with all the emotional stress that this invariably brought, also supported me.

Jimmy and I weren't the only couple to be splitting apart, it seemed to be happening all over the place as other friends' marriages broke up, often because of affairs. Lama Yeshe had spoken about there being a lack of commitment to each other in the West. He said it's as if we don't know how to stick with it and see through the difficulties anymore. There's too much wanting quick and easy solutions.

At this stage I was still wanting to keep hold of our marriage and part of me believed that despite our difficulties, Jimmy and I could find a way to transform our relationship and keep hold of the best of what we shared together. The ongoing challenge was my continuing struggle to balance my spiritual needs with the life I was living with him and the children.

As I was going through my own inner turbulence, Suzi was emerging into adolescence. In my diary I wrote:

> 'She and her friends are now looking so grown up – it is a time for them of rapid change and angst – particularly on the image and boyfriend front. Suzi is having her ups and downs with this, but so far she is weathering them.'

I was aware of Suzi, Mum and me being at different stages in the life cycle. Suzi was moving into her teenage years, me into my middle years and Mum into her old age. Three generations of women. I admired Mum for managing to meet the limitations of old age for the most part with grace and dignity. She had preserved an active interest in life well into her eighties. Our relationship still wasn't easy, but it was maturing, ever so slowly, through changes occurring in us both.

Life's difficulties sometimes act like sea-water moulding and shaping the rocks so that eventually the rough edges became smooth like pebbles. Forces work on us, just below the threshold of awareness, subtly changing, maturing and ripening us in our soul and spirit.

The forces of nature were about to consume me in a different way though as I became ill with flu. I had a dream at this time:

> 'I was driving along a road in my car...firstly the lights stopped working, then everything else seized up and I eventually had to abandon the car and get out and walk.'

This summed up very well the way that I was feeling. The flu overtook me and I felt absolutely dreadful, being completely laid low which was unusual for me. We had a family holiday afterwards and stayed in a friend's cottage, but it was awful as both Suzi and Kydd became ill with diarrhoea and vomiting. It was cold outside which added to our misery. Jimmy described this time over Easter, at one point, as circles of darkness and that is pretty much how it felt.

It was at this time that Jimmy wanted to put in an offer on a property in the south of France that he had found on one of his trips. He had shown me a video of the property and it looked lovely, but I hadn't seen it myself, and hadn't visited the area where it was located, so it was all a bit of an unknown for me. He wanted me to give him an answer, which I felt unable to do. All I could say was 'I don't know.'

Like a dog with a bone, Jimmy kept on at me, and eventually my resistance crumbled – my illness, the cold weather, wouldn't it be lovely to have somewhere in a warmer climate to escape to – it all started to look very tempting. So in the end I said, 'Yes' to this proposition. I felt starved of the sun. Having more of its warming, brightening energy, absent for long periods over the winter in Scotland, felt very appealing. It is the only time in my life that I have said yes to such a big decision, without taking the time to visit and explore this property. I regretted it later, but by then it was too late.

My spiritual life and journey had opened out into a time when I was introduced to different teachings and paths, and through this I met and was supported by friends who had become very important to me.

I was still a relative beginner, thirsty for teachings and hungry for spiritual experience, but I was finding it difficult to know which path was the right one for me to follow. Much as I tried I couldn't seem to surrender my inner authority to an outer teacher. I often felt that I would like to discuss this with somebody, but I also trusted that the answer would come in its own time. This is expressed in these words by Rilke:

> Live the questions now. Perhaps you will then, gradually,
> without noticing it, live along some distant day,
> into the answer.

*

In May of that year I had an opportunity to visit the house in the south of France for the first time. It was a very attractive house, with a swimming pool and terraced garden, with only one thing wrong with it; it just wasn't *me*. The enthusiasm I had managed to generate in Scotland for this new project gave way to a whole mixture of doubts and misgivings. Some of this had to do with my wariness about stepping into a wholly new culture. The culture was equally new to Jimmy. He at least though was completely at home when it came to talking about subjects that the French love to talk about, food and wine. His enjoyment of these contrasted with my indifference.

We were becoming more and more like chalk and cheese. I was completely out of my comfort zone when it came to meeting others in the British ex-pat community. It all reminded me too much of my own background of wealth and privilege which I had spent much of my life trying to escape. Needless to say Jimmy, Suzi and Kydd were all delighted with the house and played happily in the pool while I struggled with these conflicting feelings.

Our good friends Samra, a young Bosnian, and Florian, a photographer, came for a visit and enjoyed the house and its surrounds. The diversion of their company helped. Life seemed to be sweeping me onward with its currents. I devolved the major areas of decision making to Jimmy and opted for the path of least resistance, hoping that the charms of the house and the area would win me over in the end. I felt I just needed to be patient.

On our return home, the windstorms continued to sweep

through me and in quiet moments when I was alone, I would find myself in tears. The new house seemed to bring all the things I didn't want and created a moral dilemma that tormented me. I couldn't seem to break free of this.

I can't have been easy to live with so many negative thoughts and feelings. Jimmy and I spoke again about seeing someone together for counselling. We were in a rut and we needed to try doing something differently.

I was still hopeful that somehow we could find a way back together again. The house in France became like a wedge between us. We visited it again in the summer. Jimmy was full of optimism and enthusiasm, while I continued to have misgivings.

We visited Cannes, which I didn't like at all. I felt physically ill at the thought that I had allowed myself to be swept along by Jimmy's excitement, knowing all along that it didn't feel right to me. I didn't want to upset him and tried to keep all this to myself, but Jimmy knew that I wasn't happy.

I felt I was having to compromise myself more and more. On the surface we managed to get on well as we were, at the end of the day, good friends, but at a deeper level we were becoming increasingly remote from each other. The other issue which upset me at times was his drinking, but I couldn't blame him for seeking this readily available way to escape the negative atmosphere which was brewing between us.

Reflecting back on this now it seems sad that we couldn't face the difficulties honestly and find some middle ground. We were fortunate in so many ways, how could everything end up feeling such a mess? The answer to this was that we were wanting very different things which created increasing stress for us both.

That August, as part of the Edinburgh Festival, Jimmy had an exhibition of his sculptures at the Demarco Gallery. He was feeling excited by the prospect of having this exhibition – the last one had been about 15 years previously. Bill Beech, Sam and Lucy drove all the way from the south of England to attend this, and Bill's presence (he was at that time head of the art deparment in Brighton) in particular was much appreciated by Jimmy. The exhibition was a great success and was well attended. Jimmy received a lot of well-deserved tributes and praise for his work. Unfortunately my confidence was at a low ebb and I felt more and more as though I was losing myself, becoming invisible as the light shone brightly onto him at this time.

The help I needed would come from a different and unexpected source. An opportunity arose to participate in a weekend of North American Indian teachings, which was held at a beautiful lochside location in the hills of Perthshire and involved camping out on the land. There could hardly have been a greater contrast to my life in the city!

The essence of this work was creating harmony with all our different relationships – with ourselves, each other, with the earth and the cosmos. The teachings were very profound and beautiful and I benefitted a lot from being introduced to them. The teachers whom I met, Wind Eagle and Rainbow Hawk stood tall and spoke with a conviction arising from a deep centre within them. They were also extremely fun-loving, joyful, and in constant contact with the elements and landscape around us. As a city dweller, it was like having the walls of my house taken away and suddenly experiencing the vibrant aliveness and magnificence of nature all around me.

The weekend provided tools to build a stronger sense of self and centre, and ways to remain in balance in the face of changing outer circumstances. Putting them into practice, though, and embodying these skills of personal mastery would take many more years of practice.

At home I would find myself being brought back down to earth by the predictable ups and downs of family life. Suzi, being older now, could seem quite dismissive of me, behaving in a teenage kind of way. After one of these episodes I wrote:

> 'Tonight when I told her that I thought she didn't love me because she was being so off hand all the time, she burst into tears. She then becomes such a lovely, warm, sensitive child. Suzi's love has always been special. Kydd, as if sensing competition has stepped in fiercely proclaiming that he loves me too and that I love him more! I have to smile at this.'

After a row with Jimmy I reached a low point and wrote the following:

> 'If I think of our marriage at the moment I don't feel good at all – I feel sad, lonely, angry, hurting and exhausted. It's hard to keep up a good front on top of all of this. I just want to curl up and go to sleep. I don't know how to cope with any of this at the moment.'

Often it helped to give vent to my feelings in my journal. My regular morning practice of meditation also helped. I would sit, light my candle and watch the feelings and thoughts as they arose. Answers would arrive quite naturally in the stillness – this helped me to relax, feeling bathed in the presence of love, which brought me to a place of deeper understanding beyond the surface challenges.

At this time I received a package in the post that opened up a new possibility for me. It was a Psychosynthesis brochure – this is a therapeutic approach that includes the spiritual dimension – it felt just what I had been looking for. What made this particular course unique was that it was being offered not in London, as many courses were, but in a place called Newbold House, in Forres, which is close to Findhorn.

I remember reading it sitting outside in the sun in the garden.

Suddenly everything lit up. I saw a way forward for myself– a 'heavyweight' course would help me to integrate the spiritual dimension into my work – and it was being offered in Scotland. It seemed strange, to be suddenly experiencing after all these years, the call of Findhorn again.

I hoped that following this new course would allow me to continue developing professionally, as well as supporting me spiritually. When I spoke to Jimmy he did not respond especially positively. His doubts weren't surprising given what had happened to me on the Person Centred course. He did assure me of his loyalty and support though.

As our difficulties seemed to be continuing and we were both feeling unhappy with the state of our marriage, we finally got round to making an appointment to see a counsellor together. She was someone whom I knew of and respected. We both felt a bit strange going along for our first session. Jimmy handled himself well – he was his usual direct self, although I was surprised that he didn't admit to any feelings of nervousness, as we'd both felt this after I first made the call.

It felt helpful to begin reviewing our marriage, but we then moved on to talking about more sensitive areas. I became upset after talking about what had happened on the course – it felt like lifting a scab off an old wound and causing it to bleed again. Afterwards I felt shaky and we reverted back to a pattern of not really speaking to each other – it was as if both of us in our own ways were wanting to close the door again. The second session was a difficult experience for us both.

Afterwards when we spoke to each other at home we discovered a major area of difference. I believed strongly in the value of counselling, whereas to Jimmy the process of opening up in this way remained an anathema. He preferred to channel his emotions into creating pieces of sculpture. He became closed off and subdued, while I feared that the gap between us had become too wide to bridge.

I reached a point of understanding that Jimmy didn't want to open up what was underneath in him. Plunging into the depths isn't for everyone...there are other ways of coping and getting by, but these do have consequences. We both felt unhappy about how this session had gone and decided not to continue. Actually it wasn't really a decision, it felt more like the pattern of avoidance continuing.

At least that autumn we were able to share a relaxing time in the French house together as a family. I was beginning to see more of the positives. Although I missed the wonderful scenery of the Lakes, the warmth and light of the sun, which shone most days was a wonderful treat for us all.

I continued to hope that the deeper awareness that I was gaining would help my relationship with Jimmy. I set my intention and tried to do this. It wasn't enough to transform our diverging patterns though. Life doesn't always fit into neat packages or solutions. The two pillars that Jimmy and I were to each other were moving ever further apart.

23. Being of Light

My focus at the start of the following year, 1997, was mainly on my own inner journey and process. I began the year writing in a diary which Suzi had given me for Christmas – the image on the cover of a fairy figure with wings reminded me of an image which had emerged in my dreams of a winged figure, which I called a *Being of Light*.

This was my spiritual, creative, energetic *being* glowing with the colours of the light. The sun had often featured in my images – now it seemed that the colours of the sun were inside *me*. As sometimes happens, dreams or images like this can be predictive of changes taking place at a deep level.

Outwardly I was still feeling stuck in relation to where things were with Jimmy. There were moments which seemed to offer an opportunity to talk, like taking a walk together in the Botanical Gardens, but although he would share feelings which continued to pursue him from his prison experiences, he remained completely closed to the idea of seeking any help with these through counselling. The stuckness kept returning, like a spoke preventing our two wheels meshing and turning together like they used to. I felt restless, waiting for some kind of signpost or answer, although I had no sense what this might be.

At that point I received a letter offering me a place on the Psychosynthesis and Education Trust one year Diploma Course to take place at Newbold House – so this in a sense was my answer. In February, just before my birthday I made the first of what have by now become countless journeys north up the A9 to Forres, a small town on the Moray Firth coast of Scotland, situated close by to the Findhorn Foundation and community. My destination was Newbold House, a community retreat and workshop centre which was offering the week long Essentials of Psychosynthesis workshop.

I set off with a friend who had also signed up to do this workshop. It was a beautiful clear and sunny morning and as we drove north we had superb panoramic views of the snow covered hills which lifted my spirits. I felt a sense of space and freedom escaping the confines of the city. We were given a warm welcome when we arrived. Newbold House is a Victorian mansion, set in extensive gardens and surrounded by woodlands.

Entering the house there was an immediate sense of peace, comfort, and beauty – it was a perfect space for retreat and healing. There was a sanctuary at the top of the house and pictures which expressed different spiritual qualities. After our long journey I had a welcome sense of homecoming.

What this introduction to Psychosynthesis gave me was a map to understand better the different fields of consciousness that make up our inner world. It was helpful for me to discover this approach as it included the spiritual dimension as well as the lower self and shadow. The journey of healing or therapy aims to create a safe container to support the natural expansion of our soul's essence from within, along with the emergence of all our creative potentials in life. The Person Centred Approach had provided me with a good foundation, but Psychosynthesis promised to offer a framework, which included the powerful spiritual experiences I had been having, which I was still seeking to understand and integrate.

Newbold House and the group of sixteen of us who gathered during this week, provided a greenhouse atmosphere as we were introduced to the essentials of this approach. We were offered opportunities to engage with each other in authentic, creative and spontaneous ways. We were a mixed group, some from the central belt in Scotland like me, others from the local area and the Findhorn Foundation.

Amongst the group I met a man called Robin Alfred originally from London, who had arrived at Findhorn in the mid 1990s and had played a leading role helping the Foundation to reshape itself in what was called the Reinvention Process. Robin had worked in social work in London and had some experience of working in prisons, so it was natural that we made a connection. He had read *A Sense of Freedom* and was interested to learn that I was Jimmy's wife. He said he had a sense of knowing me before meeting me because of this.

I was keen to explore 'Findhorn' and decided to go alone. I wanted to experience it for myself. It was my first time visiting since the late 1970s when I had driven across to take a look at the community while I was working at the Royal Northern Infirmary. At that time, I had lunch in the community centre, which was thronging with people and had a lively atmosphere. There were a variety of colourful and healthy looking salads on offer attractively displayed on long wooden tables. I took a walk through the gardens searching for the legendary cabbages – I didn't see any of these, and certainly no fairies, which left me feeling mildly disappointed.

I had a foot massage from an elderly lady living in a caravan. The experience was pleasant but it didn't captivate me – I was not at a stage then when the inner doors of perception had opened. As this first visit happened before I discovered *A Sense of Freedom* on the station bookstand, I wonder if in some mysterious way I was meant to take this whole journey as a preparation before finally returning here.

I drove through Forres and took the road down to the peninsular, following the sign to Findhorn. Driving along the flat road, past the airbase with Findhorn Bay on my left, I was struck by this being an unlikely location for a spiritual community. I took a short walk through Findhorn Village, situated at the mouth of the estuary. With its attractive low set houses and modest harbour it offers pleasant views across the waters. From there I drove back along the road a short distance to what is known as 'The Park', which is the home of the Findhorn Foundation.

The first place I felt drawn to explore was the impressive pentagon shaped Universal Hall, located on the edge of the gorse covered sand dunes. Built over ten years by many volunteers it is a striking and unique venue, with a geodesic roof and many original features. I found myself standing in the entrance hall, which contained a display of photos of the history of the community for visitors. The photo I found myself standing in front of was of George Trevelyan.

George was a visionary and is looked upon as a prophet or grandfather of the New Age. He was a friend of Peter and Eileen Caddy, two of the founders of the Findhorn Foundation, and visited on many occasions. He is remembered and appreciated for his eloquent and inspiring talks, where he would expound the New Age vision.

He was a second cousin of my father's and has the characteristic Trevelyan looks with flowing white hair, a broad forehead and piercing gaze. Sadly I never met him during his life, although I had certainly heard about him. When I became aware that I was on a spiritual path I tried to contact him through Diana Whitmore, who was the Director of the Psychosynthesis and Education Trust.

She replied saying that Sir George had been one of her mentors but she was sad to have to tell me that he had died two months previously. When I received this news I had a clear awareness that if what he wrote about was true, this wouldn't matter all that much as I would encounter him in other ways, which has certainly proved to be the case. Here I was standing directly in front of a photograph of him. As I looked at his knowing smile I had a distinct feeling that he must be playing some kind of a role in guiding me here.

*

Back at Newbold House I shared this experience with Robin and said that as I couldn't meet with George in person, it would be good to hear about him from those who had known him during the years when he was a regular visitor to Findhorn. Robin suggested that I should write to Eileen Caddy and ask if she would be willing to meet with me. I did this and shortly afterwards received a note: 'Yes, Eileen will talk with you if you come to early sanctuary at the Park on Thursday.'

Early sanctuary was at 6.30am, and it was a bit of a stretch for me to make it across to The Park in time to attend this meditation, but I was delighted to be offered an opportunity to meet with Eileen, one of three founders of this extraordinary community.

When the meditation ended she greeted me and invited me to join her for breakfast. Even though it was early morning she was immaculately dressed with neatly styled white hair, glasses and sparkling eyes. She spoke with a cultured English accent and had a relaxed and easy manner. I immediately warmed to her as she offered me tea and toast.

She was clear and direct, radiating warmth, as well being practical and grounded. She had known George and spoke of him as a dear friend. She spoke to me about faith and about what she called the three Cs: Consistency, Commitment and Continuity. These she said were the cornerstones for any serious spiritual practice. I felt privileged to be sharing this special time with her. It was hard to believe that I was now entering into this legendary story through sitting with her in the early morning.

The spiritual energy, which had no doubt been dormant when I had first visited at the end of the 1970s, was now awakened and was pulsing through me. I only slept for 3 – 4 hours and got up early in the morning twice in a row to drive across to The Park. Each morning there was a different word on the sanctuary door. On the morning when I met with Eileen it was *joy*. On the second morning it was *love*. Sitting in the quietness of the sanctuary I could experience these energies like live currents, expanding and flowing within me.

*

This first visit to Findhorn and meeting with Eileen took place just before my birthday that year. Back at home, on my birthday, I had one of those moments of clear knowing, which was almost certainly a consequence of this time. It was as though a lightening bolt came through me and I knew that if Jimmy didn't change, our marriage was finished. Findhorn however had awakened in me a sense that no matter how far away it felt at that moment, one day my life could transform.

Momentarily I felt this clarity, but as family life continued, it was difficult to maintain. I sought refuge in continued visits to Samye Ling. Meditation, which I continued to practice each morning, helped me remain centred as I focused on opening to the love so strongly present within. As my own energies changed and transformed, Jimmy's remained focused in other areas. An image I had at this time was of a butterfly struggling to free itself from its chrysalis. This was how I felt. I was so much wanting to break free, and find a way to release myself into the lightness of my being – but I was caught in the web of contradictions that my life seemed to have become.

Following my meeting with Eileen at Findhorn, I sent her copies of Jimmy's two books: *A Sense of Freedom* and *The Pain of Confinement*. Shortly after this she sent me a letter dated 9th March 1997 which I have kept:

My dear Sarah,

I do want to thank you for sending me those two books, The Pain of Confinement and A Sense of Freedom, your husband's books. I felt I wanted to read both of them before writing to thank you. I have just finished both of them. Reading something like that really shook me up, but I could not put them down.

I look at the photo you sent me so I would recognize you, and I wonder how Jimmy, and you for that matter came through it all. I know he was released fifteen years ago, and I know much water has flowed under the bridge, but he looks such a lovely soul in that picture, bless him.

I do hope that all is going well with both of you, you certainly deserve peace and happiness after all you have gone through.

With love and many blessings to each and everyone in your family.

Lovingly,
Eileen

Her signature at the bottom right hand corner of the page is small and spider like, but her words express the same love and clarity that I felt when I was sitting with her. I found it extraordinary that in the short time since I had visited she had managed to read both Jimmy's books. She was turning eighty that year, but her capacity to respond in this way spoke volumes about her energy and presence.

My sense of leading a double life continued as I struggled with conflicting pulls and needs. I felt guilty about making plans to be away on retreat over Easter when it was Suzi's thirteenth birthday. When I asked Jimmy for his feelings about this he said that he was happy to give me his support. He even showed me an article he'd seen in the *Glasgow Herald* which contained an interview with Lama Yeshe. Quoting from this:

'Some accuse retreatants of the ultimate selfishness, of running away from life. Lama Yeshe disagrees: 'For me, the practice of Buddhism is giving your life to help other human beings. Everyone who comes out of retreat is more stable and calmer. They have less need, less greediness in their own mind. Their jobs and relationships are more meaningful. And for couples...the experience of being apart brings them closer.'

I appreciated Jimmy supporting me going away on retreat, as without his willingness to be with Suzi and Kydd through these times, I wouldn't have been able to do this. It's also true that he had plenty of times away pursuing his own interests.

Unfortunately though, our diverging lives didn't result in increased intimacy or closeness. When I was away I tended to feel much better – free and alive, although I missed the children and was always delighted to be reunited with them. My ongoing problem was the stuckness in our marriage, because no matter what I tried, this seemed to continue and resulted in me feeling very alone.

My conflict over where I needed to be came to a head on the day of Suzi's thirteenth birthday when I was at Samye Ling, while she and Kydd were with Jimmy in France. I thought of her all day, but I felt empty on the inside, through physically not being with her. I spoke with Lama Yeshe, who as always, gave me helpful advice, saying that if I practiced well I was doing it for us all and that having a calm and stable mind was very beneficial for the whole family – also that what counts was not physically being with Suzi all the time, but the quality of the times we were together. I could agree with all of this, but I still knew that something didn't feel right. I was a mother and it was her thirteenth birthday.

I do believe that the feminine needs to be listened to and my deepest sense was that I should have been with her. Instead what happened was that I developed a very painful tooth abscess and had to leave the retreat early because of this. My body knew what I needed to do, even though my mind had ended up feeling hopelessly confused. It ended up being a doubly unhappy outcome for me as I found myself alone at home in an empty house with no friends and no family over the Easter weekend.

It was a painful place to be, but out of it came the important awareness of how much I needed and appreciated my family. I wasn't on a solitary spiritual quest; they were, and always will be, an essential part of the journey for me. I was glad to be able to finally join them after this time. Suzi and Kydd were very loving and warm with me and to my great relief I didn't experience any sense of withdrawal or disapproval for not having been with them the previous week.

They were happy and relaxed. Jimmy was also happy and relaxed enjoying being with them in the warmth of the southern French sunshine. The sunlight and their company restored my health and good spirits.

When I returned I received an invitation to go north to meet the lead trainer of the Psychosynthesis course who was going to be visiting. His name was Arif and he had formerly been part of the London based school. I was pleased to have an unexpected opportunity to make a second visit to Newbold House. I used this opportunity to again drive across to The Park for the 6.30am meditation. Part of me felt that I was crazy to do this, but once I was up and saw the breathtaking beauty of the early morning skies, I knew that I had made the right decision.

Surprisingly I was the first to arrive. The word greeting me on the sanctuary door was *love*. Eileen appeared shortly afterwards, gave me a warm welcome and invited me to meet her afterwards again. I was delighted to be able to spend another special time with her. This time she spoke about the importance of opening to be a channel for the light. Say: *'I am light'* and send it out. Say: *'I am love'* and *be* love in all your actions. Spreading her arms out wide she embodied and radiated these qualities. She also gave me a copy of one of her books called *Waves of the Spirit*, which I still value and use.

Interspersed with these simple yet powerful teachings, Eileen shared her personal reflections and memories. She had been separated from her first five children for many years, after leaving her first husband to be with Peter. At that time this was considered to be an irresponsible and disgraceful thing for a woman to do. With Peter she had three further sons.

Reconnecting with her original family had been a long drawn out process and had taken decades. She told me that she was looking forward to celebrating her 80th Birthday with all of her eight children and grandchildren gathered together for the first time.

Eileen's inner voice had told her that she would be reunited with them one day, but she wasn't told how long she would have to wait before this happened! She also spoke about how moved she had been by Jimmy's story, which she had read straight through. My unexpected friendship with her grew from these early morning meetings and lasted until she died in 2006.

I drove back home feeling that the way had become clear again. It seemed that my future was going to centre around continuing my journeys north to Newbold House and Findhorn. The prospect of this excited me and I felt relieved that my life was finally changing.

Freedom was coming.

My own renewed optimism coincided with Kydd's tenth Birthday which he celebrated by having a sleepover with six of his friends. Jimmy needed to be around to keep things in control overnight as young boys have so much energy. Shortly afterwards he set off to London to attend Tony Blair's election party. It was an exciting time of celebrating the Labour landslide victory. After years of oppressive Conservative governments, there was a powerful sense of vision and hope for the future, which resulted in people greeting each other with the words, 'Happy New Era!'

We shared in this moment with so many others, believing in our innocence that this was a time of seismic shift and that things were about to change for the better.

24. Increasingly On My Own

Leaving Jimmy at home to continue celebrating the extraordinary Labour Party victory, I set off on another very different kind of journey. I was planning to attend a workshop with the title, Riding the Storm, which was taking place in an atmospheric castle on the island of Mull. This workshop was being facilitated by the two friends I had met through the Elizabeth Kubler Ross trainings, Nick Price and Phyllida Templeton (now Anamaire).

Nick, who I had met on my first EKR workshop also lived in Edinburgh. Dark and handsome, he used to be one of Scotland's top photographers before disillusionment with his career, combined with the departure of his wife, resulted in him taking his own spiritual quest. He has described this in his recently published book: *First Fruits and the Flower of Life*. Through pursuing his own healing he had become an experienced leader of these workshops, which offered the opportunity for emotional release, healing and transformation.

I had met Phyllida when she facilitated my first experience of this kind of deep release on the EKR workshop which I had attended in Carberry Towers in 1990. The title of this particular workshop offered a stronger than usual element of challenge, but the setting and the opportunity to work again with Nick and Phyllida immediately drew me.

These workshops are not for the faint-hearted – they require a willingness to go to the edge and to loosen the shell, or mask which most of us have acquired, which holds in place our deeper vulnerability and emotions. They are especially beneficial for those who have experienced trauma at any point in their lives, through abandonment, loss, rejection, abuse, and betrayal. These wounds leave deep imprints, which can result in life long pain and suffering. Nick and Phyllida used many different creative ways to open up this pain. It invariably turns out that the wounds themselves, despite their limiting effects, also carry some kind of gift. These so-called dark gifts are what often give survivors extraordinary abilities.

In my work as a therapist, which I don't intend to dwell on much in this account, I have accompanied many who have been subjected to the most appalling abuse. Some of the worst I have encountered has been shared with me by survivors of Satanic Ritual Abuse. I met one of these survivors on this workshop. It was brave of her to come especially as the atmosphere of the castle and the ritual elements including the use of candles, the fire and singing, ended up triggering some of her most frightening memories.

It was a real experience of riding the storm as she and others underwent deep and difficult encounters with their emotions. It takes courage to be willing to step into the cauldron and release these places of trauma and pain, but the rewards were tangible in the fresh faces, open hearts and support which emerged through it all.

When I returned home, Jimmy was in the south of France, attending the Cannes film festival. When he returned from there he shared with me an incident that happened before he left, which had affected him deeply. This involved losing his passport and having to go to Glasgow to have a new birth certificate issued. He was re-directed to Lennoxtown to obtain this and found himself pulling into a lay-by in a heavy rain storm, only to discover that he was parked outside Lennox Castle where he had been born 53 years previously in the maternity wing of this hospital. He was convinced that his Ma was in some way responsible for pulling him back there, as he had the experience three days after his birthday.

Between us I experienced a mixture of closeness and distance, as he prepared for a visit to Russia, where he had been invited to install one of his sculptures. This had come about as a result of a meeting which had taken place at Samye Ling with Thom McCarthey's brother, Tim and his Russian partner Sasha, who owned a radical bookshop in Moscow. These friendships were now creating exciting possibilities, opening us both up to new worlds.

I was pleased to be making a visit to Moscow with Jimmy for the unveiling of his sculpture, which had been installed in a courtyard in front of Sasha's bookshop. The occasion was to be part of the Inward Path Festival taking place over three days. This event provided an opportunity to meet people from many different backgrounds – artists, healers and many others, who were part of this diverse and colourful community of inward path-seekers.

There was a directness in many of these contacts – people would come up and, staring straight into my eyes, would ask: 'Do you believe in God?' 'Er..Yes...' I would reply hesitantly, taken aback by the intensity of their questioning. It felt extraordinary to be able to come here and experience such a warm welcome. At the same time I had a strong feeling of encountering a different, unfamiliar world.

In the summer there was another visit to France. We again stayed at La Fontanelle. Although I'd had to work at my relationship with the house and with this part of the world, I was starting to feel more relaxed and was discovering places and experiences there that I enjoyed. I had some lovely times with Suzi and Kydd, appreciating their quirky humour and comments, as well as getting warmed by their love and hugs.

Between Jimmy and me though, the sense of distance continued which left me with a heavy depressed feeling. In my diary towards the end of our time in France I wrote:

> 'The gap feels so large I don't know if we can ever bridge it... Have our two souls flown in such different directions that they can't come back together again?'

I also commented on our increasingly obvious differences.

> '... he likes to drive in the fast lane, I prefer to take things more slowly...he likes to eat and drink...I like walks and enjoy the peace and quiet...I like to explore the inner life, he is more interested in world events... underneath these surface differences, where are we as a couple?'

At that moment there was a growl of distant thunder. I see this now as an ominous omen of what lay ahead of us. There was a storm approaching and the air was thick with tension. There was a flash of lightning followed by a particularly loud clap of thunder. When we returned home I sank back into a trough.

> 'Our relationship just isn't working at the moment...its like a leaking ship, although both of us are doing our best to keep this stricken vessel afloat.'

Phyllida came for a visit and spent time talking to Jimmy, who she hadn't met before. She probed him about his past, which provoked Jimmy to speak with unusual depth and openness about some of his prison experiences – experiences which had left him with unhealed scars. But there was so much pain in these places that his decision seemed to be not to touch the layers of skin that had grown over it all.

When I spoke to Jimmy later he encouraged me to continue on my journey and to do whatever I needed to do as part of it, even if this meant leaving him for someone more able to meet my needs. I was partially shocked by this, but also found it an honest response. At the same time I really didn't know what it was that I wanted or needed. I felt afraid of the abyss, afraid of the unknown, afraid of not being able to find a way through this tricky patch in my life.

★

In September that year I started on the one year *Foundations of Psychosynthesis* course at Newbold House. At least as I headed north I felt a stronger, clearer sense of my identity returning and felt hopeful about what lay ahead. The course started with a mixed group of people, some of whom I had met previously. I again enjoyed the experience of staying in Newbold House.

Nearby at Findhorn I met Eileen who happily shared with me the experience of celebrating her eightieth birthday with her whole family united and together. Her life story is a moving example of the power of unconditional love and of faith. Her response when I shared with her my ongoing difficulties was to suggest I read one of her books called *Learning to Love*. I did this, knowing that I still loved Jimmy deeply, but remaining open and loving when I was experiencing him as being unavailable and unappreciative wasn't easy. I continued to draw strength from sharing our lives together, and knew that as a couple we were important to many other people. I still carried a feeling that we had been brought together for some bigger purpose.

In early October that year we received some sad news. Bobby Campbell, who was a close friend of ours and the father of triplets – Roddy, Diarmid and Fergus – had died suddenly of a brain haemorrhage. We had met this family when we were living in Abbeymount, and Suzi had briefly attended the Moray House nursery. Their mother Hon had contacted me to let me know that she had strongly supported Jimmy's release when she had read about his story in the press.

Sadly she died of breast cancer a couple of years after this when the boys were still very young. We had seen them on different occasions over the years. Bobby was an associate editor with the Scotsman newspaper. His death on the morning of the boys' thirteenth birthday was deeply shocking – a tragic loss in their young lives. His funeral, held in St Mary's Cathedral, was an incredibly sad occasion.

He was a wonderful man who had led a fully engaged life and there were many tributes. Jimmy held one of the chords as his coffin was lowered into the ground. As it came to rest someone called for three cheers. This felt a fitting way for us all to say a final goodbye.

This experience helped to put our own ongoing difficulties into perspective. I felt loved and appreciated by many of the friends who I now had in my life. I just felt sad about the continuing sense of estrangement from Jimmy.

At least in a creative sense things were going well for Jimmy. In November he signed a contract for his book and another for his play, *The Hardman*, to be made into a Broadway musical. He was delighted – it was a good boost for him. He was pleased that the Psychosynthesis course was working out well for me and seemed to be giving me what I needed. This much at least felt good.

As we reached the end of the year we left the depths of winter in Scotland behind and flew to Australia to spend Christmas in Perth. We were met at the airport by my brother, his new wife Samina, and Mum who was staying with them. They had booked an apartment for us close to the beach. They had prepared it for us and had even decorated it with a Christmas tree.

Despite the difficulties, and arguments that had happened along the way, James had bought me a very fine aboriginal painting which I greatly appreciated. It felt like a gesture of forgiveness and reconciliation on his part. We spent Christmas day with family and friends – spending part of it with James and Samina at their house and afterwards visiting Jo with her new partner Ian. Suzi and Kydd were delighted to be together with so many of their cousins all at once and we all had a wonderful day.

In the evening, before going to bed, I ended up sitting outside on the back lawn, enjoying the balmy temperature and looking up at the bright stars in the night-time sky overhead. The wind was whistling softly through the tall Norfolk pines that surrounded the house like silent guardians. My only sadness was that I was sitting there on my own. The words on Jimmy's Christmas card, which like so many others, I have kept, were beautiful:

> My Dearest Sara,
> The light now shining from you reflects on all of us. May your journey continue to reveal your truth and Self. We will always be at your side with love and support. Your man, Jimmy
> xxx

I cherished the words, but in the quiet spaces of the night, he wasn't beside me. I felt increasingly alone.

25. Approaching The Edge

Come to the edge, he said.
We are afraid, they said. Come to the edge he said.
They came to the edge,
He pushed them and they flew.
— *Guilliame Apollinaire*, French Poet

This was a verse we often used to share in our workshops. The edge is not a comfortable or easy place to be. Most of us have a fear of the unknown, and our fears can hold us hostage indefinitely if we allow them to. What I was facing in my life at that point was a sense of approaching an edge, a frightening edge, an edge which if I crossed it would mean letting go of Jimmy and of our marriage.

Identity is a strange thing. We define ourselves through the labels we acquire through life. These labels then become part of us, inextricably interwoven with our sense of ourselves, and who we are in the world. Letting go of an aspect of our identity that has been central to the picture which we have built up of ourselves can seem utterly terrifying. This was where I found myself, drawing ever closer to this edge I had always hoped I would never have to face or confront.

On New Year's morning 1998, I took the plunge. Not into the tempting aquamarine waters of the ocean, but putting pen to paper to write a letter to Jimmy. I wanted to let him know what I was feeling underneath.

'What I would like to say is that I need more out of a relationship than I am getting from you at the moment – more communication, more physical closeness, more love. Something needs to shift between us. The doors, the floodgates need to open and I don't know how to achieve this...'

I ended with three questions:

'What do we both need? Can we give each other what we need? How can we find happiness?'

Viewing the broad sweep of the ocean and the clear blue horizon, these were the questions I was holding in my heart as I sat on a patch of grass above the beach. On his way for his early morning swim, Jimmy spotted me and came and sat down beside me. I gave him my letter and we spoke for a while. There was initially a sense of touching more deeply, then the familiar confusion returned. The truth was that neither of us knew what to do. We loved each other, but we were leading separate lives, although living under the same roof. He said at the end, 'Don't ask me to give what I cannot give.' For a while after this things were easier, then he sank back into silence.

He was doing a wonderful job at living life and enjoying every aspect of it, especially Suzi and Kydd. What I was offering him was enough, or so he said. He said that he had tasted freedom and didn't want any more. This left me wondering where it left me. Although our lives contained so much that I cherished and appreciated, I couldn't bare the thought of carrying on feeling so alone.

Things between us went back to being just the way they were before. In my diary I wrote:

'This always happens, the wound closes over again and we go

back to living life on the surface, just the same...'

There was something underneath which lay heavily, like a submerged corpse, something lifeless and faceless, a dark shadow no one else could see, but I felt its presence. Lying in bed I would feel my own pain, and feel Jimmy's as well. I could recognize and name mine, his was deeper, more hidden, full of his own experience which stretched back through his nightmare years in the prison, to his early life so vividly described in *A Sense of Freedom*. His choice was not to go there, and to let the warmth and light of the present balance out this place underneath. Maybe even if he had decided to open this up, things might still have turned out the same.

The time in Perth ended with me visiting the quayside in Fremantle where I had boarded the ship to return to England twenty-seven years previously. I stood there remembering waving goodbye to everybody with a sense that I would never return and that I was leaving family and friends behind forever. I had a déjà vue sense of life moving in circles, not in straight lines. I was back in this place of departures, seeing myself approaching a threshold where it seemed I was facing another deep and life-defining decision.

Our holiday ended as suddenly and abruptly as it had begun. We jetted back across the world this time heading into winter and into the darkness of the Northern Hemisphere.

We all found it difficult to adjust to the grey skies and cold again. Suzi was amazing and as I became irritable with jet lag and tiredness, she took over in the kitchen, cleaning everything up and being very loving and supportive. I was starting to see the young woman in her emerging. Shortly afterwards I headed north to Newbold House for another module of Psychosynthesis training.

During my time there I received a card from Robin, who had become a good and close friend. Inside this there were two small blessing cards, one of which had the word 'options' on it. This provoked a time of actively wondering what my options were at that moment. I described these in my diary:

> 'It came down to two: Do nothing, accept the difficulties and wait for things to change. Or, make a change, acknowledge we are leading more or less separate lives and suggest that Jimmy takes over the upstairs space for his bedroom, while I carry on sleeping on my own downstairs.'

I was starting to see that there was a way forward, which would involve making a choice to change some of our living arrangements. It would take courage to do this, but it seemed that it would take both of us to a place of more freedom, choice and responsibility. This at least would be healthier than the stuckness we'd both been struggling with.

At home Suzi was up for change as she set about the task of redecorating her room. This meant a lot of physical upheaval and sorting out of things, but it was well worth it. She had good ideas and wanted to do things that were different and distinctive. It was an interesting foretaste of things to come, as now entering her thirties, she has developed a web-site and has a keen creative interest in interior design.

I celebrated my birthday that year at Newbold House and enjoyed being with my friends, feeling their love supporting and encouraging me. Robin wished me an ability to hold the paradoxes in my life in a loving way. I arrived home with all of this love and warmth inside me, as well as some advice from Eileen to keep things simple and not to try to look ahead. I spread out all my birthday cards in the bedroom, then sat down to read a letter from Jimmy which I'd found on the desk top in the Mews.

On the front of the envelope was written –

'SARAH – The woman of my life. My love even in the skies.

Jimmy.'

The contents of this letter were bewildering. I discovered later that he had written it in case of his death, (I didn't know that he had such a fear of flying). He had left it on the desk expecting that Anna would put it away somewhere safe. Finding the letter I had hoped that it was a conciliatory one, as we'd had a row just before he'd left a few days before on another visit to Moscow.

> **20.2.98** Dear Sarah, If you get this it means that I'm not here, except in your, Suzi and Kydd's, hearts. That means I'm alive and well and full of the most immense love one could wish for. Make the funeral classy, a good classical singer, (no pop) and a big party with lots of champagne. I know you will consider some of what I write as a deception but it never was intended that way.
>
> VILLA JERECA will come as a complete surprise to you but it is a strong investment and should be ready for moving into. Once you have broken through your anger at me do hold onto it for a few years. This place was my dream for the future. I wanted to get a place together so that I could go and just create, leave the 'Jimmy Boyle' factor behind and just be me, having you three in my life and the wonderful friends, but the burden and the scarring stigma of 'murderer' has always been a tremendous burden.

There was more but these are the essential things. My stomach turned a somersault on reading it. I felt a sense of complete confusion. I didn't know at that point that Jimmy had such a fear of flying. My emotions made it difficult for me to absorb the contents of this letter. What was this place Villa Jereca? What had he done? Had he bought a new property without saying anything to me? I found it all very disturbing and slept badly after reading it. Jimmy phoned and I tried asking him about the letter, but his voice was heavy and thick.

He said he was shocked that I'd opened it. It had been meant for Anna, not me and he had intended her to put this aside in case anything happened to him. I had no way of knowing this and had simply thought that he had left me a letter. His anger upset me as I felt I didn't deserve it. I was completely unprepared for it and didn't know how to deal with the news the letter contained.

Like a cleaver coming down, this was what really broke our marriage apart, or would in the near future. I had always trusted Jimmy completely and had left him handling our funds as he was good at this. I could never have imagined that he would take over and cut me out of the picture to such an extent. To purchase this property without me knowing anything about it, was a betrayal of the trust which I had considered to be such a bedrock between us.

My first visit to see Villa Jereca, on the Cap D'Antibes, was predictably difficult. The house, with its surrounding high wall and electronically operated security gates felt to me like a prison, albeit a very luxurious one. It was elegantly landscaped, with a large swimming pool and decorated in a style which would not have looked out of place in Vogue magazine. It was sumptuous luxury, but without soul. It didn't feel like a home to me at all.

I went out for a walk to explore the surrounding neighbourhood. Cap D'Antibes is a millionaire's peninsular. High walls, security cameras, virtually empty streets – everything spoke about keeping other people out. Having a property in such a prestigious area close by to the much- coveted Mediterranean coast comes at a high cost. Jimmy had fallen in love with the idea of this and had taken to the house like a duck to water. The children, innocent to these other realities, of course loved it as well and immediately jumped into the pool, but it all felt utterly incongruous to me.

I needed to put a high wall around my feelings as Suzi was celebrating her fourteenth birthday and friends had been invited over. Of course it was pleasant to sit in the sun, but I struggled with almost every aspect of these new surroundings. La Fontanelle had at least been an attractive and charming house, whereas the scale of this new villa was all too big for me – and in a rather absurd way for a place of its size, the kitchen was tiny. I saw faults everywhere I looked.

Jimmy said that he needed to explain how this property had come into his possession. He said that Edward, who had recently died, had left it to him in his will – and of course it wouldn't have been possible to refuse such a generous bequest. What could I say? I should have questioned him more about the discrepancy between this information and the contents of the letter which I had opened while he was away. My head just went foggy around it all and because I didn't want to believe that he could have purchased it without my knowledge, I preferred to believe the explanation that he gave me.

It was only later that I discovered that he had created a smokescreen most likely to prevent me from reacting in the way that I should have done. I tried to numb my feelings. At Findhorn I felt energized, alive, and I enjoyed relationships with friends there, which were much more basic and straightforward in terms of material possessions. This was the complete opposite to a way of life where the material side dominated.

Jimmy tried to convince me of all the positive features and was unhappy with my reluctance to agree with him. I left with a heavy heart as I flew back to Scotland to attend an Easter conference at Findhorn. The children expressed disappointment this time that I was leaving and said that they would like me to stay on with them. Kydd gave me a mild telling-off wagging his finger at me and telling me that I was 'a naughty girl!' Fortunately Jimmy on this occasion was kind and considerate as he drove me to the airport.

*

The Conscious Living, Conscious Dying conference was an

extraordinary event, which acted as a catalyst opening up this whole realm of experience at Findhorn. As the community was well into its 4th decade, many of its members had become older and there was a need to develop more experience and expertise to support people at the end of their lives.

Eileen opened the conference by lighting a candle. As she did this she said with a smile: 'I'm just doing this to show that I'm still alive!' Phyllida then gave the opening presentation, encouraging us all to celebrate the abun*dance* of life, ending with her having all of us on our feet singing, 'We are together that we can heal, We are together that we can love.' The invitation was to enter into living the spiral of life with passion and with joy.

Bridging two such different lives was becoming increasingly impossible but I was still hoping for a miracle. Jimmy and the children did come north for a visit over the Easter weekend that year. I booked us into the Golf View Hotel in Nairn, which has wonderful views out over the Moray Firth. Everything went well as the sun shone on the sparkling blue waters of the Moray Firth and Jimmy enjoyed meeting some of my friends. The conversation flowed easily as we sat discussing human consciousness, and how at this time so many different strands of the global village are being woven together.

Robin joined us escorting Jimmy and the children round The Park. Suzi noticed a lot of the original creative touches on the houses, while Kydd was more interested in the tipi, although he wondered where the TV was. Robin shared his love of football with Jimmy helping him to feel at ease. We visited Eileen. She welcomed us giving each of us a warm embrace. Jimmy said afterwards, 'She's a great woman.'

We stayed with her for about an hour as she gave us tea and biscuits. She shared with us the good news of the unexpected arrival of two cheques in the post for the combined amount of £700 – which was just the amount needed to create two new overhead kitchen windows. This is the kind of magic that has allowed everything to unfold at Findhorn.

In Eileen's words it is all the work of God or of the Christ spirit, bringing about a new age in terms of people's relationships with each other, with nature and with the planet. Jimmy seemed caught up in the energy and vision of the place as well. He seemed different – much more the old Jimmy, the original one I had fallen in love with and married, alive and bright with enthusiasm again. During this time I felt that we were in tune with each other in the way that we used to be.

As we drove home he withdrew back into himself again. I had to recognize that these visits to the north were not easy for him. He had undergone some of the most brutal years of his confinement in Inverness Prison, and the close proximity to this part of the world inevitably brought back dreadful memories.

Jimmy and I finally agreed together that the time had come to take some kind of decisive action. He had been planning to return to the South of France anyway, but we also agreed to make the change in the house, with him moving upstairs. It felt awful to be sleeping apart. I tried to numb myself and simply not think about it. I knew that I would need to use all my strength to emerge from the deadness, and the sense of failure that I was feeling about our marriage. I wanted to regain the vibrant and alive sense of myself I had discovered during my times in the north.

Jimmy had suggested at one point that I buy myself a property in Scotland that could be my place of retreat. Surprisingly a possibility to do this emerged very naturally and easily when Phyllida told me that there was a house for sale in Findhorn village, next door to the B+B that she found herself staying in. Peter Caddy, one of the Findhorn community's Founders, said that when the spirit gets hold of you, you'd better watch out because it will pick you up and pull you along by the coat tails. This describes very well my experience during that visit.

Phyllida was contemplating moving to Findhorn and we thought of sharing a cottage together – with her staying permanently while I came and went. I felt very attracted by this possibility. It seemed to offer a way to escape the difficulties of my marriage, and at the same time to deepen relationships with the new friends that I had made.

The life that I had been living was collapsing, making me very aware that I needed to create a place of safety for myself. After hearing about this cottage from Phyllida, I decided to return north to have a look at it. From the outside it had a traditional appearance and looked quite small. Inside though it was surprisingly light and spacious. I hesitated and at first wasn't sure.

Phyllida made it easy. She loved the cottage and said that she would be very happy living there. As she said this I could see what a perfect arrangement this could be with her staying to keep the hearth warm for me, (the cottage had its own open fire place), when I was able to visit. I could hardly believe the speed at which all of this was coming about, but as it felt the right thing to do I decided to seriously consider it. I felt that a new life was beckoning me.

After considering other options and with support from Robin and Phyllida I eventually put in an offer for the cottage in Findhorn village. I felt I was following my heart and intuition. The only problem was that there was another person seriously interested in buying it who had already had a survey done. I released all my attachment and waited. The message I 'received' in the sanctuary was not to think about it until the end of the week and that it would be mine.

This proved accurate when I received a call later that week at home giving me the good news that my offer had been accepted. I was pleased as well as anxious. The anxiety was provoked by my awareness that in saying, 'Yes' to this I was stepping over an edge.

With the benefit of hindsight it was indeed a good decision to buy it – it gave me a place I felt truly mine, a home with a heart and a hearth, where I would find peace; place where my inner being could be nurtured and where a new life would flourish.

*

At home though the tensions continued. Jimmy returned from a trip to France where he'd been to watch a World cup match. We had another of our kitchen talks. We always seemed to have our deepest talks there. Jimmy spoke about his Ma, Peggy and Alfie and the riches of the 'til death do us part' approach to marriage. There was a voice in me too in agreement with this. The spiritual side kept telling me to try to stick with it and find a way through, but there was a new voice wanting to risk uncertainty, aloneness and the unknown.

We slept apart, Jimmy waking at 4am and going off for an early morning run. He came back saying that he had been thinking about a two month trial separation. We also spoke about the need to be discrete in order to avoid an unwelcome wave of publicity, with all the pressure that this could bring, should any word of our marriage faltering leak out.

In my diary I wrote:

> 'This morning I'm in tears feeling the weight, the enormity, of facing the break-up of our marriage. On the one hand it's an inconceivable thought, on the other, maybe it has to happen. This is a place of real aloneness. I'm on my knees, and calling out to God, 'Help me please.'

Of course God is not a person, and at moments like this represents only our projected wish for someone to come and make everything OK. This was a passage I had to come through alone and I needed to develop the patience to wait for answers. As the cracks opened even wider between us, it seemed that the children were starting to sense something.

When we met up on holiday that Summer at Villa Jereca in France, I didn't miss the significance of Suzi and Kydd pulling us together in the pool for a family hug. A good friend of mine, Laura, an artist from Perth in Australia visited, arriving on the motorbike she'd ridden all the way from England. I was making plans to go off on another retreat but was worried about leaving the children.

When I spoke to her about this she repeated the advice given to passengers on aeroplanes – in emergencies, when the oxygen mask drops down, parents of small children are advised to put theirs on first. She suggested that I put my oxygen mask on and breathe deeply. In her very direct way she commented that she couldn't see anything of me in the house. None of my identity was represented or expressed there.

The retreat provided me with the 'oxygen' I needed at that difficult time and strengthened me in relation to the challenges I was facing. When I returned from it I continued to try to find some closeness with Jimmy, but he seemed increasingly withdrawn and, while he could be light and funny with others, he was shut down and cold towards me.

I was hurting a lot, but when I spoke to him he told me that he was dealing with us living more separately from each other and liked having his own space. It was becoming clearer that he was wanting to let go of me and that it was only the children holding him back. The edge was drawing ever closer.

26. The Broken and the Unbroken

There is a brokenness
Out of which comes the unbroken,
A shatteredness
Out of which blooms the unshatterable.
There is a sorrow
Beyond all grief which leads to joy
And a fragility
Out of whose depths emerges strength.
There is a hollow space
Too vast for words
Through which we pass with each loss,
Out of whose darkness
We are sanctioned into being.
There is a cry deeper than all sound
Whose serrated edges cut the heart
As we break open to the place inside
Which is unbreakable and whole,
While learning to sing.

The Broken - Rashani

1998 was a year of Jimmy and I moving apart from each other. Feeling full of fear at the prospect of letting go, I continued to seek ways to renew the love and affection between us that used to be so spontaneous. Towards the end of the year I suggested that we should see another counsellor together, Cathy.

Being experienced, and professional, she suggested having separate meetings with both of us first, before arranging a joint session. When we finally met together the image she offered the two of us, which seemed to sum up where we were, was of a bridge, the central part of which had crumbled. This stayed with me for a long time afterwards.

For a short while it felt as though this could be a new beginning, but unfortunately our differences continued. While I found Cathy's support helpful, Jimmy said that the sessions left him feeling bruised. I continued but he stopped coming.

It was a difficult and increasingly lonely time. We went back to previous patterns of relating, staying carefully on the surface. I was yearning for deeper contact and connection, but the spaces between us continued. I was also aware that while we might be like two pillars standing apart, there was still so much binding us together. The children, Mum, all of our friends and the public face of our marriage; it felt huge. Jimmy was much loved by everyone in our close circle, and especially by my family, as I was by his. How could we possibly separate and let all of this go?

I had a client who I was seeing at that time who said to me in a session: 'I feel that my marriage is terminal.' This resonated with the uncomfortable recognition that our marriage was in a similar place. It is difficult for me to write about this. It inevitably means having to re-experience the overwhelming feelings of loss as all the richness and colour that we had shared and created together became worn ever more threadbare. The protective bark of my life was progressively being torn away and underneath I felt raw, exposed and vulnerable.

What kept me going were my times at Findhorn. Phyllida's presence in my new cottage, which we called Aruna (which means beauty within) gave me companionship. She was warm and loving, as she encouraged me to open new places of creativity and self-expression. Each time I arrived back it felt as though I was raising my energies so that I could respond to the positive vibrations all around me. From Phyllida, Eileen, Robin and others I was being shown a new way of being. I wanted to live increasingly from the place of divine light and love within…to simply let go and trust from moment to moment.

Like a wilting plant soaking up fresh water, I found my innermost spirits expanding and springing back to life.

I enjoyed my times in Aruna. I felt calm and settled there and enjoyed simple things, meditating, planting bulbs, and especially lighting the fire. The presence of the dancing flames in the hearth always brought me back to myself. I also had the experience of 'miracles', which seemed to happen often when I was there.

These could be relatively small occurrences. For example someone I was thinking about or wanting to contact would appear with an incredible sense of timing. This ongoing experience of extraordinary synchronicity was especially apparent one day when I went for a walk along the beach and arrived home to discover that I had lost my keys. I was locked out, left standing at the door waiting for Phyllida who was nowhere to be seen. I knew that I had them with me when I started out so when Phyllida didn't appear, I eventually decided to return to the beach. Not being sure what to do, I asked my higher self for assistance and guidance. I certainly felt I needed some help.

All that came was a sense that I should keep on walking. Then literally two minutes later, I came across a young man, standing on the sea wall, who said: 'You wouldn't by any chance be looking for a set of keys would you?' To my amazement he held them up in front of me. I'd apparently dropped them when crossing one of the water channels on the beach and by some miracle he'd found them.

He'd wondered what to do – fearing that the tide would cover them, he picked them up then walked back, looking for someone who appeared to be searching for their keys. Of course this could have happened anywhere, but it seems to happen more often at Findhorn, and as a result has become part of the myth-making magic of the place.

That Christmas it snowed and despite everything we managed to have a good family day, which was much needed. Suzi and Kydd had both matured and had taken further strides towards their self-confidence and independence. They seemed to be secure enough in themselves to cope with the strains that had overtaken the two of us, but it had been a poor year socially. This resulted in Suzi, who with her loving heart wanted the best for us both, suggesting a New Year's Eve party.

This turned out to be a big success. It was an exceptionally good celebration lasting through until the early hours of the morning, with the conversations and laughter still flowing even at breakfast the following day.

The year had taken me closer to the threshold of letting go and trusting the ongoing flow of experience. Despite the tests and challenges, I knew that through the cracks, more light was shining in. As we supported each other to follow our different paths, Jimmy and I seemed to be finding a way to give each other breathing space in our marriage. At least this was how it seemed in quieter moments when I could relax and trust the currents of life.

The calm lasted over the turn of the year until another crisis was sparked in late January by an article in the newspaper Scotland on Sunday: 'Jimmy Boyle's hideaway in Antibes.' It was a full spread in the colour supplement all about the French house. I felt quite sick when I read this as it was the antithesis of all my values and I felt out of the picture completely.

When I shared how I was feeling, Jimmy said that he couldn't take any more. He said that what we were going through was a repetition of Mum and Dad and that we should separate. I felt numb as I heard him say this. Eventually one morning when I was meditating, the thought came that what I needed to do was to release him, to set him free of my expectations and demands and to trust him to follow his own heart while I followed mine.

This was shortly before our nineteenth wedding anniversary which we spent in London. The best part of the day for me being a walk, which we took together up Primrose Hill giving us a panoramic view of the London skyline. Otherwise we slept in different places and met up with various friends through the day, including Heidi who had been a witness at our wedding. How different things felt all these years later.

The focus for Jimmy at this time though was the launch of his book: *Hero of the Underworld*. This earned him recognition again for his creative talents in writing – but it was a book that had become another contentious subject between us. I won't dwell on this here. I was relieved that the reviews he received were more favourable than I had expected and he received the acclaim that he deserved.

My own focus in the north was in a very different place. I had been invited to become a trustee of Newbold House, the workshop and retreat centre where I had done the Psychosynthesis training. I had also been invited by Phyllida to join her team of facilitators to take a series of workshops for people who wanted to deal with the issues of death and dying. This was a series of five four-day modules called Death – The Final Healing. I felt delighted to be part of this as we had a wonderful group and it was a privilege to support others on their healing journey.

Our separate journeys away from home continued, and were certainly noticed by Mum who I imagine must have been becoming increasingly concerned by this time. Fortunately the children seemed to be managing alright. Suzi was getting positive reports from her school where all the teachers said what a pleasure it was to teach her. Jimmy seemed to be in lighter spirits as he left again for France – this was where he felt his soul was calling him, while mine was called back again and again to Findhorn.

My spirits continued to soar and plummet as my inner transformational journey continued. For me these were pretty awful times and I knew that I needed to strengthen myself. I heard that Samye Ling was organising a Millennium Himalayan Challenge to raise money for a stupa at Samye Ling. The thought of undertaking a trek in the Himalayas fired my imagination, and gave me the incentive I was needing to get fit. I had a goal, vision and purpose to work towards in the coming months.

Stupas are well known in the East but mysterious to many of us in the West. They are symbolic manifestations of the enlightened state of mind and are designed to generate a constant stream of blessings and of positive spiritual energy. Samye Ling was planning to build a large one and needed to raise funds for this. It seemed a wonderful way to celebrate my fiftieth Birthday to participate in this venture.

I attended another Easter conference at Findhorn – the theme of this was Peace, which felt appropriate as the Bosnian war was still raging at that time. Suzi, Kydd and Jimmy came for a short visit and heard Lama Yeshe give an inspiring talk to the conference where he shared his experience of cultivating forgiveness towards the Chinese. His essential message was that Inner Peace leads to World Peace.

One of the insights I took away from this conference was that the difference between a ceasefire and real peace is forgiveness. Real peace comes through surrendering and being willing not to know what needs to happen. I took these teachings to heart and hoped that they might help to resolve my differences with Jimmy.

We took a short family holiday to Thailand. This felt like a last ditch attempt to restore and repair the bridge between us. It gave us a chance to talk. We seemed to be in a place of more understanding and respect, but there was still a sense of distance and holding back. At least we were able to sit at a table facing each other again and this felt like a small measure of progress. Jimmy said that he loved being in France because when he was there he could unburden himself from his past. He spoke about his responsibility to the children and how he wanted to deal with our situation in a mature way.

One of the activities I most enjoyed on this holiday was snorkelling. I have always loved observing the magical world underwater, with all the incredible colours and varieties of the tropical fish. I could see evidence though of the destruction of the reef, no doubt brought about through the impact of tourism and human exploitation of these fragile environments. In my diary I compared this to the spaces between Jimmy and me, where I was experiencing so much deadness.

On the last night of the holiday Jimmy took us all out to dinner at an exclusive Chinese restaurant in the hotel. Suzi and Kydd left early and he then asked me if I'd enjoyed the holiday. I had apart from feeling that our differences were becoming ever more apparent. This had resulted in him and Suzi returning early for an extra couple of days shopping in Bangkok, while Kydd and I went on a nature safari. Jimmy took the opportunity at the end of this meal to tell me that he felt that we'd reached the end of our relationship.

As he spoke these words I felt myself numbing out, not wanting to face the finality of what he was saying. On the one hand I appreciated his honesty, on the other I was feeling the weight of the responsibility. 'What do we do now?'

I cried silent tears into my pillow that night. There is a family picture taken at the restaurant, and I treasure this, although it still causes me pain to look at it. It was the last photo taken of the four of us together as a family. We wouldn't have another one taken together for a further fifteen years.

When we returned home I felt very separate from him and very alone. Fortunately I was surrounded by many good friends and also had Cathy who offered me a safe space and supported me through this challenging time. When I told her about Jimmy saying that we'd reached the end of our marriage in a Chinese Restaurant in Bangkok, I could see the expression of concern on her face. She spoke about it as tragic and also suggested not trying to find any solutions at the moment but simply surrendering to the process.

I'd spent the first years of my marriage to Jimmy trying to make myself into the person he wanted me to be. Then I'd tried to make him into the person I wanted him to be. Neither of these strategies had worked. All we could do now was to surrender to things being the way that they were and let go of each other, trusting in the ongoing flow of the river.

*

I again headed north, this time for a Croning and naming ceremony held for me and a group of women friends by Phyllida. This ancient ritual marks the time when the woman's bleeding menses cease. She retains the blood and enters the new life phase, opening to the wisdom, which comes from within. Facing the menopause as my marriage was coming to an end could have been very difficult, but this ceremony helped me to see the ageing process in a positive light. The support of my women friends helped to carry me across the threshold as I entered a new life, stripped of my former identity as the wife of Scotland's best known former prisoner, sculptor, and author.

Eileen told me, when I saw her the morning after this ceremony, that I looked happy. In her presence I certainly had a feeling of lightness and joy. This was fortunate as when I saw Jimmy again at home he told me for the first time that he felt a need to have someone in his life. He had felt an attraction between him and another woman while he had been away.

He said that he would like my blessing in order to be able to free himself with regard to having another relationship. We agreed that we should keep the house as the base we share. We both wanted to minimize the hurt to Suzi and Kydd. He was very aware of the potential for adverse publicity and wanted to make these changes in a discrete way. We didn't talk about beginning a more formal legal process of separation at that time, we were simply taking things step by step. I felt relieved that he seemed to prefer an open marriage to separation. At the same time I felt myself being plunged into the fire of my own deep inner grief and pain at these changes. The road ahead looked empty and bleak. I felt hollow inside and very alone. I also felt a sense of inadequacy and failure, of having exiled myself.

This latter feeling proved quite prophetic as with subsequent events I found myself in an increasingly isolated and vulnerable place with none of my former identity or role to protect me. Jimmy had found a new clarity about what he needed and there was a lightness and ease in him I hadn't seen before. I felt reduced to ashes. The finality of our separation was hurting me at the deepest possible level. Even though I knew that what was happening was necessary and inevitable, my heart had finally been completely broken open. My tears flowed as I released all the hopes that things might have worked out differently.

Shortly afterwards, on one of our workshops in the north I found myself receiving guidance from the runes. This is an ancient system of divination, which has from this time on become a reliable source of guidance to me. That particular day when the runes were placed randomly by Nick in front of each one of us in the group, I received the rune Othila, which is the rune of Separation.

The meaning is:

> 'This is the time of separating paths. Old skins must be shed, outmoded relationships discarded. When you receive this Rune,

a peeling away is called for. Othila is a rune of radical severance.'

The words 'radical severance' penetrated right through me. I was at the point of no return, facing the unbearable pain of letting go, but knowing that this was the next step on my path. I was meditating shortly after this when the idea came to ask Phyllida to do a ceremony to cut the ties between Jimmy and me. The energetic emotional ties are what often make it difficult to end relationships cleanly and clearly. I asked her to do this in the small sanctuary we had created in Aruna.

This small space, with its high up windows, reminded me in some ways of his cell where we had originally met. I felt that having this ceremony would help both of us to recognize a clear ending to our marriage, which in other ways was difficult because of all the aspects of life that still connected us. Jimmy agreed to take part in this but was opposed to the idea of inviting any witnesses. I had hoped that Robin and Eileen might have been able to support us.

It would have been better, with the benefit of hindsight to ask Jimmy to suggest whom he wanted as a witness. As it turned out, although he was willing to participate he didn't really understand what this would entail. He couldn't have been expected to as he wasn't familiar with these ways of working as I was. As we moved towards this time I shed many tears, and had a sharp feeling like a dagger through my heart, inside I felt like shattered glass. This was how it felt to be breaking out of the old shell.

I knew that once the ceremony had been agreed, the next big challenge would be speaking to others. The hardest of all would be being breaking this unwelcome news to Suzi and Kydd. I was still trying to convince myself that we would just be parting as physical partners but would be continuing to love each other and support each other as friends.

It was an emotional time for us both as Jimmy also found

himself bursting into tears. I wanted to crawl into a cave. My heart felt heavy as lead. I had a sense of dread about the coming weekend. I was still hoping that some kind of last minute miracle would happen to bring us back together.

I knew that letting go of him would be the hardest thing I'd ever had to do in my life. It was also confusing because we needed to keep the outer appearances of our marriage intact for others, and most especially because we didn't want the intrusion of the press.

One by one we did tell others. Anna had seen all the signs but still hadn't guessed. She thought it would worry Suzi and Kydd to tell them and also that it would be difficult for them not to tell their friends, which would create the possibility of something being leaked to the press at some point. In all of this there are echoes of the situation which Mum faced when she and Dad divorced forty years previously.

Jimmy had made plans to head off to France for six weeks, while I wasn't sure how I was going to cope. He seemed to be able to turn almost any situation to his advantage – a skill I admire in him. At that moment I felt the wind had gone out of my sails and that I'd lost all sense of momentum and direction.

On the 18th June, the evening before our ceremony of release with Phyllida, I wrote in my diary:

> 'This feels like the most difficult step of all, the closing of a long 20 year chapter in my life and the opening of a new time when I let go of being part of a couple and step back onto my own path. At times the aloneness feels almost overwhelming, and the rawness. I've felt like a tree stripped of all its bark, standing alone, exposed in bleak midwinter winds....but I can slip back into feeling calm and steady as I do know from deep within that we are doing the right thing in letting go.'

It was difficult with Mum. She must have been hurting terribly when we told her. She rounded on me for dragging Jimmy up to Findhorn for this ceremony. 'How could I do this to him, when he's already been hurt so much?' She was very attacking at first then said that she knew when we married that we would both at some point go our own separate ways. She was very fond of Jimmy and he of her, so it was devastating to have to confront her with the news that our marriage was ending. With the benefit of hindsight she dealt with it bravely and did her best afterwards to support us both.

Jimmy spent the night before at the Clifton House Hotel in Nairn where he received a warm welcome. He'd invited one of my friends, Liza across for a meal in the evening. I felt a twinge of jealousy at this – it had been a place I had hoped we could visit together one day. Sitting in the kitchen in Aruna, I felt energetic patterning of the old pulling me back. 'This is what I'm letting go of' I reminded myself and I knew I needed to remain in my own space in order to prepare for the morning. I had brought the photo collage I had made of our wedding day – from January 31 1980. The beauty and the love of that day still shone in my heart. I had also brought along a picture of Anthony Ross.

The following morning Phyllida opened our ceremony very simply. We sat on cushions on the floor while she read words about regret that this was taking place, but of love continuing in a different way. 'The love which flows on from this moment in time is not the love of physical union but of two travelling souls.' She said that we had been essential in each other's journey. Jimmy and I appreciated each other for what we had shared together and of course for our two children.

Although the sense of finality was painful, this felt a respectful way to let go, honouring and appreciating the past. I wrote afterwards:

> 'Our love and marriage has always been about setting each

other free. We have both remained faithful to our vows, even if the temptations to break them have arisen. The reward of this deep loyalty has been a rock solid basis of trust.'

(Of course it wasn't as rock solid as I thought, as I later found out.)

This ceremony created a powerful cauldron of energy I hoped would support both of us in the early stages of letting go of each other. Jimmy left immediately afterwards. He said that he felt very good after the ceremony and that although this is not his part of the world, he loves everybody here because they love me.

I took off my wedding ring asking for fresh energy, healing and strength for the next stage of the journey. Then I joined Robin and others for a nine-mile hike over the hill tops, which offered some wonderful views but which was incredibly strenuous. The physical activity helped me to deal with emotions I otherwise couldn't have allowed myself to feel that day. I knew that the next stage would be even harder as it would involve telling Suzi and Kydd and I was expecting this to be difficult.

Back in Edinburgh I drove Jimmy to the airport for his flight to France. The parting wasn't as painful as I'd expected. We had a good talk on the way when he told me about his enjoyment of exploring life on his own. (I only understood afterwards that he hadn't had a chance to do this as we had married before his release.) He also told me about Kate, the new friend he had made and how he was hoping to invite her down to Cannes. It felt that all the pain, difficulty and stuckness of the last few years had miraculously been washed away.

I felt released into a new flow of love, which was surprising and a relief. Mum was very opposed to us telling anyone, a response I think came out of her own experiences. Jimmy and I agreed that we should let people in our inner circle know. The last and unresolved question was about finding a way to say something to

Suzi and Kydd. This left me shouldering alone the responsibility of doing this.

The hardest part was telling Suzi. I should never have undertaken this on my own as the responsibility ought to have been shared with Jimmy. We should also have told both Suzi and Kydd together. I decided that she had to know and so took her out to a café. Even now when I drive past this place I still feel the pain of that evening in my heart. I feel I owe Suzi an apology because it must have been awful for her. It was very hard to burst the bubble of her innocence and to have to tell her that her Dad and I were no longer going to be living together. It was excruciating to feel her pain and not to know how to give comfort or reassurance, as I felt responsible for causing it. It felt the worst place of all, as a mother, to find myself in. It weighed heavily on me. Suzi was very silent afterwards as we drove home.

I phoned Anna who was wonderful and said that of course she would speak to Suzi and try to help her to understand. She also told me, which was kind of her, that I shouldn't feel bad for telling her. I phoned Jimmy who said that he would phone her that night. He also said that another close friend of ours had said it was important to tell the children and to be truthful about what was happening.

Telling Kydd fortunately turned out to be less traumatic than sharing this news with Suzi. He was pragmatic in his responses. He had a friend whose parents were divorced, so he knew and understood, that things could still be OK, only different. And that was the end of it. Neither he nor Suzi wanted to talk more about it. They sought refuge in getting on with the familiar routines and preoccupations of their lives.

From now on, the only thing that I knew was that life would irrevocably change and be different. There was no going back.

27. Millenium and Divorce

'Once a chick has emerged from its shell or a butterfly from its chrysalis, there is no going back...there is a continuous unfolding into the new.'

Eileen Caddy – Opening Doors Within

Jimmy's life changed in a much clearer and more visible sense than mine. He spent most of his time in France, while I kept the routines going at home. I flew to Nice to join him for the start of the summer holidays with the children though. He greeted us all warmly at the airport and drove us to Antibes.

There was no energy or spark between, us – simply a sense of forced conversation and politeness. I felt detached, as though I was watching it all on a film. My spirits fell as we turned into the drive at Villa Jereca and waited for the huge metal gates to be electronically opened. Then we entered the world behind them, a world of opulence and comfort.

Jimmy's sculptures were prominently lit in the garden and the effect was striking. There were new objet's d'art and photos on the mantelpiece – pictures of Jimmy, Edward and Suzi, with a small one of me to the side. The one in the most central place, above the enormous stone hearth, was of Edward (The property dealer that Jimmy had formed an ongoing friendship with since our first visit to the South of France. This villa, before it transferred into Jimmy's hands, had originally been one of his properties.) Looking at his picture it seemed to me that Jimmy had taken on his mantle and made this very much his place, just as Edward would have done. I found this all quite extraordinary.

In terms of the old Jimmy, the one I thought I knew – the lavishness felt incongruous. It seemed as though he'd grown a whole new persona – one which had become more distinct and pronounced since his move here. He had stamped his identity in many places – books on the shelves, posters of his book, the sculptures – adopting a taste and style that fitted into the category of serious wealth. I felt in every sense a visitor.

It felt like staying in a hotel, but where were the staff? They seemed to be invisible. I felt relief that I had released myself because otherwise it would all have been too much for me. I had a dream image of me in a small rowing boat watching a huge ocean-going liner disappearing into the distance. Yes I was cut adrift, but my small boat would have been swamped had I remained tethered to the much larger vessel steaming on ahead.

Jimmy picked up on my discomfort and not long afterwards suggested that I should leave and let another friend visiting look after the children. This of course left me feeling hurt and rejected. I went for a walk and reminded myself that I was there for the children and would stay on –while Jimmy might not appreciate me being there, they did. So I decided to stick it out.

Jimmy left soon afterwards for Paris and told me before he left that he had invited Kate and a friend down, news which I accepted because what else was there to do. We met up with other friends who like Jimmy had been brought up in poverty in the drab surrounds of Glasgow. It wasn't difficult to see the appeal of the sun drenched south of France, but it seemed that they had all been seduced by the glamour and ritzy life style.

It would be true to say that my negative thoughts and judgements were coloured by my feelings of loss and alienation – but intrepid optimist that I am, I was still trying to keep alive a flame of hope that we could maintain at least some of our friendship and find ways to support each other in our new lives. I felt by the end of the holiday that I'd done my best and had managed to enjoy times with the children and other friends. I was determined to embrace the new and not look back so I wrote in my diary and meant it: 'Je ne regrette rien!'

I'm glad that I was able to leave with some positive feelings despite the element of strangeness about how this had all turned out. It was to be my last visit to that part of the world for 15 years and the last ever to Villa Jereca. It was not my place and the message from Jimmy was very clear, I was tolerated, but really not welcome there.

I returned home to go on a walking retreat and find a different kind of peace, one which was rooted in the natural world and in keeping faith that I would be shown step by step, the path that I was meant to walk. First though I was to be confronted with the realities and finality of the choice which we had made. Although admirable and right to let go of each other with a spirit of acceptance and of unconditional love, living up to this high ideal proved a bit more challenging.

Jimmy, on a visit home, told me that things had gone well with Kate and that he expected to be seeing quite a lot of her. Things seemed to be moving on quickly for him. I smiled to hide my hurt.

Later on there is a page in my diary which shows what I was really feeling at that time:

'TEARS, TEARS, TEARS, TEARS, TEARS, TEARS, TEARS...'

then:

'ALONE, ALONE, ALONE, ALONE, ALONE, ALONE, ALONE'

I was going into the place of my grief. The words in my diary express the hurt that I was feeling: 'Soul crushing, annihilating hurt. My marriage is over.' I tried to hold it all inside but I could no longer conceal my pain. I told some close friends – people showed their love and concern, but what could anyone do or say? Deep grief is a solitary passage, and one which I had to come through alone.

I shared what I was feeling with Jimmy who cried as well and told me that I meant everything to him. Again from my diary:

> 'He doesn't know if he could love anyone else because he loves me so much. And yet he has Kate in his life! He told me that she was coming to Edinburgh to stay with friends of his. He asked me if I wanted to meet her. I said that I didn't know. I didn't know the answer to anything anymore. All I knew was that I felt this bottomless, unspeakable hurt.'

I had another dream image: in this I have my hands joined in prayer. I am prostrate on the ground. I'm waiting for someone to shoot me through the back. I'm giving up my life. I don't know for whom or for what. But the end doesn't come.

When I was going through the worst of this Kydd was very sweet. He brought me a rug when I was lying on the couch and ran a bath for me. He was probably sensing that I needed some looking after. I felt as though my core was burning. It was hard to communicate this to others, it went too deep.

Choosing to follow a spiritual path, which I knew was right for me, had brought me to this place in my life. Others could be supportive, and even Jimmy became more affectionate, but I was alone in the deepest and darkest of places. At some level it felt like a rite of passage and a stripping away of all that I didn't need.

Jimmy was signing for film rights for his new book. My life felt empty and quiet in contrast. He was firing on all cylinders while I was in this place of deep pain, feeling a loss of purpose and direction in my life. I longed to be able to step out into the light and find my own centre, radiance and power again. The only way to arrive back in this place was to face the pain and not try to minimize or by-pass it. I'm almost ashamed to admit to it, but I reached a point where I actually felt like jumping off a cliff.

Fortunately I didn't do this – I instead jumped into something I'd never attended before, an angel workshop. This gave me exactly what I needed – a reminder of the importance of raising my consciousness in order to renew my health and well-being and ways to connect with the angelic realms. These are dimensions of higher frequency subtle energies, which are available to us if we know how to access them. I was being shown the way to raise my own energies and connect with these healing presences. I was certainly in need of all available help at that moment, and felt the benefits of being shown that there is more to life than what we can see with our physical senses.

Jimmy brought Kate across for a family meal. It was a bizarre meeting in retrospect. She was petite, blonde and bubbly, young and obviously nervous about meeting me. She was an actress and apparently they had first met when a company she was touring with performed at the Mandela Theatre in the Gateway. The biggest feeling I had was of strangeness. I felt as though I was being put into the position of being the mother, who was asked to give a blessing to the two of them.

Afterwards lying in bed, fierce grief surfaced again. The grief of letting go and of abandoned hopes. Despite this unrelenting pain, I welcomed Kate into Jimmy's life. Jimmy was touched by this gesture from me, but he felt under pressure from my emotional displays and made it clear that he wanted to have his own life. He was again leaving for France saying that it would give him a breathing space.

I can see that I was making a determined effort not to give in to my feelings of despair. At Findhorn, I felt whole again – healed by the love that I received there. I needed to be patient. The loss of my marriage was such an enormous thing to come to terms with. Jimmy had been my other half and for many years it seemed as though we fitted together. Letting go of him I felt naked. I was like a tree whose trunk had been split in two.

The question which preoccupied me was had we made the right choice? This mattered more than all the whys and hows of reaching this place. If it was right to be letting go of each other then there would be healing eventually. I didn't want to fall back into feeling a depressed victim. I needed to build my strengths and find a new way forward.

I found energy and healing in nature particularly by spending time with the tall sequoia pine trees, which stand together in a grove in the Botanical Gardens. Standing close to these trees I could feel the strength and power in their deep roots and towering tall trunks.

I visited Samye Ling and had tea with Lama Yeshe. I told him that Jimmy and I had separated, not being sure what his response would be. He said that what had happened in our relationship was a manifestation of impermanence. He said that letting go of our dream thoughts of each other was a very positive thing. The Buddhist view seems to be that if a relationship isn't working it's better to end it. People do grow spiritually at different rates. Sitting with him was like being in a clear stream of positive energy – where it is impossible to entertain a single negative thought.

Back at home Phyllida sent me a card with some uplifting words on it:

'When you can finally let go of everything, including love, then love will pour her graces into your empty spaces...' I could feel her love all around me as I read these words.

I went back to Aruna to find solace sitting beside the blazing fire. I knew that this place was where my rebirth would happen.

I was keeping up a training schedule in preparation for my

experience of trekking in Nepal early on in the new Millennium. When I told Eileen about this she felt that I was being given a push to grow my own strength. As I left she gave me a warm kiss and said, 'Bless you' as she always does when I leave. She had found it very difficult when her marriage to Peter had ended. She spoke openly about her feelings of bitterness and resentment, when Peter had left her for a relationship with a younger woman – but how the experience of emerging from being under his shadow had ultimately been healing for her.

I was growing in my spiritual strength, but as Cathy reminded me when I saw her, I needed to allow the flow of my emotions. She was a wonderful midwife supporting this process of rebirth.

That Autumn I attended a Forgiveness Conference at Findhorn, which was well-timed for me. I had discovered from reading one of Jimmy's Amex statements that he had taken Kate to Venice for a weekend and, of course, hadn't told me. This left me feeling predictably bruised.

Forgiveness is a challenge on the spiritual path. It doesn't mean by-passing the cause of the hurt. This has to be recognized and validated first. It helped me to hear that forgiveness isn't something we do – it happens through us as an act of grace. All that is needed is our willingness to let go of everything that breeds anger, resentment and hate in us. It helps to recognize that by refusing to forgive, we only cause ourselves pain.

It requires a conscious choice to commit to this path, to honour the hurt, but to know that we can move through it to a new level of truth. I was being given the opportunity to practice this.

While I wasn't immediately able to transform all my feelings, hearing of others who had been able to forgive from sometimes appalling abuses, definitely helped me. I wrote the names down on a scroll of all those in my life who I wished to forgive, beginning with Jimmy, and participated in a very deep ritual which brought me a measure of peace.

*

Jimmy left for France telling me before he left to 'Stay strong'. This brought up a rush of anger in me. I felt I'd got to the limit of showing my strength and needed to be able to show my hurt when I was feeling it. He went away looking fed up with me and I was left feeling that I'd blown it again. We were in for a bumpy ride it seemed.

As the end of the year approached I finally managed to achieve some peace of mind, on one of the many walks I took to prepare for the coming trek in Nepal. I wrote about this in my diary:

> **17.12.99:** Walking in the Pentlands last Sunday there was snow on the hilltops and it was magical to climb them. The views were spectacular and there was a beautiful radiance in the sky. I felt a great sense of freedom and expansiveness and my heart felt wide open. I would say that it was a spiritual experience to be up on the peaks and feeling so connected with everything round about me. I walked almost without stopping for three and a half hours. On the way back in the failing light, the surfaces of the reservoirs were mirror calm so that the reflections of the hills were almost perfect. A heron took off in flight a short distance ahead of me. (As I wrote earlier a heron always seemed to appear at moments like this.)

The *big* focus at the end of the year was on the Millennium. This was a time of much anticipation, hyped up, almost feverish excitement and preparations for *big* celebrations. Our household was no exception. As ever at odds with the outer flow of life, I took part in a five day silent retreat as we headed towards this threshold. This was a very beautiful experience. In the silence I could reflect on the deep inner mystery of my heart – and in that place I finally experienced a sense of rebirth and freedom.

Jimmy and I were both at home to share Christmas together with Suzi, Kydd and Mum. Despite everything, it was lovely. On Boxing Day, Jimmy and I sat down to talk. The coming time was going to be a tricky balancing act of finding ways to have our own space, while still not wanting to break up the container of the family. With Jimmy's enthusiasm for a *big* celebration leading the way, we were planning to hold a New Year's Eve party. A marquee had been ordered and a good friend Jinky Gilmour had offered to sing. The entertainment promised to make it a spectacular and special evening, and it was.

In retrospect I don't know how I managed it. Of course part of me wanted and needed to be in the spirit of celebration with the children and with friends, but Jimmy was bringing Kate so it was an awkward situation for me. My memories of the evening include having the perfect excuse to escape the main body of the party when I ended up needing to take care of some of Suzi and Kydd's friends who drank too much and threw up all over the place. Perhaps this is what I should have been doing, but I can put on a good face and bear with things when I need to.

After watching the fireworks from the top terrace I withdrew to the Mews where I sat with a small group of people. We lit a circle of candles, which surrounded a beautiful glass sphere, called Symbol for Humanity. This was a moment when I prayed for clarity, strength and courage for all that lay ahead.

There were many memorable New Year good wishes. One of my personal favourites was the Millenium resolution offered by the Dalai Lama:

'Let there be respect for the earth, peace for its people, love in our lives, delight in the good, forgiveness for past wrongs and from now on, a new start.'

This in many ways is where this time ended, and a new chapter began. Jimmy and I gave a short statement to the press about our separation, which I seem to have no record of, so I am taking the following from an article written by Jean West and published in the Glasgow Herald eighteen months later. The title of this article is: 'She taught me how to love, she absolutely taught me how to love: Jimmy Boyle faces life after marriage.'

> 'A short statement told of the strain of 'individual aspirations' as they grew in different directions, but the foundation stones of the couple's union remain steadfast. The mutual respect they have for each other is rare. There could have been bitterness and recriminations. Instead Boyle asserts 'our marriage was so dignified....Sarah was a loving person and a great giver. The more I am away from her the more I see the profound effect she had on me. She is the gentlest heart I have ever met and a fantastic mother to our two children.'

The press came to the door once, after this statement was released sometime early on in the year 2000. I answered probably looking suitably wan and pale, and gave no further comment. There were no other intrusions. I was left respectfully alone. Jimmy and I had agreed together that we would maintain the dignified public front of our marriage to protect ourselves, and most importantly Suzi, Kydd, and Mum.

The process of trying to find the best way to reconfigure our lives continued. We eventually refurbished Jimmy's studio in the Mews into a flat that he could use when he visited. When this arrangement didn't work, as we had too many stormy encounters, he eventually left altogether to make his home base in France. The process of getting divorced took another two years. It was costly and depressing, emotionally and of course financially, with expensive legal fees.

The worst moment for me was when I saw confirmation in

black and white that Jimmy had bought Villa Jereca without my knowledge. This broke the last vestiges of the trust I always believed was a constant between us. Our twenty-year marriage was annulled in two lines of print – it was a devastatingly subdued ending to what had been an extraordinary and life changing journey from start to finish.

Quest For A New Identity

'The winds of grace blow all the time. All we need to do is set our sails.'

- *Rama Krishna*

The main events of this narrative happened fifteen years ago, and much water has flowed under the bridge since then.

The ending was an ending, a door closed, the past had to be released and laid to rest. This wasn't easy. It has taken time to shed the layers of marriage, family life with the ensuing empty nest, and find the strength to transition gradually into a new chapter. The challenges of accepting Jimmy's onward passage into his new life with Kate alongside him have been many.

What has helped has been having friendships within which I could be fully myself and find the support I needed. I have also had the ongoing inspiration of my home and life at Findhorn.

Part of my quest for a new identity involved changing my name by deed poll to Sara Trevelyan. I dropped the 'h' on Sarah because for me it represented holding on. This was a small change but one which was meaningful to me. I chose Arivanna as a middle name which was a Celtic name given to me by Phyllida. More recently I have been given another name, Roshani, which means light. My inner sense of myself continues to evolve with these changes. I decided to release the name Boyle with all of its associations as none of this was 'me' anymore.

I completed my Millennium challenge, which was the trek

in Nepal. This was an uplifting experience and brought many benefits. The sheer enormity of the mountains took my breath away and it was wonderful to be part of a group led by Doug Scott, who in 1975, along with Dougal Haston, were the first British men to climb Everest. I was also humbled to experience the kindness and natural joy of our team of Sherpas who supported us the whole way.

The friendship and camaraderie of my companions helped me to find the strength to manage the physical challenges we met along the way. This provided a metaphor for the place I found myself facing in my life at that time. The lessons were all there for me, as were the rewards. This journey to the East was followed by others over the years which have taken me to, Nepal, Tibet, Ladakh, and India. These have all been pilgrimages, which have awakened and renewed my soul. The spiritual energy of these distant lands and ancient traditions reminds me that I am part of a greater inter-connected whole – a consciousness and harmony which embraces all of life.

*

I honoured Jimmy at the time of his sixtieth Birthday in 2004, by inviting a group of many of those who had supported him and me through the prison years and after, to a celebration held at our home in Inverleith. This group included people such as Richard Demarco, Joyce Laing, Kay Carmicheal and David Donnison, Betty Ferry (mother of Hugh Collins), Samra and her sister Selma, Bill and Jane Beech, Sam, Tom and Lucy, Madge Bray, Peter MacDougall and Morag Fullerton, Charlie and Janet Miller, Janet and Jimmy Flucker, Chris and Greg Boyle, Anna and many others of my family and friends who were able to be with us on that day.

The weather was beautiful as we gathered in the garden, exchanging memories, remembering and appreciating the extraordinary times we had shared together. Jimmy had not been expecting this and was overwhelmed. It was my final parting gift to him.

Shortly afterwards I sold the house in Inverleith, dividing the garden up to keep the Mews, and moved into what I called a transitional family home nearby in Newhaven. (Broken into two words 'new haven' this was exactly what this attractive traditional cottage near the water-front offered me.) Mum, who lived with us through these times, and bore the heartbreak of them coming to an end with the minimum of complaint, made an extraordinary, late in life, passage back to Australia.

She died in 2007, three years later. I was able to visit her there twice with Suzi and Kydd. On the final visit, shortly before she died, I went alone. She was frail but still had a healthy appetite and enjoyed all the different tasty dishes of food I bought and created for her. She stood steadfastly at her door, waving goodbye to me as I left in the early morning to catch my flight back to this side of the world.

A few days after I left she suffered a fall and ended up with a pneumothorax, being admitted to an intensive care unit in the Sir Charles Gardiner hospital. She died at five minutes to midnight on a Sunday evening a few days later. She was 96 when her long life ended.

My brother wanted to thank a nurse who had been especially attentive and supportive. She had sat beside Mum through her most difficult day, holding her hand and speaking gently to her. My brother had asked this nurse for her name and she had said that it was Heather. Unlike the other nurses in this specialized unit, with his astute powers of observation he noticed that she was not wearing a name badge. When he arrived the morning after Mum had died (his wife Samina was the one to witness this moment) he was told that none of the staff recognized the name Heather.

They checked and re-checked but there was no record of her presence. The words that then came blurting out of my brother's mouth – he is a professor of engineering and not noted for having esoteric beliefs or interests – were: 'She must have been an angel.' He was convinced of this extraordinary phenomenon. There were many further instances during this time that validated for me the experience of transpersonal dimensions.

The passage through the time of Mum's death touched all of us deeply, and gave me an experience of other realms of reality, extending far beyond what we can normally encounter or know. What I understood from this is that the only reality we can be completely assured of, for those who choose to believe in it, is *love*. This is the infinite and boundless source that connects, surrounds and awaits us all.

*

Suzi and Kydd both went on to graduate from University. Suzi's degree was in media studies, after which she studied journalism, then interior design. She moved to Australia and spent four years living in Sydney. Suzi is at present exploring life on the West Coast of America, as she continues creating her own interior design internet business and website. She is on her own spiritual path, combining her interests in style and health, expressing her consciousness and vision in everything she is doing.

Kydd graduated in Politics, writing his final dissertation on the political conundrum of Tibet. After spending two years participating in an internship based in New York, he spent four years living in Singapore, working for an investment company, which is an offshoot of our family business.

While based there he enjoyed getting to know the different countries of South East Asia and is keen to continue his connections with this part of the world. He has already shown an interest in the philanthropic aspect of the family, and has said that he is happy to be named as my successor for the Gateway Exchange Trust in Scotland.

Many of the skype sessions we had, took place with him sitting underneath a photograph of Sir James Scott, my great grandfather, whose inspiration, vision and hard work gave rise to the family business which has now lasted for six generations. I couldn't help but feel that the influence of this early ancestor was alive and present in the context of Kydd making his own contribution to the business as it opened a new office in Singapore.

Kydd has now moved back to London where he is involved in creating an educational project, which involves inspiring others of his generation to support social impact investing. He is conscious and in tune with the spirit and needs of this time, recognizing the opportunities, as well as the responsibilities involved in creating a sustainable future.

In my own life I have continued to work as a self-employed counsellor and psychotherapist. As the family left our home in Inverleith one by one, my therapy practice and the Mews remained the only constant strands in my life. I had the Mews refurbished and re-opened in 2004, as a centre dedicated to healing and personal growth.

I found my work with different clients, many of who had survived appalling abuses or suffered difficult losses, uplifted and inspired me. I continued to explore different therapeutic approaches, which led to me eventually embarking on a four year long study of energy healing with the Barbara Brennan School in Europe. This was a significant choice, which had a far- reaching influence on my personal well-being, as well as on my therapy practice.

My journeys to Findhorn have continued and despite selling Aruna to Robin after Mum's death, I found the warmth of the community pulling me back and bought another beautiful home called Fuaim Na Mara (which means sound of the ocean). It is on the dunes close to the beach, where the sound of the ocean waves and vast open skies create a natural sense of peace. This house had space to store some of my long neglected boxes from Edinburgh and became the place where I started finally to open up the remnants of my past.

As I said in the introduction, the catalyst for me beginning the task of writing about this time in my life was the occasion of Jimmy's 70th Birthday in 2014. This offered me an opportunity to revisit the time of my marriage. I could of course have left it there – but I have chosen to write about it to honour what I gave to it. Also to share these memorable times with Suzi and Kydd, in the hope that it will remind them too of important aspects of the story which they are part of.

Time allows for healing. The past shaped me and changed me as a person, but I didn't want it to define me. I needed to step back into my own life and values, as I had lived these before meeting Jimmy. All of our lives have now moved on and through this a new family shape has emerged. For me this has involved an even deeper appreciation of my relationships with Suzi and Kydd.

As they have become adults themselves, their sensitivity and understanding have on many occasions helped to lift my spirits and strengthen me. Jimmy has taken his own passage and my wish is that through this writing he will know how much our times together meant to me. Nothing can ever take this away.

There comes a moment when the story ceases to matter – the story is just a form which for a while contains a droplet of something much greater. The jar breaks but the space remains unbroken. I trust that if we are meant to regain some of our former closeness, then this will happen. If not we can at least appreciate what we did share, knowing that neither of us would be who we are today without having married and spent these years together.

*

What is freedom? I see freedom as a choice. It is what we experience deep inside, independent of our circumstances. Jimmy used to talk about setting himself free in prison by being able to choose his own thoughts. He developed a rich imagination, which opened up inner landscapes which helped him to deal with the drabness of his outer surroundings.

In the outside world we can allow ourselves to be driven by our habitual feelings and responses, or we can make a choice to turn within and see things differently – to see the best, understand the lessons, and welcome life as a gift – as an ongoing opportunity to grow and develop. The doorway to finding freedom lies within. Everything that I have experienced shows me that I can choose to live freely, joyfully and abundantly, trusting that the deepest healing happens in its own time and way, through forgiveness, surrender and letting go.

Having the patience to live this isn't always easy. Brian, my tutor on the Person Centred training course gave me a piece of advice, which has stayed with me: 'The wisdom of waiting is never to be underestimated.' This is not a fashionable view. We live in a fast paced world where solutions are expected NOW.

This is the era of quick fix, instant communications, rapid change and rapid response. We have less trust in the slow steady passage of time to bring about its own transformation in accordance with deeper cycles of life embedded in our own nature.

The soul works in these kinds of ways. The ego on the other hand thinks that it knows best and tries to manipulate the desired outcome.

*

Over the years I have had confrontations with Jimmy which have only led to frustration. My communications have come from a place where I have felt deeply that, 'I am right.' This belief creates its own barrier and block. Truth, as I have learned is multi-dimensional and imposing a view can be an obstacle to seeing more deeply what is needed.

In the New Story Summit, a powerful event took place at Findhorn, 2015, drawing activists and leaders from around the world to explore the new consciousness emerging at this time, there was a memorable moment when a group of participants up-ended the planned schedule, replacing it with *'we don't know'* in large letters. Not knowing leaves space for a different truth to emerge and perhaps one that at the end of the day is more sustainable, holistic and inspiring.

This is where I find myself at this moment. I am hoping that writing this account will have a positive influence on those who read it, and will contribute to the healing in our family. I hope it will touch others who have also experienced the pain and heartache of separation and divorce, and know the challenges that follow on from this.

Divorce not only affects the parents and children, it affects many other relationships, which can also become casualties of the break up if we allow this to happen. This may mean taking the time and trouble to reach out and bridge geographical or other social realities which can divide us, as well as being willing to set aside unhealed pain from the past.

My family is still Jimmy's family, just as his is mine. This has been a contentious issue at times but I choose to stay true to the relationships that were forged through these years and am touched that they continue. In a fragmenting and turbulent world I feel passionately that addressing the splits and divisions in our own families is where peace and healing begin.

The celebrations for Jimmy's seventieth in France Summer, 2015, when we were also celebrating Suzi's thirtieth, a joint event which was called 'The 100th', didn't provide much time for any intimate conversation. It did represent an opening of a kind though as it was the first family celebration hosted by Jimmy and Kate in France, that I had been invited to over the years. It was predictably generous with the hospitality provided, and a welcome opportunity to be with everyone together again – to see both Suzi and Kydd with their friends, as well as some of ours from the past, who I hadn't seen for years. It was a beginning.

More recently I had another meeting with Jimmy. This happened because I was visiting Morocco to take part in a painting retreat. I had e-mailed him to ask if he would be around. I had a short positive response from him, messaged him when I arrived and we arranged to meet for lunch on my third day there. He met me at a stone archway, which marks the entrance to one of the many alleyways leading into the warren of the old medina. Jimmy knew his way as he and Kate owned a riadh near here in their early days in Marrakech. He took me to a pleasant restaurant with a courtyard garden.

Kate was in London so it was just the two of us on our own. This was the first time, I realized, that we had sat down together for fifteen years. It was an extraordinary experience. Here we were again....facing each other....and the conversation just flowed, naturally and easily in the way that it used to. There was no awkwardness or hesitation. No strategies, no games, and no agendas. It was like two friends who have known each other intimately meeting and being pleased to see each other again. I realized that the grievances and grudges that I thought I was bringing to this encounter had disappeared.

My heart felt free to open to the person I had loved so deeply all those years ago, and in this moment, despite all the water that has flowed under the bridge, the love we shared still felt the same. I asked him to support me with this account and he said that he would. His offer of support felt genuine. Inevitably perhaps it has been a somewhat bumpy process over the past few months achieving this, as everything I have written has opened doors for him as well, some of which he might have preferred to keep closed.

At one point he wrote that he couldn't understand why having fought for so many things in his life, he hadn't fought more for me. I was touched by this. He also said that I hadn't said enough about the good times that we shared together which is possibly true. Memory is fickle and what we choose to give emphasis to can vary enormously. At the end of the day I am grateful for his support and feel that it is a measure of his courage and love that he is willing for me to put all of this out into the world in print.

I know that when two people can come together in a way which leaves space for the other, new harmonies can emerge along with deeper understandings. In this place of essence, the heart can settle into new depths of truth and find its own freedom. Finding Freedom is saying YES to it ALL, with the courage to live each day fully, and stay open to love.

These words, which come from my diary, were written in May 2000. This was the time when I knew beyond all doubt that Jimmy was leaving, and that my new life without him was beginning:

> 'Perhaps one day I will see you on the other side of it all
> And be able to smile freely again
> And be grateful for all that you taught me
> And gave me
> And we will know that love does indeed cross the oceans of time and space
>
> We tie the knot only to discover that the only way we can truly know love is to set our hearts free, and expand into the infinite.'

29. A Final Word

I continue to live with the paradox that I am happier, more content and more fulfilled in my life than I have ever been. At the same time, in terms of the past, it continues to sit within me. It has made me who I am, so I cannot strip it away. I live with the finest and best aspects of it. I also live with that which is far from resolved, and perhaps never can be.

Having been such a key player in my life, my contact with Jimmy is very infrequent these days. He has made a seemingly irrevocable decision not to return to Scotland, turning away from his past and from many of those who shared it closely with him. There is pain in this place of absence for me as well as for others.

Many would understand Jimmy's choice to stay away and to create a new identity for himself in exotic places far removed from the mean streets and confining walls of his past. Some would admire him for this. I do as well in part, but there is a question that continues to haunt me which is about the importance of the return. What is true courage? Perhaps it's about being able to face what still needs to be faced, to acknowledge the unhealed, and to find the freedom that can only come when the journey into the forgotten cracks and crevices is complete. No easy task I admit, but true freedom requires nothing less.

Jimmy's original book *A Sense of Freedom* has recently been republished with a forward by Irvine Welsh, who writes of it as a 'cultural game changer' as it was, and continues to be. Jimmy's personal story and the story of the Special Unit in Barlinnie Prison has enduring importance in terms of Scottish penal history – and there are important insights in it which continue to have relevance in terms of the ongoing crisis in prisons.

In his afterword Jimmy states that his reason for giving permission to publish it again is that in his view 'no lessons have been learned. If anything, things have got worse.' I would say that this is not entirely true, as although crises in prisons continue to erupt south of the border, there have been significant changes in some Scottish Prisons since the end of Jimmy's sentence. The underlying disconnect still exists though; we have to evolve ways of helping those who are sent to prison face and transform their inner demons. In his afterword Jimmy comments on what was at the heart of the Special Unit approach:

> 'Although they got some things wrong, the one thing they got absolutely right, even though we initially hated it, was the insistence that we all sit down as a community and talk things through.'

That such a simple thing as honest, face-to-face, straight talking, truth telling communication could be where the greatest opportunity for change and transformation lies is perhaps worth remembering. The nub of it is, that this is something that each one of us, if we are honest, can have difficulty with…it is only when there is safety, respect and faith in the freedom that can be gained through this, that we will evolve ways of making this possible.

Warders who worked in the Special Unit have admitted that it changed them as well. Training for most prison officers though remains very limited. Greater understanding of the personal reasons for persistent offending and the skills and sensitivity to work with these are still much needed. Nothing less than a transformation of attitudes both sides of the staff/ inmate divide is required to break through the self-defeating culture of not showing any weakness or not grassing.

A FINAL WORD

Encouraging and supporting family relationships, as was done in the Special Unit, can help a great deal in this respect. Also keeping the focus turned outwards onto the possibilities and supports for inmates returning to the community.

There is still much to be done, but in Scotland a climate of openness to new initiatives seems to live on. As I complete this manuscript I have found myself invited to a meeting in Barlinnie Prison to discuss an exhibition about the Special Unit and its art, put together by a group of prisoners supported by staff from The Glasgow Museum's Resource Centre.

No doubt this exhibition will revive the conversation about the contribution and legacy of the Barlinnie Special Unit. In the very active interest generated so far by this project, the mythology of the past is springing back to life again.

Spirituality is no longer the taboo subject that it used to be. It is starting to emerge in many different ways into the mainstream – classes in yoga, meditation and mindfulness, the spread of holistic therapies, opportunities to engage creatively with the natural world and to explore sustainable ways of living. The consciousness of the world is changing. Beneath the clamour of the materialist, consumer driven world there is a hunger for something that renews our faith in each other and in our all too rapidly fragmenting world. Spirituality, as opposed to religion, which paradoxically with its dogma may exclude rather than unite, holds the key to this.

I am hoping that sharing some of my spiritual journey will encourage others to trust what comes uniquely to them. The doorways are many, they exist everywhere, not just in spiritual communities – they are present and available in the heart of life, when we live from a place of awareness, openness, and enlightened presence.

The golden thread which I followed exists in us all....it is that mysterious inner light which will lead us to the open door, to the final destination, and to the soaring heights of unbounded freedom.

Acknowledgements

The process of writing this book has created many opportunities to engage in discussions about life and what it means to embark on a project like this. Writing itself is a solitary activity and needs to be, but support from others has sustained me through the ups and downs that have inevitably accompanied this venture.

I would especially like to appreciate Suzi, Kydd and Jimmy who from the beginning have all said that they would support me with my writing. Their trust and willingness for me to share these very personal experiences has meant the world to me.

Without Stephanie Wolfe Murray's courage to go out on a limb and publish *A Sense of Freedom* none of this story would have happened. It has been wonderful to meet up with her again, after many years and much water flowing under the bridge, and to discover the same depth of friendship and brave spirit. Stephanie ploughed her way through my first draft and said that she would stand by me with it. Her support made all the difference at that early stage.

I would like to thank friends who also read my early draft and offered feedback – especially Roger Graef and Susan Richards, Katherine Tetlow, Barbara Orton, Nick Price, Madge Bray, Neill Walker, Angus Marland, Alison Shoemark, Carey Morning, Phyllida Anamaire and Anna Howard. Friends are a good mirror – your honesty was sometimes challenging, but essential. Your belief in me kept me going.

Peter MacDougall I have to thank for a proper grilling during a coaching session at his kitchen table, which ended with him telling me to 'get back in the ring and knock the f...k out of my self doubts!'

Christine MacPherson for walking steadfastly with me through the whole manuscript during the early stages of editing.

Anna-Kristina Larsson and Big Sky Print for assistance with drafts one, two and three!

Micheal Hawkins for his support and skill in sensitively completing the task of editing.

Professor Brian Thorne, Helena Kennedy QC and Professor Mike Nellis for being willing to be approached at the pre-publication stage for review comments.

Jean Findlay, whom I met at the 11th hour when I had all but given up on the publishing world, and who suggested the title *Freedom Found*, (my previous working title Finding Freedom has been used by a former death row inmate whose book is now in the New York Times best seller list!) and has made it possible for this work to arrive in print. *Freedom Found* is I feel an even better title for this book, but I couldn't have started off from this place.

So many others I could mention – Anna Robb, Fay Woods, Chris and Greg Boyle, Tricia Boyle – all of those who were part of our extended family and supported our household through these turbulent years with good humour, warmth and loyalty. My family, Jimmy's family – thank you to each one of you, you have all been through this with us, but without necessarily choosing to be!

Finally I would like thank those who are no longer alive, whose freedom now lies beyond this world: in particular, both of my parents John and Joan Trevelyan, Peggy and Alfie Yule, and Margaret Boyle. Also James Boyle, and all the young people who were like family at the Gateway whose lives were tragically cut short as a consequence of the HIV virus. Finally those whose presence has illuminated my own journey in ways which are indelibly imprinted in my heart – Ken Murray, Father Anthony Ross, Eileen Caddy MBE, and Sir George Trevelyan. Your legacy has brought me to where I am today.